D1827004

A HISTORY OF CAMDEN

Hampstead, Holborn, St Pancras

Acknowledgements

I should like to thank all the staff at Camden's Local Studies and Archives Centre at Holborn Library for their professional help in the compilation of this book. In particular, I am grateful to Richard Knight, Head of the Centre, and Malcolm Holmes, Archivist, for making many helpful suggestions and for reading the manuscript at first draft stage.

I am also grateful to Roger Cline, Dr Peter Woodford, Roy Shaw, Julian Tobin and Eric Gordon for their assistance.

I also acknowledge that I have made great use of the invaluable publications of the Camden History Society and those of the Camden Local Studies and Archives Centre. These publications, consisting of one-off books and occasional papers, also include the invaluable *Camden History Review*. I am most grateful to all their individual contributors.

The Illustrations

The following have kindly given permission to reproduce the illustrations listed below:

Camden Local Studies and Archives Centre: *5, 6, 13, 14, 25, 28, 31, 33, 34, 37, 43, 52, 55, 57, 60, 61, 65, 68, 71, 80, 81, 84, 85, 88, 90, 92, 93, 101, 102, 115, 118, 120, 121, 123, 127, 128, 131, 139, 140*

Highgate Literary & Scientific Institution: *16, 51, 66, 91, 104*

London Metropolitan Archive: *107*

St Pancras Housing Association: *126*

Other illustrations were supplied by Historical Publications Ltd.

First published 1999 by Historical Publications Ltd
32 Ellington Street, London N7 8PL
(Tel: 020-7607 1628)

© John Richardson 1999

The moral right of the author has been asserted
All rights reserved: unauthorised duplication contravenes applicable laws

ISBN 0 948667 58 3
British Library Cataloguing-in Publication Data
A catalogue record for this book is available from the British Library

Typeset in Palatino by Historical Publications
Reproduction by G & J Graphics, London EC2
Printed by Edelvives, Zaragoza, Spain

A HISTORY OF CAMDEN

Hampstead, Holborn, St Pancras

by John Richardson

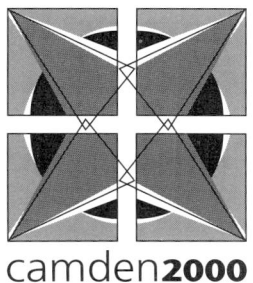

camden**2000**

Published by Historical Publications Ltd
in association with
the London Borough of Camden
to mark Millennium year

Contents

Foreword

Hampstead, Holborn and St Pancras reluctantly joined together as Camden in a honeymoon period in 1964 and were finally wed in 1965. This merger and the others which occurred that year in the London area were part of an overdue reorganisation of London government. New and larger boroughs were formed across the old metropolitan area and deep into the fringes of the Home Counties. At the same time, the London County Council, which since 1889 had governed the metropolis, was succeeded by the Greater London Council whose remit covered a much wider area – parts of Essex, Surrey, Kent and Hertfordshire were wrenched from their ancient county loyalties and subsumed into London. Poor Middlesex, a long diminishing relation of London, disappeared altogether as a governing entity and now exists primarily for the benefit of the Post Office.

The 32 new boroughs replaced the numerous borough councils and boards which had mostly served since 1900. Few of the old authorities across this swathe of inner and outer London at first approved of the mergers, but no matter how their opposition was dressed, it was primarily politically motivated or else there was a reluctance to change the old order. Hampstead, inevitably Conservative, and St Pancras, usually Labour, feared losing control in an enlarged borough. Holborn had most to lose – with a population of only 22,000, its council representation would be small in Camden. Desperately, all three boroughs claimed that they could efficiently take on the duties of the LCC which the GLC was not to inherit, without the turmoil of themselves being merged into a larger administration.

It was also contended that the bedfellows were not well met. There were few historical, social or political relationships to act as catalyst and for a time the respective parts urged the government to wed them to different partners. Herbert Morrison prophesied that in Camden's case the match was so preposterous that it would end in divorce. Only in the case of south St Pancras and Holborn, where the Parliamentary constituency covered those areas, was there cross-border familiarity.

It is still not clear how the Royal Commission finally decided on the grouping of Hampstead, Holborn and St Pancras. Perhaps it found that Islington and Finsbury (which included Clerkenwell) to the east had much in common, and Westminster, Paddington and St Marylebone to the west was a logical combination. This left a hole between, which became Camden.

Inevitably, there was some disagreement as to the name of the new borough. The larger borough, St Pancras wanted St Pancras, but in the end the advice of the Royal Commissioners prevailed, that the name should either derive from a common feature or from some central part of the new area that did not favour any of the old borough names. The only common feature that anyone could think of was the now invisible River Fleet, a stream that ran through the three parts, mostly as a drain, to disgorge into the Thames at Blackfriars. Romantic as a hidden river may be, a drain-cum-sewer is not, and in the end Camden was chosen since Camden Town is roughly in the centre of the borough.

Ultimately, the merger was conducted with little rancour and with much civility, for the three local political leaders, though quite different in background, character and views, had the essential qualities to see the thing off to a dignified start. There was a muted yet keen jostling for position, understandable in the circumstances, on the part of officers and councillors, but there is no doubt that for all Morrison's gloomy apprehension, Camden began with harmony.

The reluctance to merge and thus relinquish up to 1000 years of identity was not wholly political. There was a genuine belief in the three areas that each had a unique character that could and should not be diminished or fudged. It may be argued, with some justification, that Hampstead had always had a particular and recognisable nature – a generally affluent, educated and artistic population, some fine domestic architecture and a glorious Heath. To point out the exceptions to this rosy assessment would be pedantic, for there was a great deal of truth to it. But St Pancras had no such uniformity. It included half of picturesque Highgate Village

1. *The Fleet river was suggested as a name for the London Borough of Camden. It is shown here in 1815, above ground near Old St Pancras Church.*

and the comfortable houses on its southern slopes. On the other hand the slums of West Kentish Town were in the hinterland and further south still were the grimy and not yet gentrified terraces of Camden Town, the vast Utopian council estates near Albany Street and, south of Euston Road, the faded terraces and squares of Bloomsbury and Fitzrovia. This was not a borough to be summed up in a brief description – it was a London mix writ large.

As for Holborn, much of it had always been an adjunct of the City and the legal profession, while its western part, Bloomsbury was notable for its professional institutions, the University and British Museum hinterland. Its small resident population lived mainly in blocks of what were then sub-standard housing and was somehow masked and hidden away.

These characteristics have been changed enormously by the strength of market forces since the creation of Camden. The borough has become more affluent in its nooks and crannies and ostentatiously so in its broad avenues; it is one of the most sought-after locations by middle-class people, and yet paradoxically it has at the same time become a seemingly impregnable Labour Party stronghold at borough council elections.

With the belief that each old borough had a distinctive nature, often came an assertion that old villages lay there somewhere. But only Hampstead may claim to be a 'village' in this sense (I exempt Highgate for the moment, for only part of it is in Camden). St Pancras was a fragmented parish from Tudor times onwards, and modern Holborn was a mix of parishes which included the uncared-for elegance of Bloomsbury and a gradually expanding commercial annexe to London.

However, it is possible to say that of the new boroughs Camden has in its past fully experienced almost all the strands of London history. It really is a true microcosm of the capital and is one of the richest seams for social historians to mine. A few examples – it has been at the heart of transport history in the capital; it has one of the most fascinating political histories; it has had and has magnificent houses and the most degrading slums; it includes many major institutions such as hospitals, museums and libraries; it has been home to innumerable artists, writers and scientists; it contains some of the best public open space in the country and has been at the heart of the battles to preserve such spaces; and it has been famously involved in social reform.

The merger of the three former boroughs may have dismayed Herbert Morrison, but it was never in doubt, given its background, that it would be a vibrant local authority.

CHAPTER ONE

Parishes on the edge of London

The three boroughs that were later merged into Camden were created by an Act of 1899; their first councils were elected in 1900 when the boroughs assumed responsibility. All three areas had previously been in the County of Middlesex, and now became metropolitan boroughs instead. Of the three, Hampstead and St Pancras had retained almost the same shape and size since Saxon times during their progression from parish to vestry to municipal borough. Hampstead had been, until the nineteenth century, a conventional parish, its social influence and ecclesiastical activity mostly concentrated in the town centre and the parish church. But St Pancras parish was unusual and since medieval times had been fragmented into several centres of settlement and parochial power. What eventually became the borough of Holborn was a concoction, a joining together of several parishes and other administrative areas. The one thing the three parts of Camden had in common was a reliance on trade and connections with the cities of London and Westminster.

Hampstead is first noted in 986AD when a grant of the estate (similar in area to the subsequent manor, parish and borough), was made by Ethelred the Unready to the Abbey of St Peter – today's Westminster Abbey.[1] The heavily wooded slopes of Hampstead, then visible from the monastery by the Thames, supplied the monks with timber, pigs and the produce of farms in the clearings. Hampstead's character was forged by its hill, the top of which is 440 feet above sea level. The village, however, did not sit on an ancient and heavily used highway, but as roads and transport improved then its commanding position on the Northern Heights and its adjacency to the Heath made it an enticing place for Londoners who wanted a summer house to buy or rent. Its fresher air and its spa, developed in the 1690s, attracted visitors in search of cures. Gradually, land was enclosed from the Heath and the 'New End' of Hampstead was developed, so that by the middle of the eighteenth century, at least to judge from John Rocque's map of 1746, Hampstead was larger than any

2. Part of the AD986 Charter granting the Manor of Hampstead to the Abbot of Westminster. The original is now in the British Library.

neighbouring centres of population.

The Hampstead section of the Finchley Road was completed by 1829, thereby opening up the potential of land on either side. This was long unexploited, however, due to complications over the manorial ownership (*see pp.105-112*). Consequently, much of western Hampstead is late 19th century and Edwardian, although by then the Church Commissioners and Eton College had already developed much of their Belsize and Chalcots estates.

St Pancras parish took its name from the church in Pancras Road. It has been suggested that a church on this site, dedicated to the Phrygian martyr, St Pancras, was one of the earliest in London. Evidence of Roman occupation in the area and the dedication of the church to St Pancras (a saint popular with early Christians) suggest a very old foundation indeed, perhaps 4th century. Though a settlement of sorts surrounded the old church in medieval times, the hub of the parish by the 13th century was Kentish Town, a mile to the north. Early that century a chapel-of-ease was built there so that the residents, what few there were, did not have to travel to the official parish church. This relocation of the usual place of worship is, so far as I have been able to discover, the earliest such occurrence in Middlesex (see p.36). Another advantage of having a chapel in Kentish Town was that it was more accessible to the residents of the south side of Highgate Village, which fell within St Pancras.

In this way the parish of St Pancras was early divided between the old church area and Kentish Town, and as Highgate developed, a third and affluent neighbourhood also made its mark. New developments – on either side of Tottenham Court Road and Euston Road from about the middle of the 18th century, and in Camden Town from the beginning of the 19th century, also vied for parish influence. By the end of the 19th century Kentish Town, outvoted by a population increase elsewhere in the parish, and overwhelmed by burgeoning railway lands and a swathe of third rate housing within its own area, had lost its cachet and parochial dominance.

The oldest of Holborn's components was the parish of St Andrew, Holborn 'above the Bars', a term which indicated the area of St Andrew's that was *not* part of the City of London. Very

early, Holborn and its Saxon wooden church was the first settlement on the route which led west out of Newgate in the City wall. But in 1130 the City was permitted to extend its boundaries (though not its wall) westward and boundary bars were erected in Holborn at the corner with Gray's Inn Road. Obelisks mark those bars today. Because of this the parish church of St Andrew became included in the City of London, although the greater part of its parish remained in what was then Middlesex. This was of little consequence until the work of parishes increased in the 18th century, when St Andrew's felt it expedient to hold separate parish meetings for areas above and within the bars.

The church itself, now in the shadow of Holborn Viaduct, then overlooked on its east the valley of the Fleet river which ran on the line of today's Farringdon Road/Street. This unpredictable waterway was bridged at Holborn by St Andrew's, but there were steep inclines either side of the bridge, and it was a hazardous crossing in winter.

Holborn's population and reputation was augmented by the first settlement of the Knights Templar at the northern end of Chancery Lane (see p.13), by the presence of 'inns', in which

3. *A reconstruction of the St Giles and Drury Lane area as it might have appeared in 1570 (published in 1818). The triangular plot formerly belonging to the leper hospital of St Giles is to the left, showing the rebuilt parish church.*

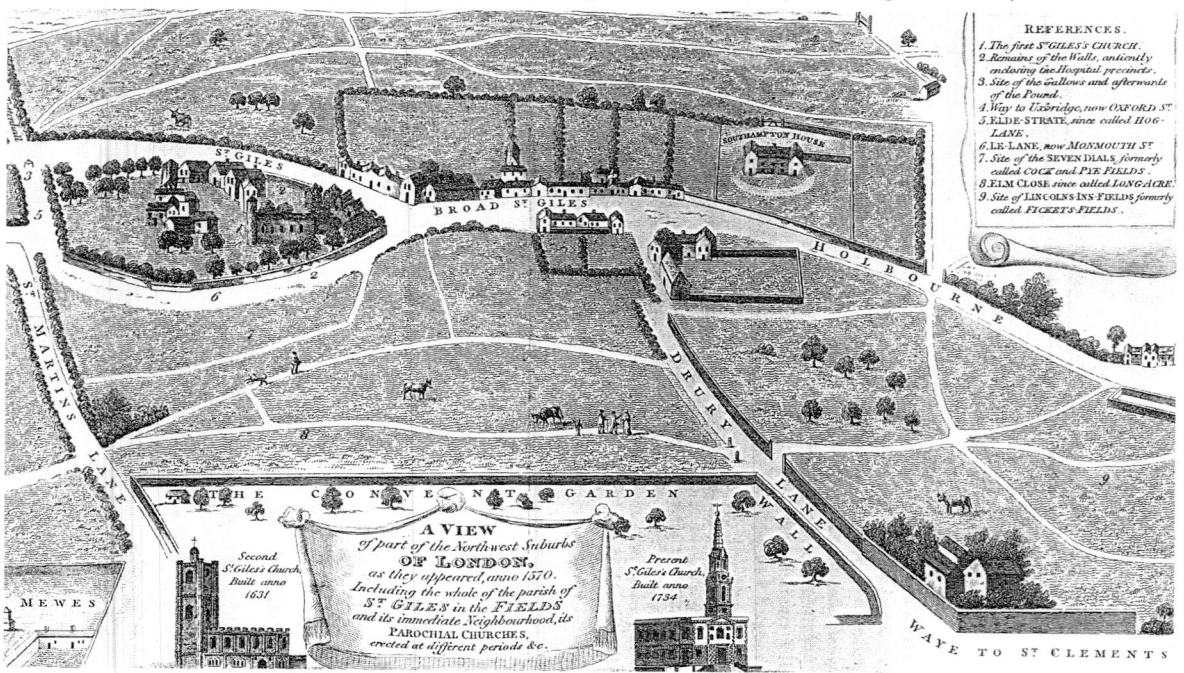

law students resided, and by the gradual expansion of Ely House. In the 17th century, building development extended north of the main highway – most notably to include Red Lion Square – and it became necessary to build a chapel of ease for that neighbourhood. What became St George the Martyr, Queen Square, opened as a chapel in 1706, but was provided with a parish of its own in 1723, when it was carved out of the parish of St Andrew above the Bars.

The early intrusion of the City and the creation of St George the Martyr parish were not the only reductions of the parish of St Andrew. The Liberty of Saffron Hill was also outside the authority of the parish. This encompassed an area between Leather Lane and Saffron Hill that had contained Ely House and its gardens. Indeed, when Holborn borough council met for the first time on 6 November 1900, officers who attended included the Clerk to the 'Vestry of the Liberty of Saffron Hill, Hatton Garden, Ely Rents and Ely Place'. The precincts of Lincoln's Inn and Gray's Inn were also separate parishes and because of this Holborn borough also inherited an 'Overseer of the *Ville* of Lincoln's Inn'; the councillors also found that they employed a medical officer who served the area of Staple and Furnival Inns 'as much as are in Holborn'.

It will be seen from this that what was regarded as Holborn proper, was a patchwork of ancient and somewhat arcane administrations. It was joined in the creation of the borough of Holborn by the parishes of St Giles-in-the-Fields and St George, Bloomsbury.

The parish of St Giles takes its name from the leper hospital established *c.*1118 by Queen Matilda, though it is possible that the area constituted a separate parish, name unknown, before that, under the aegis of the Abbot of Westminster. By 1222, when the limits of Westminster Abbey authority were more closely defined, the parish of St Giles existed.

Recent archaeological discoveries have revealed that St Giles included an even older settlement, for remains of the Saxon port of Lundenwic have been found, particularly in Kingsway and Shorts Gardens, Covent Garden. It is now apparent that sometime after the abandonment of London by the Roman legions in 410AD, a Saxon port grew up to the west of the City. It stretched along the Strand, but also extended northwards on the axis of Aldwychstrate, a road which became Drury Lane and which joined the old Roman road of

High Holborn.

The leper hospital chapel stood roughly on the site of today's church of St Giles-in-the-Fields. The parish also contained today's Lincoln's Inn Fields, Seven Dials, part of Covent Garden and land east of Tottenham Court Road (south of Torrington Place), most of which was the old manor of Bloomsbury.

St Giles was reduced in 1724 with the creation of a new parish to be served by St George's church in Bloomsbury Way, though for civil purposes the two parishes were joined. The ecclesiastical parish of St George consisted of most of what we now think of as Bloomsbury proper, although St Giles was left with a ribbon of land to the east of Tottenham Court Road. This arrangement was made before the development of the Bedford Estate, so that when building did begin in the 1770s the boundary between the two parishes went untidily through one side of Bedford Square and left such roads as Malet Street and Great Russell Street in two parishes.

The manors
Until the end of the 16th century lords of the manor probably held more power in the London area than did the parish authorities. But with the passing of the Highways Act 1555 and the Poor Law Act of 1601, the decline of the manor and the rise of the parish was hastened. By these two Acts the parishes became responsible for any king's highway within their boundaries, and for the upkeep of the poor from the proceeds of a poor rate. In St Pancras the functions of the manors quietly faded away, but because of the long battle to prevent development on the Heath, the presence of the Hampstead manorial lord was of significance until the end of the 19th century.

The manors were, in medieval times, land management bodies having the power to regulate agricultural policy in any large, strip divided fields that still existed. They permitted and recorded any change of occupancy of holdings whose freeholds were still in manorial hands, and they and the manor courts authorised any development on 'waste' or common land. They also dealt with minor criminal offences, the blocking up of streams, the stopping up of footpaths and the quality of local ale.

It is difficult to be precise as to when manors lost their authority in matters which touched both manor and parish. For example, in 1725, St Pancras Vestry condemned the policy of the lord of one of the St Pancras manors which permitted the enclosure of part of the waste or common land for development. The Vestry ordered enclosure fences to be taken down, since in its view they diminished the land available to landless parishioners to graze their animals. Despite this, development did take place on those parcels of waste, but one suspects that manorial authority was by then on its last legs.

The principal manors of St Pancras – Cantelowes and Tottenhall – were, until the Reformation, owned by the Dean and Chapter of St Paul's Cathedral. Briefly described, Cantelowes stretched from Highgate High Street to what is now Agar Grove in Camden Town, on the east of the ancient highway now represented by Highgate West Hill, Highgate Road, Kentish Town Road and Camden High Street, though it also included the Kenwood estate. Its Islington boundary was the important road out of London today called Brecknock Road and Dartmouth Park Hill. There was another patch of Cantelowes to the south of King's Cross, in the area of Gray's Inn and King's Cross Roads. Tottenhall manor included most of the area to the west of Cantelowes but also ran further south, on both sides of Hampstead Road and part of Tottenham Court Road, down almost to Oxford Street.

Each of these manors fell into lay hands after the Reformation. About 1670, the lease of Cantelowes was in the possession of the Jeffreys family one of whose descendants in the first part of the 18th century married Charles Pratt, later to become Baron Camden. In 1768 Tottenhall manor was obtained by the Hon. Charles Fitzroy, the later Lord Southampton, with the aid of an Act of Parliament – the prime minister then, the Duke of Grafton, was Fitzroy's brother.

4. Tottenhall manor house, at the corner of today's Hampstead Road and Euston Road, painted in 1743.

There were three smaller St Pancras manors. Rugmere (Regent's Park area) crossed the parish boundary into Marylebone and was largely acquired for Henry VIII's Marylebone Park. A prebendal and a lay manor of St Pancras lay south east of Agar Grove, the latter including the site of the Foundling Hospital and part of the parish of St Giles.

In Hampstead the pattern was simpler. The manor, which belonged to Westminster Abbey before the Reformation, was the same area as the parish, except that at some time a sub-manor of Belsize had been formed – this is first named in 1334-35. Both manors were taken by the Crown at the Dissolution of the Abbey in 1540. Hampstead manor was granted to the new bishopric of Westminster, but when this too was dissolved ten years later, the land reverted to the Crown, which sold it into lay hands. Notable lords of the manor since then have included Viscount Campden, the Earl of Gainsborough and Sir Thomas Maryon Wilson. (The Viscount Campden is not to be confused with the later Lord Camden whose lands were in Camden Town.) Belsize manor was reinstated to the Dean and Chapter of Westminster Abbey and by and large remained with them until it was vested in the Church Commissioners in the later 19th century. A notable landholding outside of the manor lands was that of Eton College – the Chalcots Estate in the south of the parish and the Wyldes estate – mostly over the Hampstead border in Hendon and Finchley. These properties, previously belonging to the leper hospital of St James, Westminster, were granted to Eton College in 1449, soon after its foundation.

The manor of Bloomsbury was in the northern part of the parish of St Giles and made up most of St George's Bloomsbury parish when it was created in 1724. The name derives from William de Blemund, the landowner in 1201. In 1375 the estate was bequeathed to Charterhouse by the then owner and thus, on the dissolution of that monastery, became the property of the Crown. But only briefly, for in 1545 Henry VIII gave it to Thomas Wriothesley, later created Earl of Southampton. This title was extinguished in 1667 when the 4th Earl died without male issue and his daughter Rachel inherited the estate. She married William Russell, eldest son of the 1st Duke of Bedford. Much of Bloomsbury is still in the possession of the Bedford Estate.

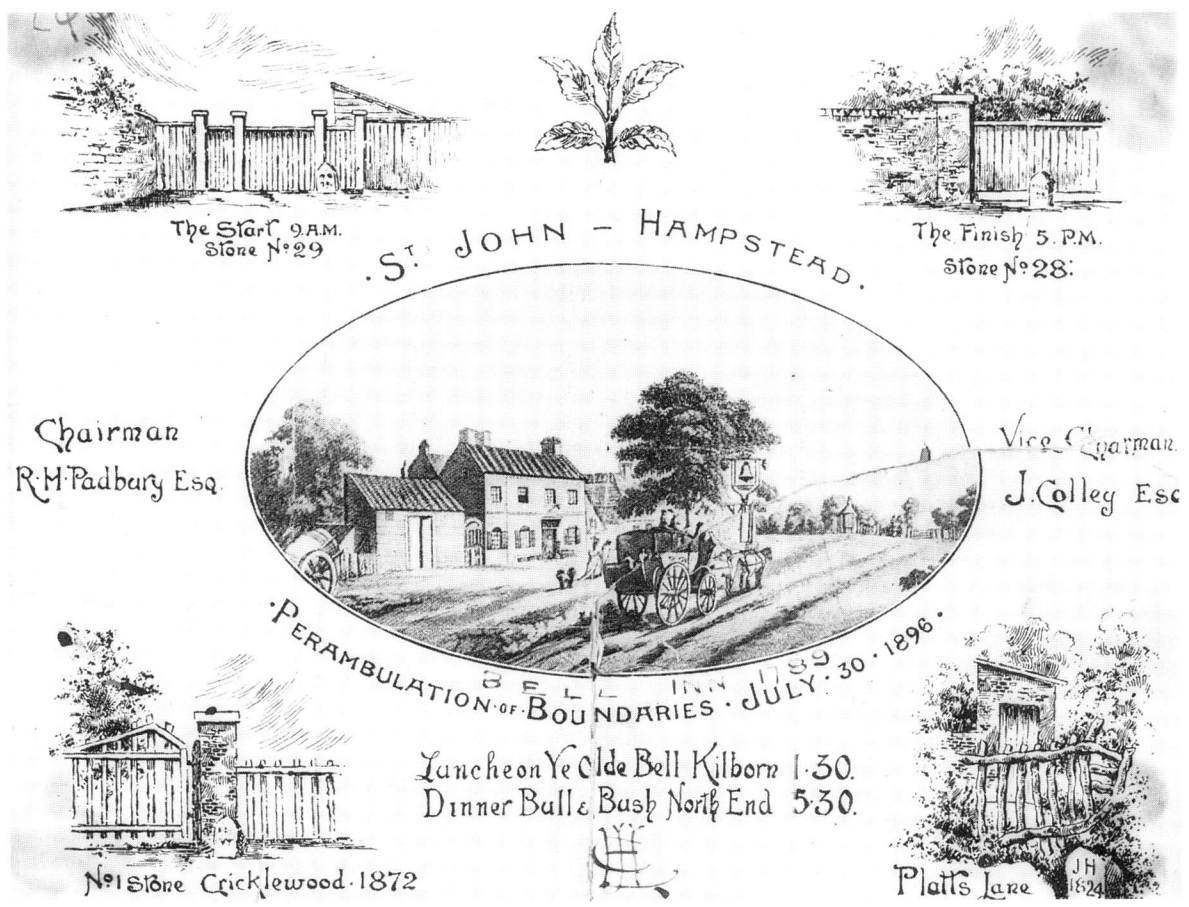

St John – Hampstead.

The Start 9 A.M. Stone No 29

The Finish 5. P.M. Stone No 28.

Chairman R. H. Padbury Esq.

Vice Chairman J. Colley Esq

Perambulation of Boundaries · July · 30 · 1896 ·

Luncheon Ye Olde Bell Kilborn 1·30. Dinner Bull & Bush North End 5·30.

No 1 Stone Cricklewood · 1872

Platts Lane

5. *Announcement, or perhaps an invitation, to one of the later Perambulations of the Bounds in Hampstead in July 1896. The event, starting at 9am, was to finish at 5pm, punctuated by lunch at the Old Bell at Kilburn.*

The vestries and boroughs

The parishes were administered by the vicar and two churchwardens, aided by overseers of the poor and of highways, perhaps assisted by a clerk and a few prominent residents. There was not a great deal of work to do – the doling out of parish charities, the care of the church and the churchyard, and the granting of poor relief, which usually took the form of direct grants to parishioners who remained in their own homes. Meetings took place in the church vestry or else at a local inn such as the King of Bohemia in Hampstead, or the Black Dog in Kentish Town.

The Vestry also organised a periodic 'perambulation of the bounds', a walk around the boundaries of the parish to ensure that boundary stones were still in position and that no encroachments had taken place. This event, usually on Rogation Sunday (the Sunday before Ascension Day), involved the vicar and other leading citizens, together with charity school-children who were obliged to insert or refurbish boundary stones, the whole business being rounded off or interrupted by a meal. This traditional procedure continued until at least the end of the 19th century. Many of the stone markers survive today, either built into walls or else in the open. Some are to be found in the Parliament Hill and Kenwood area where the boundary between St Pancras and Hampstead strides across open fields.[2]

In theory, early vestry meetings were open to any resident assessed for poor rate, but in practice, as the early records of Hampstead and St

Pancras show, attendance was usually sparse. But this changed, particularly in St Pancras. As population increased from the 1750s, the rise in the poor rate became a contentious issue and vestry meetings were well attended. Much of the expenditure and business of the 18th-century vestries was indeed concerned with the poor rate – early that century Hampstead, for example, used 90% of its rate income on poor relief, but a hundred years later, when the vestry had many more functions and a larger paid staff, this figure was reduced to 42%.

The dramatic increase of resident poor in the 19th century transformed vestry politics, for the handling of affairs was not manageable in a large open vestry which had no sub-committees. In 1800 Hampstead obtained an Act for the appointment of a Board of Guardians to supervise the work of poor relief and by 1834 there were 60 guardians, all of them prominent residents. In St Pancras the 19th century began in great discord, when in 1804 a number of residents, incensed by disorderly conduct in the open vestry, applied to Parliament for an Act to create a body called the Directors of the Poor. This was obtained and the Directors were able to demand a poor rate via an open vestry which could do little to vary it. This was a sure basis for friction.

Some years later another group of St Pancras ratepayers applied to Parliament to adopt the Select Vestries Act. This proposed the elimination of the open vestry altogether to be replaced by a self-perpetuating vestry. This may seem undemocratic now but present standards of democracy were not then established at national level, let alone locally, and Select vestries were common throughout the country. The Directors of the Poor, fearing their own abolition, also applied for the creation of a Select Vestry which would include most of their own number. Their application prevailed and on 29 April 1819, St Pancras Open Vestry met for the last time.

The Select Vestry of St Pancras was not an improvement, for it mostly represented the interests of the larger landowners who included the Marquess of Camden, the Duke of Bedford, Lord Calthorpe, the Earl of Dartmouth and Lord Somers. That the ratepayers had greater expectations is indicated by a meeting of some of them in 1829 which formulated a petition to Parliament praying for the abolition of the Select Vestry whose powers 'excluded the Parishioners from exercising any control over the receipts and expenditure of monies collected, the disposal

being wholly confined to the Select Vestry themselves, who were their own auditors' and that 'the Select Vestry was self-elected, and that a needless and extravagant expenditure existed in the disposal of the funds for the relief of the poor'. We see here a continuation of the ratepayers' obsession with the poor rate – its increase and distribution became the nub of a long-running tussle for power in St Pancras.

The ratepayers were successful in putting an end to the self-elective powers of the Select Vestry in 1832, but the Vestry also had other problems. It had allowed the spread of what were known as Paving Boards. In short, these Boards were nominees of local landowners, empowered to raise from residents a paving rate to spend on roads and pavements, drainage and lighting. They held sway throughout most of the parish so that in effect the local authority had little power to supervise the streets.

The social problems which beset St Pancras in the 19th century could not be solved by its parish administration. It was an extreme case, but the problems were common to much of London and were made intractable by the opposition of the City of London to the reformation of London government: the City itself feared diminishment of its own importance in any solution.

The forces for reform, however, could not be withstood. In 1855 the Metropolitan Board of Works was formed which had powers, mainly relating to drainage and sewerage at first, over the whole of metropolitan London *excluding* the City. At the same time the old interlocking authorities of vestries, burial boards, district boards, paving boards and other miscellaneous bodies were largely abolished and vestries were reconstituted with extended powers and responsibilities. In this new form vestries governed St Pancras and Hampstead until 1900, though in the Holborn area the MBW formed two district boards to carry out much-needed sanitary and slum clearance work, one for the combined parishes of St Giles and St George Bloomsbury, and the other for Holborn itself which covered the parishes of St Andrew above the Bars, St George the Martyr and St Sepulchre Without.

---

[1] David Sullivan, *The Westminster Corridor*, pp100, 109 (1994).
[2] See *A Walk Along Ancient Boundaries in Kenwood* by Malcolm Stokes, published by the Hornsey Historical Society in 1995.

Chapter Two

Settlements in the South:
early Holborn

The Knights Templar

As from 1095, a number of Christian princes in Europe engaged in a protracted campaign to conquer and retain the city of Jerusalem, and in particular keep control of the city's Church of the Holy Sepulchre, built on the reputed site of Christ's burial. Previous Muslim regimes which had controlled the city permitted Christian pilgrims to visit Jerusalem, but in 1071 the Saracens were replaced by the Seljukian Turks who made pilgrimage hazardous. On the urging of the Pope, militant Christians undertook Crusades to recover the territory and this was achieved in 1099. Thereafter it was thought necessary to maintain a military presence to safeguard pilgrims. In 1119 two French knights founded the Order of the Temple in Jerusalem, a band of 'fighting monks' dedicated to the protection of pilgrims, and were granted headquarters on Mount Moriah where Solomon had built his Temple and where stood the great mosque, the Dome of the Rock. From this organisation evolved the Knights Templar. To the south of them was the hospice of St John, from which developed the Order of Knights Hospitaller, a less militant organisation with an emphasis on the care, rather than the protection of pilgrims, which at first co-operated with the Templars before becoming their bitter rivals.

The Templars, with their distinctive banner featuring what became the red Maltese cross, were a formidable force, and in that period of fierce and romantic attachment to the Christian holy places became heroes in much of Europe. They were recipients of thousands of grants of land so that it was possible for them to build a network of round churches – a shape derived from the rebuilt Church of the Holy Sepulchre in Jerusalem – across the continent. In London the Templars built a round church on the south side of High Holborn, between Staple Inn and Chancery Lane, a site now occupied by Southampton Buildings (since boundary changes in 1994, in the City rather than in Camden). During excavations in 1875 to build the London and County Bank, remains of this building were discovered which indicated a diameter of 45ft.[1] The Old Temple, as it was subsequently called, was consecrated in about 1135, but approximately 25 years later the Templars sold it to their neighbour, the Bishop of Lincoln, and moved to south of Fleet Street by the Thames. That location, of course, is where the Inner and Middle Temple Inns of Court are today, and where the Templars' new round church, The Temple, was consecrated in 1185. Parts of that building remain today.

The Knights Hospitaller predated the Templars in their London settlement, for in c.1100 one, Jordan de Bricet, granted the Order a site in Clerkenwell which today is crossed by the Clerkenwell Road. St John's Priory was built there at about the same time as the Templars were erecting their headquarters in nearby Holborn. The crypt of the present church of St John's Clerkenwell is part of that priory, and in St John's Square the outline of the Hospitallers' round church is picked out.

The Knights Templar have left echoes elsewhere in Camden, for they owned an estate in the Shoot-up Hill area: Temple Fortune Lane and other local street names are reminders of this.

The two Orders continued to be rivals until 1307 when the Templars were suppressed and many of their lands and possessions, including the Shoot-up Hill estate, were given instead to the Hospitallers.

The lawyers move in

Much of the Chancellor's legal work had moved by about 1338 to what was referred to as 'Chauncelleres Lane'. Chancery Lane was called New Street (1227) when it was formed by the Templars to connect their Old Temple in Holborn to their new headquarters off Fleet Street, but in 1278 it is noted as 'Convers Lane', a reference to a building on the east side of the road which housed Jewish converts to Christianity. In 1377 the *'Domus Conversorum'* was assigned to the Keeper of the Rolls in Chancery, and became a record repository and a lawyers' chapel; this was replaced by the Public Record Office.

Why was Chancery work, previously performed at Westminster, transferred here so that the road became Chancery Lane? No certain answer can be made, but it is possible that the work was actually done in the Bishop of Chichester's house on the west side of Chancery Lane – John de Langton had twice been Chancellor of England (resigning finally in 1308), but he was also Bishop of Chichester up to his death in 1337. Furthermore, the Chancellor's court was held in later times in the hall of Lincoln's Inn, which had taken over the Bishop's premises by 1422.

As we shall see, the transfer of Chancery work to Chancery Lane appears to have occurred *after* the burgeoning of residential inns for lawyers in the area. Henry III had closed law schools within the City in 1234, but in 1292 Edward I ordered that no one should act as a pleader in the courts unless he was properly qualified to do so, and so some educational establishments were required. Holborn was a popular location for lawyers' inns (originally hostels), probably due to its nearness to the City and Westminster and yet with freedom from the City's authority. Similarly, when *c.*1377 lawyers occupied the Temple area south of Fleet Street, they may have chosen it because it was an extra-parochial liberty within the City of London. That autonomy is reflected in the status of today's Temple church, which is a 'Royal Peculiar', owing fealty to the Crown and not to any bishop. Unfortunately records of the early Inns were lost in the bonfires of the Peasants' Revolt of 1381 and it is not possible to resolve some questions about this period.

The four London Inns of Court have the exclusive right to call prospective barristers to the English Bar. They were once related to nine Inns of Chancery which served as their preparatory schools. Why they were called Inns of Chancery is unclear, though they may have trained Chancery clerks. In any event, they appear to have lost that function by the end of the 17th century, and in their later days mostly provided accommodation and social facilities for solicitors. Five of these Inns were in or off Fleet Street and the Strand, and four were in Holborn.

Two of the Inns of Court are in Holborn. Gray's Inn derives its name from the Grey/Gray family which owned the Holborn manor of Purtpool from the early 14th century (today, a road called Portpool Lane runs into Gray's Inn Road opposite Verulam Buildings). About the middle of that century the manor house came to be an 'inn' and in 1397, when Henry Gray died, it was leased to several lawyers.

The Gray's Inn hall dates from *c.*1556, though it was badly damaged in the last war. But the magnificent screen, allegedly made from the timber of a Spanish Armada galleon, had already been removed before the bombs fell. As with the Inner and Middle Temples, dramatic performances were often held in the hall. These included the first performance of Shakespeare's *Comedy of Errors* in 1594 – the playwright's patron, the Earl of Southampton, was then a Bencher at Gray's Inn. Until the Interregnum of the 17th century, masques, revels and dramatic performances were an important feature of life at the Inns of Court which were not then entirely given over to the teaching of law, but were in many ways finishing schools, where social graces and contacts might be acquired. They were London's equivalent of the Universities of Oxford and Cambridge, but with the background to enter the legal profession if required.

A chapel at Gray's Inn was on its present site in 1315; this was rebuilt in 1689, and the stained glass from that period still survives.

It is thought that the origins of Lincoln's Inn lie with Thomas of Lincoln, the King's Serjeant, who by 1331 possessed property on the south side of Holborn which he leased out to lawyers. There is a 1339 record of four apprentices killing two chancery clerks who resided in 'the rent of Thomas de Lyncoln'. However, Henry de Lacy, 3rd Earl of Lincoln (*d.*1311), is also thought to be associated with the foundation of Lincoln's Inn – his crest appears in the arms of the Honourable Society of Lincoln's Inn and on the early 16th-century gateway.

The location of the first Lincoln's Inn is uncertain, though it may have been the house which became Thavie's Inn (the site of today's Bartlett's Buildings). Sometime between 1412 and 1422, the Society of Lincoln's Inn took possession of the Bishop of Chichester's house on the west side of Chancery Lane, at its northern, Camden end; the Bishop's premises contained a hall, chapel and brewhouse. A library is mentioned by 1475, and the hall was rebuilt 1490-92, though the Society did not obtain the freehold of the land until 1580.

6. South Square, Gray's Inn. An undated watercolour by T.C. Fraser.

The lawyers of Lincoln's Inn were largely responsible for the preservation of much of Lincoln's Inn Fields. In the 16th century that area consisted of several fields, mainly used for pasture, which stretched from the little lane called Whetstone Park down to the later Royal Courts of Justice; in the west they extended across today's Kingsway towards Drury Lane. It is thought that somewhere on these fields Anthony Babbington and his fellow conspirators were barbarously executed in 1586. In 1613 the then lessee of one of the fields, Sir Charles Cornwallis, applied for a licence to build a house there. This provoked a quick response from the Society of Lincoln's Inn, which protested that the Fields were essential for the leisure of its members. Indeed, the Society pressed James I, the owner of the land, to follow the example of the City of London at Moorfields, and improve the land so as to make it better suited for recreation. The Society was successful on this occasion in preventing development, but market forces in the end prevailed when Charles I, reminded that he received only just over £5 per annum for his land

7. The gateway of Lincoln's Inn. Lithograph by T.R. Way in Reliques of Old London (1896).

here, agreed to the proposals of a new tenant, William Newton.

Development began soon after. Newton Street was built early, though its location *west* of today's busy Kingsway disguises its previous topographical relationship with Lincoln's Inn. Despite losing to Newton, the Society was able to extract an agreement that there should be an open square in the centre of any development. Today's Lincoln's Inn Fields is the consequence.[2]

The four Inns of Chancery in Holborn were, from east to west, Thavie's, Barnard's, Furnival's and Staple. In the 1349 will of John Tavy, an armourer, he described an inn 'wherein the apprentices used to dwell'; evidently, before his death, they had moved out of this into another house on the site of Bartlett's Buildings and then once again towards the end of the 14th century to premises off Shoe Lane by St Andrew's church. By the early part of the next century Thavie's Inn was closely associated with Lincoln's Inn which, in 1549, bought its freehold. Thavie's Inn was dissolved in the 1760s.

Barnard's Inn lay to the west of Fetter Lane. It consisted of about a dozen houses around a quadrangle and derived its name from the lessee, Lionel Bernard, who had let it out to law students by the time its owner, John Mackworth, Dean of Lincoln, died in 1451. In the middle of the next century it had a hall made of timber, later replaced by a small red brick structure, only 36ft x 21ft, eventually used by the Mercers' Company for a school dining room. Though subordinate to Gray's Inn, Barnard's Inn remained an independent body until it was dissolved in 1888, the last of the Inns of Chancery to survive.

On the opposite side of the road lay Furnival's Inn which appears to have been used by lawyers as early as 1385. The property then was owned by Sir William de Furnival and leased by a manciple (an inn of court bursar) called John Noreys. It consisted of two houses and thirteen shops. This was rebuilt in 1587-88 and in 1638 it received a new frontage to Holborn, possibly designed by Inigo Jones. The lease of the Inn, which had been owned by Lincoln's Inn since at least the 16th century, was surrendered in 1817 and the property was rebuilt in 1818-20 by Henry Peto – a grand neo-classical building which, although no longer an Inn of Chancery, was usually let to members of the legal profession. Charles Dickens lived there 1834-37. The Peto building was shortlived for in 1878 it was

demolished to make way for the beginnings of Waterhouse's impressive office block for the Prudential Assurance Company. The Prudential building, when fully built, was in both the City and in what is now Camden: boundary changes of 1994 put it all into Camden.

The remaining Holborn Inn of Chancery was Staple Inn. The site of this is fronted by the picturesque façade of 16th-century shops facing Gray's Inn Road that are such a tourist attraction. Staple Inn was the largest of the four Holborn Chancery inns. Originally, it appears to have been, as its name suggests, a place where merchants dealt in the staple commodity of wool, but a corporate body of lawyers probably occupied it *c*.1407, and by 1528 the freehold was owned by Gray's Inn, for which it acted as a junior partner. The hall of the Inn dates from 1580, but the rest of it was rebuilt in the 18th century. Staple Inn was in decline in the 19th century when it let out its premises to the Patent Office, and in 1884 the remaining members dissolved the organisation and sold the property to Prudential Assurance who, instead of tearing the premises down, restored them. They are now used by the Institute of Actuaries.

A different kind of legal inn existed to the east of today's Ely Place, its site now covered by the western end of Charterhouse Street. This was Serjeants' Inn, which occupied a house owned by Sir John Scrope in the second half of the 15th century. Serjeants-at-law were superior barristers, part of a fraternity from which judges were chosen. By 1497 they had moved to Chancery Lane where they rented property from the Bishop of Ely.

8. Staple Inn Hall.

Ely House

While the Inns of Court and Chancery developed in Holborn a number of bishops acquired estates nearby on which to build their London residences. These palaces, some of which fronted Fleet Street and the Strand, were judiciously placed between the City and Westminster, between trade and court intrigue and influence. We have already seen that the Bishop of Chichester had a house on the west side of Chancery Lane, occupied in 1422 by the Society of Lincoln's Inn. The Bishop of Bangor had a town house just south of St Andrew's churchyard; the Bishop of Lincoln acquired the premises of the Old Temple and built his next door; the Abbot of Malmesbury had a residence just southeast of Staple Inn on the line of today's Furnival Street. On Fleet Street and the Strand were palaces of the bishops of Salisbury, Exeter, Bath & Wells, Chester and Worcester, and the Abbots of Cirencester and Peterborough.

Most importantly for Holborn was the purchase of some property on the north side of Holborn highway opposite St Andrew's church, probably in the 1280s, by John de Kirkeby, Chancellor of England. Created Bishop of Ely in 1286, he left the property to the See of Ely when he died in 1290. It included a vineyard of seven acres, a garden and some arable and pasture land. The buildings by then included a great hall and a part-built chapel which appears to have been finished by his successor, William de Luda (Louth). This was dedicated to the patron saint of Ely cathedral, St Etheldreda.[3] A later bishop, John de Hotham (d.1336), added another forty acres in the Saffron Hill area, but these he left to the Prior and Convent of Ely so that the Ely House estate as a whole was partly owned by the bishopric and partly by the chapter of Ely.[4] By virtue of its ecclesiastical ownership the estate became extra-parochial, outside the jurisdiction of St Andrew's parish. It was not only a Liberty but also had the right to grant sanctuary to those, particularly debtors, sought by the law. A nearby area, Baldwin's Gardens, somehow also acquired this facility when it was developed near the end of the 16th century, but an Act in 1697 abolished the right of sanctuary held by many places, including Ely House and Baldwin's Gardens.

Ely House was large, boasting a great hall lying east to west between other chambers, with the chapel just north west of it. The site of the house is today covered by Ely Place, though the chapel, now the Roman Catholic church of St Etheldreda, survives. The house was further enlarged by Thomas Arundel, Bishop of Ely from 1373. John Stow, in the 16th century, remarked: 'he did not only repaire, but rather new builded, and augmented it with a large Port, gate house, or front towards the streete or highway: his arms are yet to be discerned in the stone worke thereof.' After Arundel's improvements the building was much larger than a Bishop of Ely could possibly require as a London house, but it was desirable enough for John of Gaunt to occupy in 1381, when his own house – the Savoy Palace in the Strand – was sacked by rioters during the Peasants' Revolt, and in subsequent years the bishops let out parts of the premises to nobility. The gardens had a good reputation and – reshaping a conversation between Richard III and Bishop Morton of Ely, recounted by Hollingshead – Shakespeare had Richard say:

> 'My lord of Ely, when I was last in Holborn
> I saw good strawberries in your garden
>   there.'

In 1531 the house was the scene of a five-day banquet, attended by Henry VIII and Catherine of Aragon, which marked the installation of eleven new serjeants-at-law. It is said that in this series of meals 51 cows, 100 sheep, 91 pigs, 24 oxen, 720 chickens, 444 pigeons, 168 swans and over 4,000 larks were consumed.

Such a house attracted covetous eyes. Both the Earl of Warwick and Thomas Wriothesley, Henry VIII's Chancellor tried to acquire a part of it against resolute opposition from the then Bishop of Ely. But he could not withstand the pressure of Elizabeth I, whose favourite, Christopher Hatton, was given a lease on the gatehouse and most of the front courtyard, together with gardens and orchards. This was in 1576 but by 1578 Hatton had used his royal favour to such effect that he had built his own house to the west of Ely House and was pressing for a freehold interest.

Hatton died in 1591 and Hatton House descended to his nephew's wife, who vigorously resisted the efforts of the bishopric to obtain possession. In 1659, encouraged by property developments in Covent Garden and Bloomsbury, the owners of Hatton House demolished it and streets were formed on the Hatton part of the estate. These included the road Hatton Garden; by the time of the Great Fire, which the area escaped, other parts of the estate were developed.[5]

9. The Hall of Ely House, as depicted in 1772, shortly before demolition.

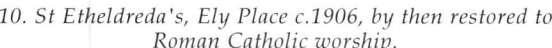

10. St Etheldreda's, Ely Place c.1906, by then restored to Roman Catholic worship.

Ely House survived much longer than the intruder, Hatton House, for it was not until 1772 that the bishopric sold the property, after which the house and its hall were demolished. The site was developed *c.*1778 by Charles Cole, who built the double row of houses known as Ely Place, separated from Holborn as today by an iron gate and lodge, and until modern times restricted to people with legitimate business there. Cole was not permitted to demolish the chapel, which was used by the inhabitants of this exclusive enclave. This was later occupied by the National Society for Promoting the Education of the Poor, and leased to the Welsh Episcopalians in 1844 until its return to Roman Catholic ownership in 1874. St Etheldreda's shares, with part of Westminster Abbey, the distinction of being the only surviving London building erected in the reign of Edward I (1272-1307).[6]

A reminder of the separation of the Hatton and Ely estates is the passageway, Old Mitre Court, which links Hatton Garden and Ely Place. Here, the Mitre was built in the 18th century on the site of a tavern allegedly erected in 1546 by Bishop Goodrich for palace staff. A stone mitre, painted bright blue, which may have come from the old Ely gatehouse, adorns the present building.

11. Ely Place with its lodge, in the 1930s.

Lepers in the Fields

Leprosy was a scourge of the Middle Ages and recognised as sufficiently contagious for its victims to be ostracised and isolated.[7] As we have seen earlier, the parish of St Giles-in-the-Fields derives its name from a 12th-century leper hospital founded in the same period as the leper hospital of St James, Westminster – St James's Palace is on the site of that. Others, in Mile End, Kingsland Road, Hackney and Tabard Street, Southwark, were established in the 13th century. There was, perhaps, a resurgence of the disease in the 15th century, for two new leper hospitals were founded near London, one at Highgate (1473) on the western lower slope of Highgate Hill (now covered by the Whittington Hospital), and one at Knightsbridge (1475).

The St Giles Hospital was established by Queen Matilda (1080-1118), consort of Henry I, probably in the last year of her life. Using rent income from Queenhithe, the quay she owned in the City, she granted sixty shillings annually for the maintenance of a hospital large enough to house fourteen lepers. The hospital was built, together with a chapel, in open fields well away from the City, in that triangle of land today delineated by St Giles High Street, Shaftesbury Avenue and Charing Cross Road, with a gatehouse in the High Street. The administration of the hospital was placed in the hands of the City of London.

The annual gift of £3 was not enough to sustain the hospital, but it was supplemented by alms from passers-by, and by other gifts. In 1346 Edward II granted the hospital a toll for two years on 'the road from St Giles to Temple Bar' – possibly Drury Lane.[8] Henry II and Edward III

added to the hospital's landholdings so that by the time it was closed in the 16th century, it owned a good deal of what had become the parish of St Giles-in-the-Fields. In 1299 the Crown had granted it, for reasons of economy it seems, to the Hospital of Burton Lazars in Leicestershire and under its jurisdiction St Giles mostly remained until 1536 when the Burton Hospital was obliged by Henry VIII to hand over to him the property of St Giles in exchange for some less valuable estates in Leicestershire. At that time, St Giles also held the manors of Feltham and Heston in Middlesex.[9] Three years later the Burton Hospital itself was dissolved and its estates taken by the Crown anyway. By this time leprosy was a rare disease, though St Bartholomew's had some cases in the 1550s which it farmed out to the leper hospitals at Highgate, Hackney and Mile End.

After the Dissolution, the St Giles property was divided between Lord Lisle and Katherine Legh and the hospital, by then probably housing infectious but not necessarily leprous inmates, closed. It is probable that the hospital chapel had also, with appropriate division, been used for a parish church, but there is no record of any clergyman being presented to the living there until 1547.[10]

[1] W.H. St John Hope, *Archaeologia*, Vol LXI.

[2] *Survey of London*, Vol. III, St Giles in the Fields pt I, p.10

[3] In the judgement of George Gilbert Scott, the chapel was built 1290-99. Quoted in *A History of Ely Place* by Stephen Eyre Jarvis, p.4 (4th edition, 1907).

[4] *ibid* p.4

[5] Much detail about the Hatton estate is given in 'The Survey of Hatton Garden in 1694 by Abraham Arlidge' by Penelope Hunting *in London Topographical Record*, Vol XXV (1985).

[6] Paper by Charles Lee, *St Etheldreda's Church and Ely Place*, prepared for the visit there of the Camden History Society in 1974.

[7] For a survey of London's leper hospitals see Marjorie Honeybourne, *Transactions of the London & Middlesex Archaeological Society*, Vol 21, pt 3.

[8] Recounted in *Notes and Queries* 1853, Vol. 1, p.223

[9] *Survey of London*, Vol. V, St Giles-in-the-Fields pt II, p.123.

[10] *Ibid*, p.127

CHAPTER THREE
Villages in Middlesex

Early St Pancras

The parish of St Pancras contained three villages during the medieval period. One, sparsely populated, was by the old parish church in what is today Pancras Road. A second was at Kentish Town and the third in Highgate, or at least that part of Highgate included in St Pancras parish on the south side of the High Street. By the 18th century there are frequent references in the parish registers to residents at St Giles' Town End – near the junction of Tottenham Court Road and Oxford Street – and others in the area of the Pindar of Wakefield public house in Gray's Inn Road. The construction of the New Road (today's Euston Road) in the 1750s encouraged development on both sides of it.

As we shall see (*p.36*), the old parish church in Pancras Road was neglected as from the 13th century when a chapel-of-ease was built in Kentish Town – even the vicar had moved northwards soon after 1250[1]. The likely reason

for this decampment was the inundations of the river Fleet. Silted up over the centuries, the river frequently burst its banks after heavy rains, and at Pancras Wash – an area by the church – it flooded the road and surrounding land, making it unpleasant or impossible for residents to get to church services. Given anyway that the larger part of the parish population lived in Kentish Town, where fresh water supplies and soil quality were better, the construction of an alternative place of worship there was inevitable. But despite the convenience of the new chapel at Kentish Town, the old St Pancras building remained the parish church.

The existence of two churches and therefore two centres of social influence possibly affected the siting of the two nearest manor houses. Instead of being located near to the parish church as was usually the case, that for St Pancras manor was as far away from the church as it could be within its own manor – to the east of St Pancras

12. The junction of today's Royal College Street and Kentish Town Road, looking south. The apex of the two roads was demolished in the 19th century for road widening and Dunn's warehouse was built on the site. The Castle Inn is on the right.

13. The Assembly House, at the junction of Kentish Town Road and Leighton Road, is one of the oldest established pubs in Kentish Town. This view of it was probably drawn in c.1750, when it was temporarily named The Flask.

Way, roughly where Camden Garden Centre is today in Barker Drive. And that for Cantelowes was almost opposite.[2] These houses were, therefore, conveniently half-way between the old church and the lure of the village of Kentish Town. The Tottenhall manor house (*see ill. 4*) was at the junction of today's Tottenham Court Road and Euston Road, where the Prudential office block now stands.

In medieval and later documents, the names St Pancras and Kentish Town are often interchangeable. This has caused many problems in locating early properties, one of which is the house owned by William Bruges (1375?-1450), the first Garter King of Arms. Bruges, whose function was the administration and granting of coats of arms in an age when they were of great significance, had spent some years in the service of the Crown, and in 1416 was responsible for entertaining Emperor Sigismund at his house in Kentish Town. It was no small occasion, for the guests also included the Lord Mayor, representatives from London's livery companies, officers-at-arms, esquires and knights, the Bishop of Ely – no doubt staying at the time at his Holborn house – the Prince of Hungary and the dukes of Briga and Holland. Bruges knelt bareheaded to receive this cavalcade and escorted it to his house where minstrels and sackbuts diverted them.

The food consumed included nine pigs, seven sheep, one hundred pullets, one hundred pigeons, thirty capons and twenty hens, hares, rabbits, kids, salmon, eels, crabs, oysters, wild boars and red deer. If they stayed the night – and such a feast would have rendered them reluctant to ride back to London – Bruges' house probably sheltered the titled, while the rest slept in the open. The location of the house is not clear – it could have been on St Pancras Way, or just south of today's Kentish Town underground station.[3]

Dr William Stukeley, an 18th-century clergyman and noted archaeologist, who had a rectorship at St George the Martyr, Queen Square and a house in Kentish Town Road, claimed that the St Pancras church area had been the location of a Roman encampment. To the south-west of the church was an area once commonly called The Brill – from a local farmhouse. Stukeley thought, wrongly, that this name derived from a Roman military station. Further south, it was long purported that Battle Bridge, the old name for King's Cross, marked the spot where Boudicca lost a major battle against the Romans. There is no documentary evidence for this and in any case the earlier, and more mundane, name for Battle Bridge was Bradford Bridge. Queen Boudicca features in another Camden legend –

14. *A drawing by William Stukeley of the Parliament Hill tumulus, 1725.*

that she was buried beneath the tumulus at Parliament Hill. This was always an unlikely suggestion, for why would she be buried so far from her own Iceni tribe territory? A thorough excavation in 1894 revealed no traces of either burial or burial goods.[4]

The southern entrance to Kentish Town was the junction of today's Royal College Street and Kentish Town Road (*ill. 12*), where roads from the City and Westminster met. Here, the Castle Inn (now called The Verge) was the landmark. The village of cottages, farmhouses, barns, houses and pubs straggled northwards up the main road. By the 1450s, the chapel-of-ease had been re-erected on the west side of the road, where the Owl Bookshop now stands. In the 16th century a prominent farmhouse stood where Caversham Road joins the main street (*see ill. 82*). There are a number of prints of this building, which was not demolished until the 19th century, as well as detailed drawings of some of its interior rooms.[5] Before Junction Road was constructed *c.*1814 to link Kentish Town to the new Archway Road, the village was an unremarkable last watering and drinking place before the long climb to Highgate Village. Alternatively, northbound travellers could use the older road that lay on the parish boundary between St Pancras and Islington, a route today marked by York Way, Brecknock Road and Dartmouth Park Hill. Whichever route was chosen, it would be tedious for man and beast in wintertime, and the inns of Kentish Town and Highgate were welcome stopping places.

Early medieval travellers would have continued along the route of Hornsey Lane and on to Crouch End, but at the end of the 13th century the Bishop of London, who owned much of the parish of Hornsey, cut a toll road (North Road-

North Hill) from what is now the Gatehouse in Highgate Village as an alternative.

People bought provisions from local inns or direct from farmers who might also be butchers. Only one (unnamed) public house in Kentish Town is noted in the Sessions Rolls during the time of Edward VI and that was in 'Grene Street' (Highgate Road), but there were undoubtedly others. When the Castle was rebuilt in 1849 a Tudor fireplace was discovered; in a survey of Cantelowes manor in 1599 mention is made of The Bull, an earlier name for the Assembly House; and in a panoramic drawing of Kentish Town made in the early 19th century, the artist depicts the White Lion and Bell, which is certainly 16th century or even earlier.[6]

On Highgate Road were farmhouses, notably that bequeathed to St John's College, Cambridge in 1637. This was on the site of Denyer House, just north of the railway bridge. Along the east side of Highgate Road was waste land, used by landless tenants of the manor. This was gradually enclosed so that by the end of the 18th century very little remained in common use. That waste land can be envisaged today between

15. *A gate to the Bishop of London's new north road, constructed in the 13th century, was transformed over the years into an inn called The Gatehouse. The old building was taken down in 1769.*

Highgate Road and the narrow back way called College Lane, originally a footpath at the side of the waste. This path continued in front of today's Grove Terrace and then veered off at the Bull and Last pub across the fields to Highgate. Crossing and recrossing Highgate Road was the Fleet river (*see pp.27-28*).

The village green was opposite today's Grove Terrace – remnants of it survive in front of the Edwardian mansion blocks. The original size of this is not known, but it probably extended back to the field which contains the present public swimming pool.[7] The location of the green, *north* of the village, suggests that Kentish Town was very early the principal settlement of the parish – there is no record of a green near St Pancras Old Church.

The Cantelowes manor court rolls, which date back to the 15th century, provide evidence of a substantial village at Highgate. We know about a property in 1480 called 'le Swan', probably an inn near the Angel, and another called 'le Cornerhows' on the site of the Angel, its name suggesting the existence of South Grove. In the 1380s Crouch End is described as being 'juxta Highgate', implying that Highgate was a signifi-

cant settlement. The village green and its ponds, now covered by Pond Square, are referred to many times in the court rolls.

No large house in the St Pancras part of Highgate is referred to until 1536 when a 'capital messuage' on the site of Fairseat (backing on to Waterlow Park and now used by Channing School) became the property of Sir Roger Cholmeley, the future founder of Highgate School. The forerunner of nearby Lauderdale House was built *c.*1582. By 1553 there were five licensed inns in Highgate Village, an abundance reflecting not a large local population, but the passage through Highgate of many drovers persuading their herds and flocks to Smithfield.

The Kenwood estate may be traced back to 1226, when it was owned by William de Blemont, of the family which gave its name to Bloomsbury. Held by the Convent of the Holy Trinity in Aldgate until the Dissolution, it was then disposed of by the Crown. In 1616 John Bill, the King's printer, bought the land and built a house here, traces of which may still be found in the basement of the present Kenwood House.

16. *Dr Coysh's house in Swains Lane in the mid-18th century. Dr Coysh, of Dutch nationality, was well-known for his treatment of plague victims.*

Hampstead

'The story of Hampstead's development ... is dominated by three recurring aspirations – its hill, its heath and its healthiness.'[8] The geological upheavals which created the hill also ensured that the soil on the Heath, largely sand and gravel, was unsuitable for agriculture but good for grazing cattle. Hampstead's reputation for healthiness was demonstrated in 1349 when the Abbot of Westminster retired here to escape the Black Death, and in the 16th century John Norden commented on the good quality of air. Such a reputation had its drawbacks – at plague times citizens of London and Westminster fled north to Hampstead's heights and there died in hundreds, bringing contagion to the local population. In the 1603 plague – so serious that it delayed the coronation of James I – Sir William Waad of Belsize wrote of people from town dying under hedges, and in the Great Plague there were 260 deaths in Hampstead where there were only 100 houses. The rush to elevated places was fortuitous for the little village of West End, which is on low land: this had no deaths at all in its thirty or forty houses.[9] Defoe was of the opinion that Highgate escaped the Great Plague, where a Dr Coysh, who lived in Swains Lane, tended a number of victims free of charge, and this is supported by the fact that interments in the burial ground of Highgate Chapel were of normal numbers that year.

The Heath was common land, encroached upon only when the lord of the manor and his copyhold tenants colluded. But when Hampstead expanded from the beginning of the 18th century with the popularity of Hampstead Wells, it was from the common that the New End of Hampstead was carved, changing Hampstead from a village to a town. The earlier village had a different aspect. In 1653 local residents asked the Parliamentary Commissioners responsible for taxation, 'to remember [the] poverty of the place. Many are poore labouring men on wages at the Tyle-kilns and other places, and their wives washing clothes for London. Divers houses are occupied by citizens of London, who pay there.'[10] This plea suggests that the use of Hampstead for holiday rents had already begun.

Hampstead was centred originally around Frognal – a place name whose derivation is still not certain – and the early manor house was at the junction of Frognal and Frognal Lane. The 1664 Hearth Tax return lists 161 houses in Hampstead, of which twelve had ten hearths and

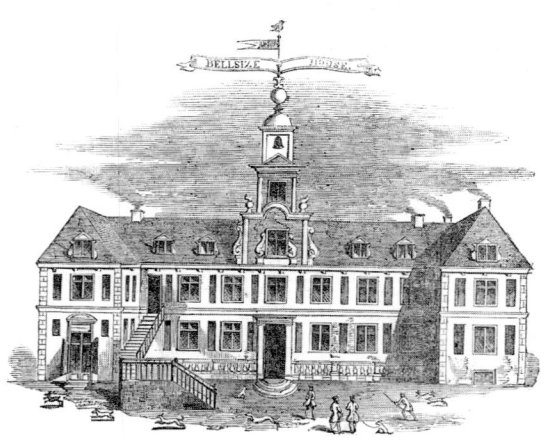

17. Belsize House, c.1721.

18. Fenton House in 1911, drawn by A.R. Quinton.

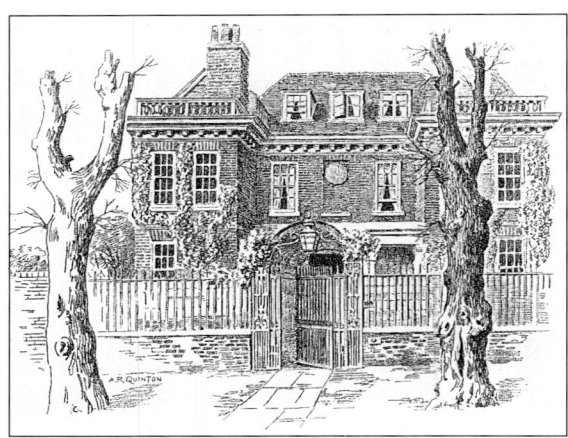

over, the largest having 24. Ten years later the return shows 225 houses.

The first Belsize House (from the French *bel assis* – beautifully situated) is referred to in 1317 when the Lord Chief Justice, Sir Roger le Brabazon, left his house and 57 acres to Westminster Abbey. The Abbey muniments of 1496 reveal the production of 400,000 bricks at Belsize – a Brick Field on the estate is still shown on 18th-century maps. But as Professor Thompson points out,[11] it would seem unlikely that the Abbey used those bricks in central London since the inconvenience and labour of carrying them there from the heights of Hampstead would have made them too expensive. More likely, they were used to rebuild the mansion and there was, in fact,

19. South End Green and Pond Street in 1828.

a large house in existence there by 1550. Elizabeth I visited it in 1593, when the occupant was her Chief Clerk of the Privy Council, Sir William Waad. In the 17th century Pepys praised the gardens and their 'brave orange and lemon trees', but Evelyn found them ill kept.

The house, on the north-east of today's Belsize Square, was reputedly rebuilt in 1663 by Colonel Daniel O'Neill, a man made rich by a gratefully restored King Charles II. It was assessed for only 7 hearths in 1664, so presumably rebuilding was still under way. Ten years later the house is assessed for 36 hearths, by far the largest number in Hampstead.

On the east side of Rosslyn Hill stood the oddly-named Chicken House. We have a precise date when this house was visited by James I and his favourite, the Duke of Buckingham, because a sketch exists which depicts a stained glass window, now lost, which was inserted in the house and inscribed to mark the date of the occasion – 25 August 1619. Originally, the house was probably a hunting lodge, but later became a tavern whose lodgers included the future Lord Chief Justice, Earl Mansfield. Almost opposite, on the west side of the High Street, was Vane

House, probably built in the middle of the 17th century. It is associated with Sir Henry Vane, a zealous Puritan of the Civil War period, but who paid for it with his head upon the Restoration. 'He is too dangerous a man to let live' said Charles II, and despatched soldiers in July 1660 to bring Vane into custody. But it was not until 1662 that he was charged with treason and brought to execution at Tower Hill, an event witnessed by Pepys. It is not certain that Vane House was his home or if instead he lived in a property just slightly to the north, called Slyes.[12] This latter house was large enough to be split into four separate residences early the next century.

Vane was not the only man to be prised from his Hampstead home to retribution at the Restoration. Colonel John Downes, who occupied Belsize House during the Interregnum, had been one of those who had sat in judgement on Charles I and was a signatory of the king's death warrant. That could hardly be overlooked at the Restoration and in June 1660 he was taken to prison. At his subsequent trial he denied supporting the execution of Charles I, asserting that he was intimidated into signing the warrant. He was

20. Remains of Kilburn Priory in 1750.

sentenced to death, but eventually allowed to serve the rest of his life in the Tower prison.

Other large houses of the 17th century included Holly Hill House, on the site of today's junior University College School: its door and staircase were incorporated into the present school building. Off Frognal, on the site of a tennis court that recently belonged to the Medical Research Council, was a building which became the parish poorhouse in 1729. This, according to Barratt, was used by actors for summer holidays. A 1693 addition was what became Fenton House – the oldest surviving mansion in Hampstead. Originally called Ostend (or East End) House, it was owned by Joshua Gee in the 18th century – his initials appear in the gate leading on to Holly Bush Hill. It was given its present name when it was bought by a Riga merchant, Philip Fenton, in 1793. (The house is now owned by the National Trust.) Other survivors from that period are the house called Cloth Hill on The Mount, erected in 1694, and Burgh House in New End Square, built in 1703.

Hampstead village today surrounds a busy crossroads by the Underground station, but until the later 19th century no road on the line of Fitzjohns Avenue existed. Heath Street terminated to the west of the High Street in a squalid arrangement of courts until Church Row was encountered. Most through traffic went north up Holly Hill to Childs Hill and thence to Hendon. The parish church of St John (dedicated to St Mary until the rebuilding of 1747) was thus at the western extremity of the village.

Other Hampstead settlements were at Pond Street (mentioned in 1607), Kilburn and West End. By the first decade of the 18th century there were about 24 houses around Pond Street, though some were of the 17th century. The pond was where the buses now turn round; it became a rather unsavoury feature and was filled in 1835 when a public green took its place.

Kilburn, on both sides of Kilburn High Road (and therefore partly in the parish of Willesden) grew up around the old Kilburn Priory. The Priory and its 224 acres, under the auspices of Westminster Abbey, succeeded a hermitage on the site. It was not an affluent convent as an inventory of 1535 showed. Attached to it was a *hostium*, used by travellers and in particular by pilgrims on the road to Edgware (Watling Street) journeying to the shrine at St Albans. This ecclesiastical lodging house is thought to be the forerunner of the inn on the site, the Red Lion.

The village of West End was isolated from the main Hampstead Village by virtue of the considerable hill to climb and the lack of a good road. It was near enough, however, for the church bells of Hampstead parish church to be heard.

[1] Charles Lee, *St Pancras Church and Parish*, pp.14-16 (1955).

[2] John Richardson, *Kentish Town Past*, pp.20-23 (1997).

[3] *ibid*, pp.23-26

[4] See report on excavation in *Middlesex and Hertfordshire Notes and Queries*, January 1895.

[5] Heal Collection in the Local Studies Centre, Holborn Library.

[6] See *Kentish Town Panorama* by James F. King, facsimile edition by the London Topographical Society (1986)

[7] The Tottenhall Court Rolls, dating from the 14th century, are at present being transcribed under the auspices of the Camden History Society; these may provide some information about the Green.

[8] Christopher Wade, *Hampstead Past*, p.8 (1989).

[9] Walter G. Bell, *The Great Plague in London 1665*, p.185 (rev. edn 1971)

[10] Parliamentary Assessment of landholders in Hampstead, 12 December 1653. BodleianLibrary MS, Rawlinson D715 (8), reprinted in Thomas Barratt, *Annals of Hampstead*, vol. 3, p.363 (1912).

[11] F.M.L. Thompson, *Hampstead: Building a Borough 1650-1964*, p. 8 (1974).

[12] *Victoria History of the County of Middlesex*, Vol IX, p.16 (1989)

CHAPTER FOUR
Water, Everywhere

Rivers and wells have featured large in the history of several parts of Camden. This is certainly the case in Hampstead, in which three rivers rise and where the sale of medicinal waters from about 1700 encouraged the expansion of the town and a subsequent influx of affluent residents.

The Rivers

West to east, the rivers are the Westbourne, Tyburn and the Fleet. Numerous tributaries converged near the old Kilburn Priory to form the Westbourne where it then crossed Maida Vale and traversed Paddington – Eastbourne and Westbourne Terraces mark the banks. The stream that gave Kilburn its name was part of the Westbourne river: early spellings include *Cuneburna* or *Kyneburna*, meaning either 'royal stream' or 'cows' stream', though an alternative interpretation is 'cold stream'. The Westbourne was once harnessed to form the Serpentine lake in Hyde Park, and it then disgorged into the Thames east of the Royal Hospital, Chelsea.

The Tyburn rose at the corner of Fitzjohns Avenue and Akenside Road, where a plaque today records the existence of Shepherds Well – Spring Path and Shepherds Path are reminders of this well, an important source of fresh water for Hampstead. The river was joined by a tributary rising on the Belsize estate, just west of Haverstock Hill. The two streams merged in St John's Wood, and further south the river was used in the formation of Regent's Park lake before it went through Mayfair and beneath Buckingham Palace. At Westminster it divided into two arms, one of which also split into two around the Abbey and the Palace of Westminster, forming what was called Thorney Island, before flowing into the Thames.

The Fleet has left a large literature behind it, mainly because it flowed for much of its course through populous areas. The Hampstead source rose near the Vale of Health, and the main Highgate source is still visible today at Kenwood. From Hampstead it flowed along the line of Fleet Road and then through part of West Kentish Town; the Highgate stream was channelled

21. The Fleet river just south of Battle Bridge (King's Cross) in 1810

through Highgate Ponds, crossed Highgate Road by Swains Lane, and then recrossed at Burghley Road (where Bridge House recently stood) to join the Hampstead branch somewhere beneath the new commercial estate opposite Kentish Town station. It flowed almost to Camden Town but instead crossed beneath Kentish Town Road to St Pancras Way, past Old St Pancras Church to King's Cross, and along the line of Farringdon Road where it formed a boundary to Holborn. Finally, on the line of Farringdon Street, it went to Blackfriars.

In medieval times, the Fleet was navigable up to Holborn Bridge (where Holborn Viaduct now crosses). The Earl of Lincoln, petitioning in the reign of Edward I against a mill erected by the Templars on the bank of the Fleet, noted that at one time the river was of such breadth and depth that ten or twelve ships at once, with merchandise, often came to Fleet Bridge (Ludgate Circus), and some went to Holborn Bridge. Certainly the Fleet formed a substantial inlet at Blackfriars. This has led a number of authorities to derive the river's name from the word *fleot*, meaning tidal inlet or creek, for it was believed that the river was called Fleet only from Holborn Bridge southwards. However, a map of an area east of

Highgate Road *c*.1547, which depicts a piece of land given to charity, calls the stream 'Fleete'.[1] This appears to support the contention of John Ashton in 1888 that Fleet means a brook, or tributary to a larger river.[2]

Sometimes, the Fleet was called the River of Wells or Holebourne for much of its course. It is marked as the River of Wells in a map of Kentish Town for 1638, although in the Cantelowes Court Rolls it is always referred to as the 'ditch'. In Kentish Town it is remembered in Anglers Lane. An old resident, writing in 1909, remembers his boyhood days on the banks of the river at this point.

> '...it was one of the loveliest spots imaginable – so deserted in the early hours of the morning that, when the anglers were not there, some of the youngsters from the cottages around, and some who were not youngsters, used to bathe in the river.'

The river, was not always that idyllic. Any sewer worker will tell you that when there is a heavy fall of rain over Highgate and Hampstead, he exits the Fleet drainage system quickly. The force of the river is illustrated in the memoirs of Samuel Bagster.[3] In the 1780s, as a boy, he sometimes went to his uncle's tile works at King's Cross (then called Battle Bridge) to see the fires stoked up in the kilns. In winter homeless young people were often permitted to sleep overnight in the warmth generated by the kiln. But this warm lair was to be their misfortune, for the Fleet was suddenly inundated with rain: '... the flood rapidly filled the base in which they were reposing not conscious of danger and so suddenly and so high did it arise, they could not escape; it extinguished the burning mass above, scattering the red hot chimney pots and tiles in ruinous overthrow ... That night I was roused from my sleep by voices crying loudly for help, all I could make out was, "Two boys are drowned."'. In 1826 the Fleet at flood was 65ft wide where it crossed beneath Kentish Town Road roughly opposite today's car park entrance to Sainsbury's in Camden Town.[4] Here, incidentally, it ran *beneath* the Regent's Canal, a startling demonstration of how levels have changed over the centuries.

As we have seen the Fleet's inundations at Pancras Wash in the 13th century had probably caused the residents to build a chapel-of-ease away from the old parish church in Pancras Road. In 1317 a prolonged drought was broken by a phenomenal thunderstorm. The river flooded, causing serious damage to both Holborn and Fleet bridges. The areas most affected by any Fleet flooding were around King's Cross and in the low-lying pocket of land behind today's *Guardian* offices in Farringdon Road – a wretchedly poor and brutal part of London called Hockley-in-the-Hole. In 1809 the land between Old St Pancras Church and the slopes of Pentonville Hill was covered with water for a time, and there was a serious flood in 1818, when the water rose several feet overnight and swept southwards while people slept. Even when the river was restricted to an underground pipe it was strong enough to burst out. This happened in 1862 during the construction of the Metropolitan Railway at King's Cross, causing havoc there.

The current of the Fleet moved machinery. Turnmill Street, on the eastern side of Farringdon Station, is a reminder of when the Fleet at this point was called Turnmill Brook. We know that the Knights Hospitaller at St John's Gate, and the nuns at St Mary Clerkenwell, had mills on the river, but John Rocque's map of Farringdon in 1746 shows no mills surviving, though the Fleet is shown halfway between Turnmill Street and Saffron Hill, wending its way between malodorous alleys. Probably such mills as existed by the time of Rocque's survey were small enterprises. In *the Daily Courant* in 1741 a property in Turnmill Street is advertised as having 'A good stream and current that will turn a mill to grind hairpowder or liquorish or other things', and in 1750 there was a snuff-mill still working further north up stream at Bagnigge Wells in King's Cross Road.[5]

Another name for the Farringdon stretch of the stream was the Holebourne, meaning a stream in a hollow. Where the Holborn Viaduct now crosses, the river lay very deep, and Holborn Bridge, which carried the main road out of Newgate, presented travellers with a sometimes perilous challenge. Most probably Holborn derived its name from this part of the river, though it is also suggested that it could have come from a tributary of the Fleet hereabouts called the Oldbourne.

Water Supplies

The springs, wells and rivers of north London were of great interest to the City of London whose fresh water supplies were inadequate to meet the needs of a growing population in the

16th century. Much of the City's water came from the Thames, but was extracted *below* the outfalls of the Fleet and Walbrook – rivers which had for centuries been used as sewers by City residents. John Stow's *Survey of London* (1598) observed that a number of traditionally used City wells were either stopped up or contaminated by then. The City also conveyed water from Paddington springs and the Tyburn, and tapped wells and springs in Highbury, Hackney, Hoxton and Bloomsbury. Other sources included Lamb's Conduit in Bloomsbury. A worn plaque in the wall of Rokeby House in Long Yard off Lamb's Conduit Street still records the ownership by the City of Lamb's Conduit, but does not mention the generosity of a wealthy member of the Clothworkers' Company, William Lambe, who in 1577 spent £1500 renovating a medieval conduit system. Lambe's conduit used water from a Fleet tributary near Guilford Street and from local springs; it was conveyed by lead pipes to a restored conduit house at Snow Hill, just by Holborn Bridge.

Inevitably, the City had to look further afield. In 1543/44 it obtained an Act to allow it to make use of 'dyvers great and plentyfull sprynges at Hampstede Hethe, Hakkney, Muswell Hill and dyvers places within fyve miles of the Citie'. In 1589 it made an effort to marshal the waters of Hampstead Heath by constructing Hampstead Ponds, but this seems to have been a failure. The City renewed its interest in water supply schemes when Edmund Colthurst proposed to supply London with water from springs in Middlesex and Hertfordshire. The City took over the scheme but did nothing to forward it, and Colthurst and his richer partner, Hugh Myddelton, were permitted to take the scheme back into their own hands. The result was the New River Company, which brought water from Amwell and Chadwell in Hertfordshire to a reservoir at Clerkenwell (Amwell Street) and from there by gravity to parts of the City. The grand opening was in 1613.

Though not initially a success, as London expanded so did the network of the New River Company – many of its pavement plates with the initials 'N.R.' may still be seen in Camden. The Company constructed reservoirs in The Grove, Highgate, in Hornsey Lane, Camden Park Road and on the site of Tolmers Square.

The New River made the exploitation of springs at Hampstead and Highgate superfluous for the time being, but in 1692 the City leased its right to develop them to William Paterson, a founder of the Bank of England. It is not known for certain when work commenced on the construction or enlargement of the Highgate Ponds (it is possible that at least one of them was a medieval fish pond), but there is a reference in the St Pancras parish register for 1698 which notes 'a poor labouring man at the Waterworks at Cane Wood'. And in 1703 there is a reference to Wat Daventry, 'the Hampstead Watermen's servant at the foot of Highgate Hill' (West Hill), who probably lived at Millfield Cottage which in later years is identified as housing the water company's officers. A sale notice of 1789 states that the leased land contained 'three spacious lakes … which supply Kentish Town and a great part of London'.

Using the water from springs and the tributary of the Fleet which rose at Kenwood, six reservoir ponds had been constructed by the end of the 18th century – these are today's Highgate Ponds, one of the glories of Parliament Hill Fields. The Hampstead Water Company, as Paterson's enterprise was called, was not an important source of water supply. In 1814 it still supplied houses at the southern end of Tottenham Court Road, but thereafter it reached no further than Camden Town, and in 1840 it supplied 4490 houses with an average daily distribution of 427,468 gallons.[6] The water was adequate for domestic use, but it was not particularly drinkable and the Company was probably relieved to be taken over by the New River Company in 1859 for a perpetual annual payment of £3,500. In 1934, water from the system was being used to flush the Metropolitan Cattle Market in York Way, and the last recorded use of the ponds for water supply was in 1936.[7]

Bagnigge Wells

Several medicinal wells in the St Pancras area were on the course of the Fleet. The best known was Bagnigge Wells west of today's King's Cross Road – the Fleet flowed through the grounds. On the basis of a pronouncement of Dr John Bevis that the waters in two wells here had chalybeate and purgative properties, the owner of the land, Thomas Hughes, opened them to the public in 1759. Dr Bevis also published a paper which mentioned that on a chimney piece in the main house the Royal Arms were carved and there was a bust of Nell Gwyn. Legend has since persisted that she lived there. Indeed, when the lease was reassigned in 1762, it was referred to as the 'copyhold House at Bagniggs called …

22. A Sunday 'Ordinary' at Bagnigge Wells in 1793.

Bagnigge Wells was popular (though never so fashionable as Hampstead Wells) until about 1800. Ornamental gardens were planted, music was played and tea was served. A rustic cottage and a grotto were provided for a public eager to enjoy bucolic pleasures in town, though genuine countryside then was not too far away. Three bridges spanned the Fleet, which meandered through the grounds, and there were seats on the banks for those who 'chuse to smoke, or drink cyder, ale, etc., which are not permitted in other parts of the garden.'

Popular or not, it had a quickly changing series of proprietors, suggesting that it did not make money, and by 1820 the land west of the river had been disposed of. The Fleet river became a dubious and malodorous asset and the house a cheap concert room for 'visitors of an inferior class'; in 1841 the last entertainment was held there. In a history of Islington published in 1842, the building was described as a ruin, and much of the grounds were taken by Cubitt for a building yard.

Chads Well and Pancras Wells

A narrow turning called Fifteen Foot Lane, east off the northern end of Gray's Inn Road, led to a lesser known medicinal well, St Chad's. The alleyway was a cul-de-sac, at the end of which lay the river Fleet as it turned south-east from King's Cross, and the entrance to a small establishment with the sign 'Health Restored and Preserved'. Visitors were charged 1 guinea a year, or 9s 6d quarterly, 4s 6d monthly and a single visit 6d, for a large glass of warm well water. These days, St Chad's Place, as the turning is now called, is over the complex of station and tracks of the Metropolitan Railway and it is tempting to think that the water which habitu-

23. St Chad's Well, probably early in the 19th century.

Nell Gwins' etc. In 1779, ladies and gentlemen could 'enjoy the benefit and pleasure of drinking these waters for threepence each morning, or be entitled to drink either of the purgative or chalybeate waters at their pleasure, during the whole season, upon subscribing 10s 6d. ' As late as 1885 the 'springs and purging chalybeate and other mineral waters and a pump room' are noted in a mortgage of the property described in the Cantelowes Court Rolls. The only evidence of Bagnigge Wells today is a stone in the wall of today's 61 King's Cross Road, a later building, on which is inscribed: S T THIS IS BAGNIGGE HOVSE NEARE THE PINDER A WAKEFEILDE 1680. The stone has been recut, and the 'S T' is probably a mistake for 'S P' meaning St Pancras. The Pindar of Wakefield was a well known inn which originally stood nearby on the west side of Gray's Inn Road. It was badly damaged in a thunderstorm in 1723, in which the daughters of the publican perished, and was subsequently rebuilt on the east side of the street. The successor to that still stands at no. 328 but is now called The Water Rats after the entertainment charity which owns it.

ally drips on to the eastbound platform is from the well.

St Chad's flourished at the same time as Bagnigge – in 1772 it advertised that 1000 persons a week visited it. These would have included the pupils of Gordon House Academy in Highgate Road, whose headmaster from 1788, Andrew Mensal, marched them down to the Well once a week in the hope of saving on doctor's bills.[8] Other devotees were the surgeon, John Abernethy, who lived in Frognal, and a well-known comedian of the time, Joseph Munden, who lived in Croft Lodge, a house now part of La Sainte Union Convent in Highgate Road. A new pump room was built in 1832, but the establishment declined as belief in medicinal waters waned; in 1841, when William Hone published his *Everyday Book*, he noted that it had ceased to be frequented, except by a few 'locals' and 'old cronies'. In 1860 it went altogether as construction of the Metropolitan Railway began.

Pancras Wells was an earlier establishment, trading from about the beginning of the 18th century. They were located south of Old St Pancras Church, a site occupied today by the railway bridges emanating from St Pancras station and the gasholders of the old Imperial Gas

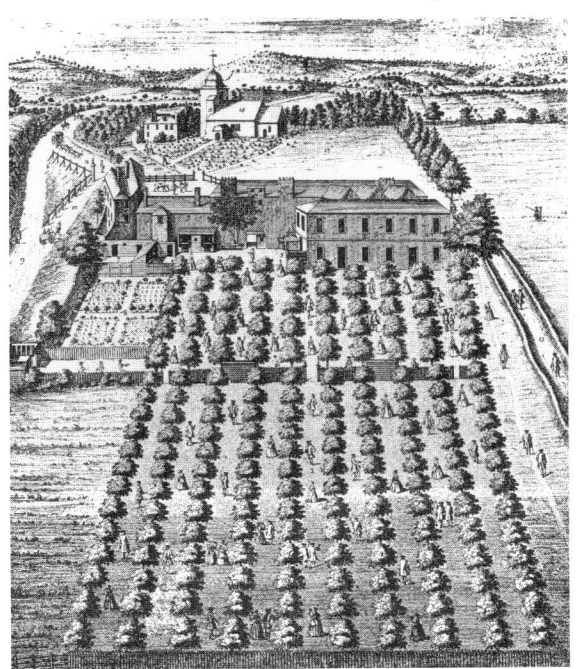

24. *St Pancras Wells, laid out with trees in 1730. Old St Pancras Church is in the background.*

Company. In 1697 a handbill extolled the virtues of the waters, which were 'a powerful antidote against rising of the vapours, also against the stone and gravel'. In 1722 the proprietor admitted that some of the patrons were not respectable and promised to do better, and in 1730 they had recovered their reputation. A print of that year shows that the grounds had been considerably enlarged, with a boringly landscaped plantation of trees, but they did have an almost uninterrupted view of Hampstead and Highgate. Other attractions included a Long Room and two pump rooms, plus a house of entertainment – an obligatory addition at these establishments, and as with Hampstead Wells, bottles of the water were sold in central London. But by about 1795, the Pancras Wells had closed.

Hampstead Wells

The best-known and most fashionable wells in the London area were those at Hampstead. They were among the first generation of London wells – at the time of their early exploitation those belonging to Thomas Sadler, near Islington, were also popular with Londoners.

In December 1698 the lord of the manor of Hampstead, the 13-year-old Earl of Gainsborough, granted through his mother six acres of land including 'the wells lately made there for medicinal waters' to the poor of Hampstead. The estate, partly swamp, sloped steeply down from what is now Well Road, and included a medicinal well whose qualities were already well-known. From this rather unpromising gift developed a charity which recently celebrated its 300th birthday. It also helped to transform Hampstead from a village to a town.

In the 1650s the well rivalled as a curiosity the Hollow Elm, a large tree near what used to be called the George Inn on Haverstock Hill. Into this had been cut a spiral staircase of 42 steps which led to a viewing platform upon which a school for 'twelve young gentlemen' gathered on occasions.[9]

Hampstead waters were endorsed by Dr William Gibbons of Burgh House who had, of course, a professional interest in rich people flocking to Hampstead. They were, he proclaimed, 'full as efficacious in all cases where ferruginous waters are advised'. In other words, they had plenty of iron: the rump of a fountain on the path that extends to Kenwood from Millfield Lane, raised in memory of Henry Goodison who had a role in the saving of Kenwood

25. The first Long Room of Hampstead Wells, in Well Walk, 1879. From a watercolour by J.P. Emslie.
Nowadays, Gainsborough Gardens occupies the gardens to the rear.

fields, is stained orange from similar water.

The Hampstead Wells Charity had the responsibility of exploiting the water and the adjacent acres for the benefit of the poor. But as a recently published book on the charity points out, the Trustees were of that class of society who were too busy for such menial duties.[10] They were able to note in their minutes of 1700 that bottles of the water were sold in Fleet Street, though this does not seem to have been profitable. Water for this operation was taken from the head spring which George Potter, writing in 1904, described as a rectangular pond, 'about 40 feet long by 20 feet wide, and rather deep'.

The spa, as it became, owed its celebrity to John Duffield. He was granted a lease on the land (though not of the well itself) and proceeded to build the first Long Room in Well Walk, opposite the present drinking fountain. The water was conveyed from the spring and across Well Walk to Duffield's building, where it was drunk in the Pump Room section. Visitors could then recover from this in the adjoining Assembly Room in which food, concerts, gambling and other enter-

tainments were provided. The site of that building is now marked by a plaque on a house adjacent to Gainsborough Gardens, a housing development which forms part of the old grounds of the Long Room.

The spa was celebrated in prints and plays, and occasionally associated with Mother Huff's, a teahouse near the Spaniards Inn with gardens and a fortune-telling service. The poor, who must have expected some windfall from all this were, however, disappointed for in the first thirty years the Trustees neglected to collect any rent from the proprietors.[11] *The Postman* newspaper in 1707 advertised that there would be 'very good musick for dancing all day long...and there is all needful accommodation for water-drinkers of both sexes, and all other entertainments for good eating and drinking ...with convenience of coach horses, and very good stables for fine horses with good attendance...'. Nearby was a new tavern, some booths and the newly-established Sion Chapel in which marriages could be performed discreetly: 'five shillings only is required for all the Church fees for any couple that are married there – provided they bring with them a licence or certificate according to the Act of Parliament'. A clergyman was always available and, indeed, if the couple had their wedding dinner at the nearby tavern, then no fee for the marriage was charged. And at Drury Lane in 1705 a comedy called *Hampstead Heath* by Thomas Baker highlighted 'Hampstead's variety of diversions'. A lady extols the place: 'To dance all night at the Wells; be treated at Mother Huff's, have presents made one at the raffling shops, and then take a walk in Cane Wood with a man of wit that's not over rude.'

The heyday was a short one, for the crowds attracted, inevitably, bad company. A travel writer in 1714 observed that Hampstead 'brought so many loose women in vampt up old cloathes to catch the City Apprentices that modest Company are ashamed to appear here even with their relations.'[12] Things became so bad that an armed guard was formed in 1718 to accompany visitors back to London. It is not clear when the Long Room closed, but in 1725 it was converted into a chapel by Joseph Rous to the advantage of New End residents who didn't care for the journey to the crowded Hampstead parish church in Church Row. The descendants of this congregation in Well Walk went on to build Christ Church in 1852; the chapel was then taken by Presbyterians and later on it became a Drill Hall. It was demolished in 1882.

Meanwhile a new Long Room opened its doors. Alexander Pope, in a letter written in 1734 about a visit to his Hampstead friend, Dr Arbuthnot, says: 'I spent a whole day in Hampstead. He was in the Long Room half the morning and has parties at cards every night.' The new Long Room, about a hundred yards to the west, and on the other side of the road near Burgh House, also had a ballroom attached, and it was this version of Hampstead Wells that was visited by Dr Johnson, Fanny Burney and Mrs Thrale. It appears, however, to have been less reliant on the properties of the water. Supplies of this could be had in a room beneath the Wells Tavern, but the main attractions were the increasingly sophisticated offerings of the Long Room, which are described in Fanny Burney's novel, *Evelina*.

But fashion waned and the new Long Room was converted to a private residence in 1803 and the ballroom to several houses. These were damaged in the last war and despite protests were demolished in 1948. The Council development, Wells House, is on the site.

Belsize House

Hampstead Wells had a rival, albeit without the attraction of medicinal water, from 1700. About that year, Charles Povey, a retired coal-merchant and inveterate inventor, became a sub-tenant of Belsize House. He opened the house and gardens to the public and, in addition, provided yet another Sion quick-marriage chapel. In 1720 he sub-let his tenancy to a Welshman called Howell, who with great flair and style vulgarised the place. It began well enough and was endorsed by a visit of the Prince of Wales in 1721. Howell proclaimed in 1723: 'Bellsize House is open every day... with a good concert of Musick in the Long Gallery during the whole season. The Proprietor is now provided with a Pack of good staunch Hounds, and a Huntsman, ready to show the Diversion of Hunting whenever the company pleases; the Walks in the Garden and Parks are made very pleasant, where Gentlemen and Ladies have frequent Egress and Regress to Walk without any Expense. Any company that stays late,' he added, 'there are Servants with Fire-Arms to see them safe to London.'[13] In addition, there was a small race-course on which both horses and footmen were raced to the encouragement of keen gamblers.

The facility for frequent walks in the gardens led to a bad reputation and a falling off of respectable popularity. A satirist as early as 1722 makes plain the problem:

> 'The scandalous lewd house that's called Belsize,
> Where sharpers lurk, yet Vice in publick lies,
> Is publicly become a Rendezvous,
> Of Strumpets, common as in common Stews...'

Kilburn Well

Not to be outdone, in 1714 a speculator began to exploit the mildly chalybeate spring at Kilburn, by the Bell inn – the site today is marked by a plaque on 42 Kilburn High Road. The landlord of the Bell sold flasks of water and a tea house was set up. It was more sedate, but no longer lasting than Hampstead Wells. In 1733 an advertisement claimed that: 'The Whole is now opened for the reception of the public, the great room being particularly adapted to the use and amusement of the politest companies, fit for music, dancing or entertainments.'

26. Shepherds Well, at the junction of today's Fitzjohns Avenue and Akenside Road. Published in Hone's Table Book, 1827.

Water Carriers

If the provision of medicinal water went in and out of fashion, the supply of fresh water for drinking and washing clothes and people was a constant preoccupation. Just as in the City of London, where the poor made a living carrying pails of water from the public conduits and wells to the more affluent in their houses, so there were local water carriers. Notable among these was Jack Foster who lived in a hovel of a cottage in Townsend's Yard, the little turning off Highgate High Street leading to the Garden Centre. According to the 1851 census Foster, who died in 1865 aged 79, shared the tiny house with his wife, son, two grand-daughters and a female servant. In Hampstead a number of men and women earned their living carrying water from Shepherd's Well, at the junction of today's Fitzjohns Avenue and Akenside Road – a fountain until recent years stood near the site. This well was the only one in Hampstead which provided soft water in any quantity, without the taste of iron common to many local springs. 'Among the carriers was a harmless and good-natured idiot called Jack Rough. A well-built man, he walked around swinging his buckets in time with a ditty he was crooning; this acted as a street cry. The last of the Hampstead water carriers died about 1868 in the workhouse at New End.'[14]

This spring was a reliable source: it did not freeze in winter and still produced water in the worst droughts. To make it more accessible to local people, pipes were laid to take a supply to a cistern in Rosslyn Hill opposite Pond Street. The use of Shepherd's Well declined after the New River Company built its reservoir to serve Hampstead (to the west of Whitestone Pond), and in 1874 the well was reported as being 'in ruins, and nearly choked up with weeds and rubbish'. The remains were demolished in 1878.

[1] John Richardson, *Kentish Town Past*, p.49 (1997)
[2] John Ashton, *The Fleet, its river, prison and marriages*, p.2 (1888).
[3] *Samuel Bagster of London 1772-1851*, published by Samuel Bagster & Sons (1972), quoted in 'Adventures in Old St Pancras' in Camden History Review 5 (1977).
[4] Nicholas Barton, *The Lost Rivers of London*, p.23 (rev. edn 1992).
[5] *Ibid*, p.103.
[6] Charles Lee, 'Plentyfull Sprynges at Hampstede Hethe' in *Camden History Review* No. 3 (1975).
[7] *Hampstead and Highgate Express*, 2 May 1936.
[8] William B. Boulton, *The Amusements of Old London*, 66 (1901).
[9] For fuller description see Christopher Ikin, 'Where was the Great Hollow Elm of Hampstead?' in *Camden History Review* 19 (1995).
[10] Christopher Wade, *For the poor of Hampstead for ever: 300 years of the Hampstead Wells Trust* (1998).
[11] *Ibid*, p.25.
[12] John Mackay, *A Journey through England*, (1714-23).
[13] *Daily Post*, 17 June 1723.
[14] Much of the information in this section about Shepherd's Well, and this quotation, are derived from Roy Allen, 'Shepherd's Well' in *Camden History Review* 15 (1988). He points out that the small buckets in Hone's wood cut (ill. 26) were hardly suitable since water would easily be spilt. No doubt tall pails were used. It would have been difficult to sell a bucket singly, and in 1850 water was sold in double buckets, the charge being three-halfpence or twopence according to distance.

CHAPTER FIVE

Overcrowded Churches

Rebuilding in Hampstead

The popularity of Hampstead and the consequent surge of new houses and summer residents found the old parish church wanting. It sat only 366 people in pews that were all rented except those owned by the rector. By the 1740s there were about 600 families resident in Hampstead, aside from summer visitors. The church was, in any case, in a very bad state.

A chapel for the manor of Hampstead is first noted c.1244 as being part of the parish of Hendon – both Hampstead and Hendon were estates of Westminster Abbey. A relationship with Hendon was still evident in 1826 when an Act for rebuilding Hampstead church protected the rights of the vicar of Hendon, but by then Hampstead was to all intents and purposes an independent parish. Until the 18th-century rebuilding, Hampstead church was dedicated to St Mary (as was that of Hendon).

Parishioners in 1709 petitioned the lord of the manor to remedy 'the ruinous condition of your chappell'. Their hopes must have been raised when in 1711 an Act was passed for the building of 'Fifty New Churches in the Cities of London and Westminster', an attempt to provide more church space but using funds supplied by central government. However, Hampstead was not chosen and civic pride was probably dented when parishes such as Bethnal Green and Shoreditch were. Undaunted, the parishioners made an application for government assistance in 1744, which noted that the present building was 'in so dangerous a condition, that the inhabitants cannot come to divine service without apparent hazard of their lives'. Funds, however, were raised by a lay committee and the project for a new church began.

Two architects were approached. One was Henry Flitcroft of Frognal Grove, who had rebuilt

27. South-east view of the new church of St John's Hampstead, designed by John Sanderson, soon after its completion in 1747. Engraving by Chatelain, 1750.

St Giles-in-the-Fields and St Olave, Southwark. The second was James Horne, who had a number of churches to his credit; he had also supervised the building of the Foundling Hospital in Bloomsbury. Flitcroft, however, declined to produce a plan if there was a competitor in the offing, and the trustees with great resolution resisted this condition. They were left only with Horne, whose designs did not arouse much enthusiasm, until another local resident, John Sanderson, who lived at a house called Parkgate near the Spaniards, volunteered a design which met with general approval. Sanderson found that to put the tower in the conventional position at the west end of the church would involve considerable expense because the land fell away in that direction and too much foundation work would be necessary. The tower was therefore placed at the east end and, as a result, the church today forms, with the houses of Church Row on either side, a most picturesque setting.[1] It was not until 1878, during substantial alterations, that the altar was moved from the east to the west end. The church was consecrated, dedicated to St John (but which one was not made clear), on 8 October 1747.

Hampstead's population continued to grow at a considerable rate. In 1801 it totalled 4343 inhabitants and in the next ten years a further 100 new houses were built. It was evident that another church, even a chapel-of-ease, was needed, especially for the area around South End Green where a good many of the houses were of a substantial size. A new church was indeed built there in 1823 – St John's in Downshire Hill – but it was from the outset a proprietary chapel, outside the control of the parish. Such chapels, fairly common at that period, were often owned wholly or partly by the clergyman in charge. They sought the custom of residents in newly built areas who were reluctant to go to over-crowded parish churches and were, as a consequence, an irritant to parish vicars whose incomes from pews and services were affected. The architect of this handsome classical building, which still adorns Downshire Hill, is not known, but most likely it is the work of the builder, William Woods.[2] St John's, Downshire Hill, opened on 26 October 1823.

A North-South Divide

More extreme overcrowding made for contention in St Pancras. As has been noted, the old parish church in Pancras Road had been super-seded as the customary place of worship in the 13th century by a chapel in Kentish Town Road. The chapel was rebuilt in 1456 and despite enlargement in 1633 was still, by the middle of the 18th century, only 53ft by 26ft. So complete was the shift of worshippers from St Pancras Church, that in 1593 John Norden described its isolation in memorable language:

'Pancras church ... standeth all alone as utterly forsaken, old and wether-beaten ... about this church have been manie buildings, now decaied, leaving poore Pancras without companie or comfort: yet it is now and then visited with Kentish towne and Highgate, which are members thereof, but they seldom come there, for they have Chapels of ease within themselves, but when there is a corps to be interred, they are forced to leave the same in this forsaken church or churchyard'. He added, 'although this place be as it were forsaken of old, and true men seldom frequent the same, but upon devyne occasions; yet it is visited by thieves, who assemble not there to pray, but to wait for praye, and manie fall into their hands, clothed, that are glad when they escape naked. Walk there not too late.'

There must have been some recovery, for during the Civil Wars St Pancras church was regarded as a centre of loyalty to the non-puritan church and the monarchy. A news-sheet dated June 1649 (five months after the the execution of Charles I), reports that: 'On Saturday last there was in Pankridge Churchyard a great congregation met and a parson with them, that did read the booke of Common Prayer and all the parts thereof ... and prayed for the late Q' of England.'

The minister appointed in 1655, Randolph Yearwood, was controversial. He was, despite his appointment during the Interregnum, opposed to puritans and presbyterians and was at loggerheads with local zealots. He frequently complained of the lack of funds to run the parish, and that the Trustees of the St Pancras Church Lands had refused to expend income in support of the poor. His own lack of income no doubt encouraged him to officiate at weddings which might have been illegal. One can only deduce that from the figures in the parish register: in the first five years of the 1660s, the average number of marriages was about 21; in 1668 the figure was 175 and in 1690 when he had been succeeded by John Marshall, the number was

28. Kentish Town chapel-of-ease in Kentish Town Road. It was on the site of today's Owl Bookshop.

29. The new Kentish Town Chapel (later St John's parish church), built in 1784, in Highgate Road. It has since been enlarged and refronted.

three. The parish register compiled by Marshall in 1690, laconically and just a little smugly notes 'Marriages now Regular since my coming to this Vicarage AD1690.' Certainly Yearwood was found guilty in 1674 of marrying a couple in the churchyard without publication of banns, and in 1676 was imprisoned for debt in the Fleet Prison. Long after he died it was noted in the *Freethinker* journal in April 1718, that: 'St Pancras church in the Fields where a great many who necessity puts them upon frugality are marry'd at Under-rates, and save the expense of a Licence. We found the little Church crowded with lovers.'

In 1708 it was noted that all services were held at Kentish Town chapel except on the first Sunday in every month, when the inhabitants re-sorted 'to their Mother Church of St Pancras.' A declaration by the vicar, Benjamin Mence, in 1794 that henceforth the old church would be open for divine service only once a month in-dicates that since 1708 more frequent services there had been resumed. But by 1794 circum-stances were vastly different, for in the 1750s the New Road (today's Euston Road) had been constructed with a consequent large increase in the population of the south of the parish. the vicar, by his pronouncement, was courting a strong reaction, and it came in the form of an unsuccessful appeal to the Dean and Chapter of St Paul's. During the turmoil Mence died and the incoming vicar agreed to the parishioners' demands.

In the meantime a furore had arisen over the decision to rebuild Kentish Town Chapel. There was no doubt that it needed rebuilding – it was 'by length of time greatly decayed, part of the walls bulged, the timbers rotted and broke, and the roof so much sunk, that it hath been for some time propped and cramped … and was danger-ous for the inhabitants to attend divine service therein'. But the residents of the south of the parish, who by then paid the larger proportion of the rates collected, were not at all pleased that their own needs were neglected while those of Kentish Town warranted attention. The levy of a special church rate to pay for the rebuilding was hotly opposed and delayed the new church for some years.

The new chapel was built in Highgate Road in 1784, dedicated to St John the Baptist, to the designs of James Wyatt. It later became a parish church in its own right and was substantially enlarged by J. Hakewill in 1845. Due to falling attendances, it was made redundant in 1993, was briefly occupied by a group of ecological activ-ists, and is now used by the evangelical Christ Apostolic Church UK.

The residents of the south part of the parish did, however, have access to some proprietary chapels. One was at the Middlesex Hospital (first established in Windmill Street in 1746), which was licensed to conduct baptisms. More importantly, Percy Chapel in Charlotte Street was built in 1766. Twelve years later Fitzroy Chapel was opened in Maple Street – this was later used as the parish church of St Saviour's – and in 1801, Woburn Chapel was opened in Tavistock Place. Residents also used the chapel in the Foundling Hospital (*see pp.49-50*), and another chapel was attached to the St James's Burial Ground just north of the junction of Euston Road and Hampstead Road. Each of these chapels was outside the control of the ecclesiastical parish of St Pancras.

The demands for a new parish church were not, however, to be frustrated much longer. In 1811, when a new vicar was appointed, the population of St Pancras was 46,333 and the old parish church accommodated only about 150 people. In 1812 St Pancras Vestry agreed to apply to Parliament for an Act to erect a new building. It was not a popular decision, despite the obvious need and the support from residents in the south, but at the time the parish was not in a good financial position. Four years later an Act was obtained to borrow up to £40,000 and to levy a rate not exceeding 4d in the £ for its repayment.

The architect chosen was William Inwood, who

30. Percy Chapel in Charlotte Street.

31. St Pancras New Church in Euston Road, designed in Greek Revival style by William and Henry Inwood.

was born at Kenwood where his father was bailiff to Lord Mansfield. His later churches in the area were Camden Chapel in Camden Street in 1824 (now used by a Greek congregation), St Peter's in Regent Square in 1826 (destroyed in the last war), and St Mary's in Somers Town in 1827. In the design of each of these he was assisted by his son, Henry William Inwood.

St Pancras New Church, designed in Greek Revival style at a time when most architects were turning to neo-gothic, still dominates Euston Road. Its attractive caryatids of artificial stone,[3] modelled on those of the Erectheum in Athens, were an expensive but attractive landmark. The church was consecrated on 7 May, 1822.

An unusual situation pertained in Highgate where the residents of the village lived in the parishes of St Pancras, Hornsey or Islington. Whatever the case, they were a considerable distance from their own parish church. But for centuries they had had the facility of a chapel attached to Highgate School, and even before the school's foundation a hermitage there had a small chapel attached. William Phelippe, a hermit,

was granted in 1364 the tolls for traffic using the North Road and in return for the upkeep of local roads. In 1387 a chapel for wayfarers is noted, and by 1464 it was dedicated to St Michael, a patron saint often associated with churches on hills. In 1503 the then hermit took refuge in the chapel steeple when he was allegedly assaulted by the vicar of St Pancras and others during the annual perambulation of the bounds of the parish.

Highgate School, founded in 1565, began c.1571. Its chapel, administered by the school governors, served both the school and the village. The schoolmaster was also the reader at the chapel. But confusion existed as to whether the chapel was an integral part of the school or a chapel-of-ease for the village. This imprecise relationship was to lead, in the 19th century, to controversy and a court case.

In the 17th and 18th centuries the school was a neglected and unimportant enterprise, its function the education of poor boys at the smallest possible expense. In contrast, expectations of standards at the chapel rose. It was enlarged twice in the 17th century, and from 1617 it was

32. *The old Highgate chapel, part of Highgate School.*

licensed to perform marriages, and burials were permitted in the chapel yard. In 1615, when the villagers were dissatisfied with the schoolmaster's inaudible services, they secured the services of a preacher to visit the chapel every now and then.[4]

During the Interregnum the six governors of the school, and therefore in charge of the chapel, were strongly Parliamentarian as indeed was most of the village population. They included Sir John Wollaston, founder of the almshouses in Southwood Lane, and John Ireton, brother of the Army general.

The conflict of interests between school and chapel developed apace in the 18th century. The schoolmaster Horton, nominally the minister in charge of the chapel, was denied income that went instead to the brought-in preacher, the formidable Dr Lewis Atterbury, but by 1731 a compromise was reached whereby the master took the revenue for baptisms, marriages and burials, but the preacher was to administer the sacrament alternately with the master.

The school, however, remained a sub-standard institution far removed from its present status, and a very poor relation to the chapel. In 1771 the master complained of school funds being used for chapel and poor relief purposes. In 1772 the chapel was re-roofed and enlarged by taking in three rooms from the schoolhouse.[5] In 1819 a report of the House of Commons found that the forty boys at the school were actually taught by the sexton – a parish official often poor and illiterate himself. The master stated that he himself did not teach them because he was fully

taken up with pastoral business. When a headmaster retired in 1838 there were only 19 boys in the school, such was its attraction.

Matters came to a head in 1818 when there were plans to further enlarge the chapel. Some residents complained to Lord High Chancellor Eldon (a resident of Hampstead) that income which rightly should be spent on the school was being used to maintain and develop a parish chapel. Eldon's verdict in 1827 agreed with this view, so that the Ecclesiastical Commissioners were bound to provide alternative accommodation for Highgate residents. This resulted in the opening of St Michael's church in South Grove in 1832, to the designs of Lewis Vulliamy.

Holborn

Since 1130, when the City of London was permitted to extend its western limit across the valley of the Fleet to the junction of today's Holborn and Gray's Inn Road, the church of St Andrew, Holborn has been within the City, though the greater part of its parish remained in Middlesex and is now within Camden. It is noted in a document of 959 as being 'the old wooden church of St Andrew'; by the late 13th century it had been replaced by a stone building and was rebuilt again c.1440-68

The surge in London's population in the 16th century, probably an increase of 500%, inevitably affected Holborn, one of the closest outparishes. The Dissolution of the Monasteries made available for development the lands of nearby monastic estates, such as those at Clerkenwell, Whitefriars and Charterhouse. Expansion of London moved mainly northwestwards from the City, a trend accentuated by the Great Fire of London in 1666, which also stimulated development in St Giles-in-the-Fields parish.

St Andrew's was not damaged in the Fire, but by then needed rebuilding anyway. Christopher Wren, despite his workload elsewhere, was the architect for a new building, in which the old tower was retained. Rebuilding took place 1684-87, with an interior much the same as St James, Piccadilly, another Wren church. The living was a rich picking for any clergyman. The most famous of St Andrew's rectors was Dr Henry Sacheverell, a High Tory with strong views against religious toleration and the proposed Hanoverian succession. In 1709 he delivered a virulent sermon incorporating his views at St

Paul's in the presence of the Lord Mayor, and the Whig government imprudently brought impeachment charges against him. After a celebrated trial in which Sacheverell was supported by the mob and popular opinion, he was found guilty but merely suspended from preaching for three years. He was rewarded by Queen Anne in 1713 with the rectorship of St Andrew's and spent a comfortable last four years of his life in South Grove House at Highgate.

Seven years before Sacheverell came to St Andrew's, a chapel-of-ease for the new and on the whole better-off residents who had occupied the new developments in and around Red Lion Square, was built. The new building, dedicated to St George the Martyr, was funded by private subscription. It was then at the northern end of Holborn's expansion, but such was the rush of speculation early in the 18th century that it was soon engulfed by buildings and found itself a part of Queen Square. It was 'adopted' by the Commissioners for Building Fifty New Churches during the reign of Queen Anne, improved and beautified, and made a parish church in 1723, its territory being detached from that of St Andrew's. St George's too had a famous rector, Dr William Stukeley, who had a summer house in Kentish Town Road opposite today's Prince of Wales Road. He was also a competent antiquarian and archaeologist, but his theories on the extent of Roman activity in the St Pancras area were to dog his reputation thereafter. He was appointed to St George's in 1747 and was an unconventional clergyman – in 1748 he postponed a service for an hour so that his congregation could witness an eclipse of the sun.

If St Andrew's was intimately related to the City of London, then the other main constituent of the later borough of Holborn was in a similar relationship to Westminster. The residents of St Giles-in-the-Fields, just outside the environs of the court at Whitehall, must have been progressively influenced by trade and the wealth of residents in Covent Garden (developed in the 1630s), the noble houses in the Strand and the vast demands of the court until William and Mary left to settle in Kensington at the end of the 17th century.

The name of the parish (especially taking into account the adjacent St Martin-in-the-Fields) indicates just how rural this area was in the medieval period. The chapel of the leper hospital (see p.19) was used not only by the inmates but by local residents, separated by a wall which

ran through the main aisle.[7] The church was so dilapidated in 1623 that it was replaced altogether; in any case, with the population then of about 2,000, it was far too small. A new church (architect unknown) was consecrated by Bishop Laud in January 1630. By 1664 the social status of the area must have risen, for the Vestry petitioned the Bishop of London to erect a gallery in the church 'for the better accommodation of the nobility and gentry coming to church'.

The new St Giles was relatively short-lived as less than a hundred years later it was found to be very decayed, and perhaps as a consequence of the many burials in the adjacent churchyard, it was sunk several feet beneath the level of the land and very damp as a consequence. The passing of the Act to build fifty new churches persuaded the parishioners that they might well get a new church without the responsibility of paying for it. The Commissioners in charge of implementing the Act declined their application however, saying that it was their function to pay for new churches not to rebuild old ones. The Commissioners were eventually overruled and in 1718 Parliamentary approval was obtained to rebuild St Giles. But no new church, or money to build one then materialised and to make matters worse the Commissioners then funded the building of St George, Bloomsbury which would have its own parish carved out of that of St Giles. Since the territory concerned was the more affluent part of the parish, this meant that St Giles, still without money to build its own church, was left with a district containing many of the poorest people in London. Eventually, the Commissioners did pay for a new St Giles church. The architect chosen was Henry Flitcroft of Hampstead (see p.35) who began work in 1731. The church was finished by the end of 1733. This classical building, much influenced by Wren and Gibbs, still survives, but its once pivotal setting at a junction of roads has been obliterated by the formation of New Oxford Street in the 19th century, and the more recent building of Centre Point.

The church of St George, Bloomsbury, consecrated in January 1731, is on a very small site indeed. Designed by Nicholas Hawksmoor, it is unusual in at least two ways. First of all, it is square. Secondly it has a tower, the upper part of which is a representation of the Mausoleum at Halicarnassus, topped by a statue of George I, the gift of a local brewer. This is nowadays regarded with affection, but was the object of

33. An 18th-century view of the new church of St Giles-in-the-Fields, designed 1733 by Hampstead resident, Henry Flitcroft.

derision at the time. Horace Walpole, there to comment on anything, wrote:

> When Henry the Eighth left the Pope
> in the lurch
> The Protestants made him the head of
> the Church;
> But George's good subjects, the
> Bloomsbury people,
> Instead of the Church, made him head
> of the steeple.

Dissent

When the High Church Dr Sacheverell moved up to Highgate in his later years he moved to a village that was popular with dissenting ministers because it was outside the restrictions imposed by the Five Mile Act of 1665. Modern

Dissent springs from 1662, when an Act of Uniformity was passed which deprived clergymen of their livings unless they swore 'unfeigned assent and consent' to a common form of service and prayer. This was augmented in 1665 by the Five Mile Act which precluded nonconformist clergymen from preaching within five miles of any corporate town. In these circumstances clergymen found the socially acceptable villages of Hampstead and Highgate attractive. One of these was William Rathband, late vicar of South Weald, who possibly helped to found a Presbyterian meeting house in Southwood Lane on the site of the later Baptist Chapel (now part of Highgate School). Another Presbyterian, John Storer, a preacher at Stowmarket, came to live in a cottage on the site of Church House in South

34. *St George, Bloomsbury, a view published 1799 by Thomas Malton.*

and their descendants today occupy the Rosslyn Chapel. Their most famous early minister (c.1787-1802) was the Rev. Rochemont Barbauld, husband of the poet Anna Barbauld; during his term here he became insane.

The increase in Anglican churches to house the vastly increased London population in the mid-18th century was matched by the spread of Methodism, a movement which began in earnest when both John Wesley and George Whitefield were barred from Anglican pulpits. Both men were reluctant to form a sect but the success of their evangelical approach to Christianity eventually made one inevitable. Whitefield, banned from preaching at St Mary's Islington in 1739, resorted again and again to open-air preaching. He records in his diary in 1750 that speaking in the open air at Mayfair he had 10,000 people to hear him. In November 1756, with the support of the Countess of Huntingdon, he opened his own chapel in Finsbury and later another on the west side of Tottenham Court Road. Whitefield was immensely successful, attracting not only thousands of ordinary people, but nobility and royalty. With awesome energy he travelled regularly to America to preach, and it was there that he died in 1770. In his chapel in London, draped in black for six weeks, John Wesley conducted the memorial service.

Whitefield's Tabernacle in Tottenham Court Road sat between 3000-4000. It was nearly sold for commercial use in 1827, but after renovation was reopened in 1831. After a serious fire in 1857, the site was bought by the London Congregational Building Society and a new chapel erected; this became unsafe due to faulty foundations and a new building was erected in 1899. This building was destroyed in 1945, one of the last London buildings to be damaged in World War II. The present building on the site is used by the American Church in London.

Grove. William Mead, a prominent Quaker, bought Lauderdale House in 1677 and there entertained George Fox, his father-in-law. Mead, together with William Penn, had been arraigned in 1670 for disturbing the peace and unlawful assembly at a meeting house in Gracechurch Street in the City. They pleaded the right of free worship and in a famous judgement were found not guilty by a jury which refused to be intimidated by the Recorder, the future Judge Jeffreys. Both jury and defendants were then committed to Newgate prison by the authorities.

In Hampstead, Ralph Honeywood kept a Presbyterian preacher at his house in Red Lion (Rosslyn) Hill and this was probably the beginning of the congregation granted a licence in 1692 for a meeting house in the residence of 'Isaac' Honeywood. The Honeywoods were wealthy City merchants who moved to Hampstead during this period, possibly for religious reasons.[8] They met in an outbuilding of what became Carlile House near the junction of today's Willoughby Road and the High Street. In the 1760s the congregation became Unitarian

[1] See Michael H. Port, *Hampstead Parish Church: The Story of a Building through 250 years* (1995).
[2] *A Short History of St John's, Downshire Hill, Hampstead* (n.d. but c1973).
[3] Charles E. Lee, *St Pancras Church and Parish*, p.41 (1955).
[4] Thomas Hinde, *Highgate School. A History*, p.20 (1993).
[5] *Ibid*, p.31
[6] Caroline M. Barron, *The Parish of St Andrew Holborn*, pp.32, 38 (1979).
[7] John Parton, *Some Account ...of the Parish of St Giles in the Fields*, p.193 (1822).
[8] *Rosslyn Hill Chapel 1692-1973*, p.20 (1974).

CHAPTER SIX
The Darker Side

Charities

The poor and the illiterate leave few markers in local history. Some occur in the records of bequests that provided them with bread or clothing. Most of these gifts were based on so small a sum of capital or revenue that their usefulness did not later keep pace with the rise in prices, let alone expectations and need. Others were based on pieces of land that were developed profitably. This was particularly so with the Hampstead Wells Charity. This derived, as we have seen (*p.31*), from a 1698 bequest of six swampy acres and the water from a relatively unexploited chalybeate well. The Trustees, local worthies, neglected their duties initially, but by 1730 there was an appreciable revenue to pass on to the poor. What with the proceeds from the waters, and the development of the land over the years (it stretched from Well Road to the southern end of today's Gainsborough Gardens) the bequest became a fruitful asset.[1]

It was not the first large charity in Hampstead, for in her will of 1643, Elizabeth, the Dowager Viscountess Campden, left £200 for the poor of Hampstead. This was to be invested in land to produce £10 per annum, half of which was to go to 'the most poor and needy people that be of good name and conversation' and half to the apprenticing of one or more poor boys. The Viscountess was the widow of a former lord of the manor, Sir Baptist Hicks, who had been created Viscount Campden in 1628, his title deriving from his country estate at Chipping Campden. Fourteen acres were bought at Childs Hill and by 1855, the year of the first surviving Minute Book, about £20 annually was being used to fund apprenticeships and the rest was doled out in bread or money. But the charity's income was too small to have much impact and in 1880 the two old Hampstead charities merged and pooled their assets as the Wells & Campden Trust.

35. Well Walk c.1905, showing the 19th-century fountain opposite the site of the first Long Room. Well Walk is on part of the former Hampstead Wells Charity land.

The size of these charities may be compared with some other 17th-century Hampstead bequests, such as that of Thomas Cleave who left 56 shillings to fund an annual gift of thirteen penny loaves to the poor, and that of Thomas Charles who left 24 shillings to provide bread for the poor forever.

Similar small charities existed in the parish of St Pancras where land was far less valuable and, moreover, developed much later than in Hampstead. The same Thomas Cleave bestowed penny loaves upon the poor, based on income from land at first, but later from the rent of the Boot public house in Cromer Street. William Platt in 1632 not only left his property at Kentish Town (an estate between Highgate Road and Brecknock Road) to St John's College, Cambridge, but created a fund that doled out to the poor of Kentish Town and Highgate. Also, nos. 17-21 Highgate High Street formed the basis of a bequest by Lady Gould for the poor of Highgate from the 18th century. But the main St Pancras charity was the Eleanor Palmer Gift (1558), based on about three acres of land that extended from Highgate Road across today's Fortess Road, a plot which now includes Kentish Town fire station. The land was called Fortys Field (hence Fortess Road). Two thirds of the income was for the benefit of the poor of Chipping Barnet and one third for those of Kentish Town. Before 1852 the income was distributed annually to individuals via the parish Directors of the Poor, but after that it was used for the work of the St Pancras Almshouses until modern times; more recently it has been administered by the Fortys Field Housing Association. The land was not of particular significance or value until the laying out of Fortess/Junction Road across it early in the 19th century.

Workhouses

Until the Dissolution of the Monasteries the monastic houses were a usually reliable source of poor relief all year round. Their abolition in the 1540s led to the passing of the Poor Law Act of 1601, which obliged parishes to appoint (unpaid) Overseers of the Poor to look after the local poor out of a poor rate, and to set them to work where appropriate. Later in the century restrictions were placed on the movement of paupers away from their home parish and it became an obsession with parishes to move out of their area any poor stranger who was likely to be a charge on the poor rate. In 1723 a Workhouse Act

empowered parishes to erect workhouses in which the poor could be housed and employed.

A St Pancras workhouse was established in 1731– the Vestry minutes imply that this was the first. However, a journal kept in the early 18th century by a local magistrate, William Woodhouse, who lived in St Pancras Way, suggests that a local workhouse existed well before the 1723 Act. His journal[2] for 1703 records the local mob-killing of a 70-year-old woman accused of witchcraft. The woman and her aged husband were secretly moved for safety from their cottage to St Pancras church by parish officials, but the mob 'demanded these unhappy wretches at the workhouse' and 'on being acquainted that they were not there, they pulled down the pales and walls, broke all the windows, and demolished a part of the house'. The poor couple were eventually found and ducked in a stream, presumably the Fleet, and the woman died from the effects.[3]

Whatever the significance of this journal entry, the workhouse noted in the Vestry minutes opened in a house in St Pancras Way[4] with a matron to supervise the inmates. Most likely the house was in poor condition already, and in 1772 it was declared unsafe. But it was not until 1775 that the Vestry considered the conversion of a house called Mother Black Caps, a tavern or inn on the site of today's Camden Town Underground station, and it was another three years before inmates moved in. In 1787 the wards were so overcrowded that five or six people might sleep in the same bed, and there was always the danger of fever breaking out. In 1809 it was reported that 'On examination of the bedsteads, the number is 224, 52 of which are single and 97 double bedsteads, all of which be fit for use if they be cleansed from vermin.' The remaining 75 were said to be useless. It was also noted in 1802 that the cellars, only 4' 8" high, 'were overflowed with water, for which there is no drainage.'

In that same year controversy raged in the St Pancras Open Vestry about the cost of the poor and the inadequate resources of the Vestry to pay for them. At that time the Vestry had not much more than a paid parish clerk to conduct its business – most other functions were carried out by unpaid residents, chosen by rote. These included the Overseers of the Poor, who were not permitted by law to pay others to collect rates despite the fact that St Pancras parish by then was a populous one and the collection of rates a sizeable chore. In 1802 it was reported that the annual deficiency in rates collected was nearly £2,200, a very large sum indeed. This led to the appointment of a body called the Directors of the Poor (see p.12) to manage poor relief in the parish, and who also had powers to pay collectors of the rates.

The first meeting of the Directors was held at the Adam and Eve public house in Hampstead Road in June 1804. One of their first jobs was to fund, construct and manage a new workhouse. They chose a site north of Old St Pancras Church, backing on to its insalubrious burial ground, and a new workhouse was opened in 1809, accommodating 500 people. At first the inmates were allowed to leave the building during the day, but the Directors, indignant that some of them did odd jobs while out, then made them stay in the workhouse all day doing work for the parish, or else work outside only if the money they earned was returned to the parish authorities. An infirmary was also built in 1812.

The passing of the Poor Law Amendment Act (1834) brought more order, but more stringency, into the support of the poor. It emphasised confinement in workhouses, making no distinction between those who were 'impotent poor', such as the old or infirm unable to work, and those who were able bodied but who could not or did not find work. To deter the second category, workhouses were made as unpleasant as possible, which of course was unfortunate for those in the first category. Husbands and wives were housed in separate wings, and children were taken away from both. The Act also appointed Poor Law Commissioners to oversee local poor relief. St Pancras spent many years fighting their governance through the courts. Representatives of the Commissioners, called Guardians of the Poor, were appointed but the Directors continued to meet and function in opposition. The matter rumbled on for years until the Guardians eventually assumed control.

Meanwhile, though the population of St Pancras had increased from 45,000 at the beginning of the century to about 120,000 in the 1830s, the workhouse remained the same size, except for the excavation of a basement to form a girls' schoolroom. A building meant for 500 often housed 1000, and children sometimes slept 6 or 8 to a bed. Not only was the place overcrowded, it was dangerously unhealthy. Percolations of an unpleasant nature came from the adjacent burial ground; what proper lavatories there

were emptied into a cesspit in the children's playground; other privies were below stairs without ventilation. Nearby were also the dungheaps and pig sties of Agar Town – there were even 27 sties within the workhouse walls. Even more unpleasant, it was common to burn old corpses in the burial ground adjacent to make more space, and the smell from this was unbearable. In the Infirmary there were no trained nurses, but there was the help of a surgeon-apothecary and a midwife. Wages paid to staff were very poor indeed, and it was reported that scullerymen worked from 4am to 7pm for $5^3/_4$ d per week and a pint of beer daily.

The administration of St Pancras was in chaos for some years. In 1858, for example, the Vestry Clerk absconded with funds and the Vestry was obliged to advertise for his whereabouts in Europe so that he might be brought back. At the same meeting it was reported that the Clerk to the Directors of the Poor had also absconded with funds and in the same month a Collector of Rates also defaulted. In another month an assistant surgeon at the workhouse was dismissed for immoral conduct with a female inmate – he had also procured an abortion for her. Criminal proceedings against him were instituted but he disappeared and while absent he wrote to the chaplain of the workhouse to come and see him to 'console his disturbed mind and give him spiritual aid'. This the good chaplain did, but he then declined to reveal to the Vestry where the poor man was hiding because, he said, he had learnt it in privileged circumstances. So the Vestry fired the chaplain as well.

Hampstead had a poorhouse in Pond Street in 1670 and another at New End in 1705. In 1779 three cottages for the poor were built 'at a place called Gangmoor or Hatches Bottom'. This place, to the east of East Heath Road, had been a malarial swamp until drained by the Hampstead Water Company in 1777; its later name, no doubt a wry comment on its previous nature and with an eye to selling a cheap piece of land more expensively, was the Vale of Health. A will dated 1801 is the first known document to use this name, but this has not prevented numerous residents and tourist guides stating as fact that the Vale was resorted to during the Great Plague of 1665.

Such cottages for the poor were additional to the parish workhouses, the first of which had been opened in 1729 in a large Tudor house in Frognal near the junction of the later road called Mount Vernon. A report in 1732[5] noted that in

36. *Hampstead Poorhouse in a Tudor house in Frognal. Drawing by W. Alexander, 1801.*

the cottages the poor had lived 'in nastiness as well as in poverty'. It is unlikely that conditions in the house were much better: in 1734 hop sacks were hung against the lathe and plaster to absorb rain and in 1757 the landlord of the property complained that the Vestry was not looking after it properly; by 1800 it was regarded as unsafe. The work imposed on the inmates was tedious: in 1731 they mainly spun mop yarn. But older inmates were rewarded for sitting up with the sick, or for collecting holly from the Heath, and in December 1735, Mary Godward was rewarded for doing (an unspecified task) for a vagrant that nobody else was prepared to do, and later for washing some unpleasant blankets and cutting corns and nails of an inmate. Between 1734 and 1739 about 130 persons are recorded as having been in the workhouse at some time or other. Some were strangers to the parish, usually sick or pregnant.

In 1757 it was acknowledged that the house could no longer be used as a workhouse without the expense of repairs and it was decided to revert to the old system of housing the poor in cottages. This turned out to be more expensive and within a year the workhouse was reinstated, but contracted out to whoever thought they might make a profit from it. Early in the 19th century a new workhouse was built in New End, the future site of New End Hospital.[6]

St Giles parish appears to have been in union with other parishes, such as Stepney, in the 1660s in establishing a poorhouse in Clerkenwell Green for the aged and infirm.[7] A workhouse was opened in the Seven Dials area in the 1670s, which had to be moved once Seven Dials was laid out; consideration was then given to taking

37. *St Giles' Workhouse in Endell Street.*

some houses in Whetstone Park, near Lincoln's Inn Fields, the most infamous street in the parish. But it was not until *c.*1725 that a proper workhouse was opened on the east side of what is now Endell Street, with a burial ground attached (full by 1755). This building was rebuilt in gothic style in 1879 and was named Dudley House; its site, on the corner of Endell Street and Shorts Gardens, is now covered by local authority housing.

A Holborn Union of poor law authorities was established in 1836 which included the parish of St Andrew above the Bars, St George the Martyr and the Liberty of Saffron Hill. The Union was later extended to include St Sepulchre, Furnival's Inn, Staple Inn, St James and St John, Clerkenwell and St Luke, Clerkenwell. Gray's Inn opted to pay the Union a sum of money to care for any poor that lived within its precinct, but preferred not to be part of the Union itself.

The Plague

One part of St Giles was an infamous resort of the poor – its 'rookery', sandwiched between Great Russell Street and St Giles High Street, an area today cut through by New Oxford Street. The rookery had a long history – its early form may be seen in Hollar's 1658 panoramic map of London and by the time of John Strype's map of 1720 it was built with courtyards and alleys as, indeed, were the neighbourhoods just south of St Giles High Street, where the poor also found shelter. The area was blamed for the spread of the Great Plague of 1665. Sir Thomas Peyton wrote then 'That one parish of St Giles at London hath done us all this mischief'. This was an exaggeration since plague, in one form or other, visited the City of London frequently, and in any case there were casualties in the City and Westminster the year before. It was possible as well that plague had appeared already in the City but had been hushed up. In London at that time, and in the outer parishes such as Holborn and St Pancras, women 'searchers' were employed whose task it was to assess the cause of any deaths and report them to the sexton, but most particularly to notify him if a person had died of plague. A frequent consequence of positive plague identification was that the family of the deceased were isolated in their own house until found to be free of the contagion themselves. The searchers, usually illiterate and without medical knowledge, could be easily bribed by families anxious to avoid this stigma. The searchers were, at plague times, outsiders themselves, just as were those who picked up the corpses at night, or those who buried them in hastily dug pits.

The year of 1665 began with extreme cold – ice stopped traffic on the Thames. Plague appeared in London and the out parishes as soon as March was out, but it did not gain a substantial foothold until May. However, there was a reluctance of parish clerks to report plague deaths in what were called the Bills of Mortality. These weekly statistical surveys, culled from parish records, were woefully inaccurate and may only be taken as an indication of what happened. In the week commencing 15 August, St Giles is noted as having 175 deaths from plague, but even worse, St Andrew, Holborn had 220. St Giles was lucky in having a local apothecary, William Boghurst, with extraordinary courage. Unlike other apothecaries and officials of all kinds, he stayed on in St Giles and tended those

with plague sores. 'He commonly dressed forty Plague sores a day, and in diagnosis would test the pulse of a patient, sweating in bed, for five and six minutes. He upheld in their beds those threatened by strangling and choking, often for half an hour together, the breath frequently falling upon his face.'[8] Despite Boghurst's efforts the deaths in St Giles were so many that adjacent parishes set guards to prevent its residents fleeing across the parish boundary.

The Rookery

Hogarth had the St Giles Rookery in mind in his famous *Gin Lane* drawing. Its lodging houses particularly concerned Henry Fielding, the magistrate of Bow Street. Saunders Welch, High Constable of Holborn, then wrote:

'In the parish of St Giles there are a great number of houses set apart for the reception of idle rogues and vagabonds, who have their lodging there for two pence a night; in the above parish and in St George's Bloomsbury one woman alone occupies seven of these houses, all properly accommodated with miserable beds from cellar to garret for such twopenny lodgers, several of which are for men and women, often

38. St Giles Rookery

39. William Hogarth's 'Gin Lane', with the distinctive spire of St George, Bloomsbury, in the background.

strangers to each other, being together promiscuously, the price of a double bed being no more than threepence as an encouragement to them to be together; gin is sold at one penny a quartern; in the execution of a search warrant Mr Welch rarely finds less than twenty of them open at a time. In one of these houses he hath numbered 58 persons of both sexes...'

Gin Lane illustrated the devastating effects of the cheap gin era. But St Giles was not the only neighbourhood affected – Seven Dials, another part of the parish, was rife with gin shops.

Many in the rookery were Irish, particularly from County Cork and the west of Ireland. In 1796 a parish poor rate of £2000 supported 1,200 Irish people, and in 1819 an Overseer of the Poor stated that of a total parish rate of £32,000, £20,000 went to destitute Irish.[9] The completion of New Oxford Street in 1847 dispersed much of the problem, but did not erase it altogether in the neighbourhood, as there were pockets left untouched by the line of the road. When a survey of the remnants of the rookery was made that year, it was reported that in a lodging house in Church Lane just north of St Giles High Street, two rooms on the ground floor contained 4 families, consisting of 8 males and 9 females. In all, the house of three floors contained fifty people, all of them Irish. There was no privy and no running water and the yard was strewn with excrement.

Child mortality was very high as was infanticide, and many of those that did survive were sent on to the streets where parish and church authorities turned a blind eye to their plight.

The Foundling Hospital

This institution, whose grounds now house the Coram's Fields Playground in Guilford Street, was founded by a sea-captain, Thomas Coram (1668-1751), retired about 1719 from a lifetime at sea, but still with an interest in colonial development. He was distressed not only by the numbers of children he saw abandoned in the streets but by the waste of potential English settlers in the colonies. He may well have read Joseph Addison's article in the *Guardian* in 1713 in which the author urged a:

> 'provision for foundlings or for those children, who through want of such a provision, are exposed to barbarity of cruel and unnatural parents. One does not know how to speak on such a subject without horror; but what multitude of infants have been made away with by those who brought them into the world and were afterwards either ashamed or unable to provide for them!'

Addison had in mind the awful fate of many illegitimate children. A later historian of the Foundling Hospital commented on the mothers of such mites:

> 'Neither she nor the offspring of her guilt appear to have been admitted within the pale of human compassion; her false step was her final doom, without even the chance, however desirous, of returning to the road of rectitude.'

Often young children were despatched by parish authorities (as is evident from the St Pancras burial registers) to wet nurses, who themselves were poor and unhealthy. In the case of St Pancras an enormous number died in their new homes. A Dr Cadogan, writing in 1750, remarked that 'the ancient Custom of exposing them to Wild Beasts or drowning them would certainly be a much quicker way of dispatching them than the lingering deaths they had' in the homes of wet nurses.

Coram's efforts to interest George III or the government in the matter were largely unsuc-

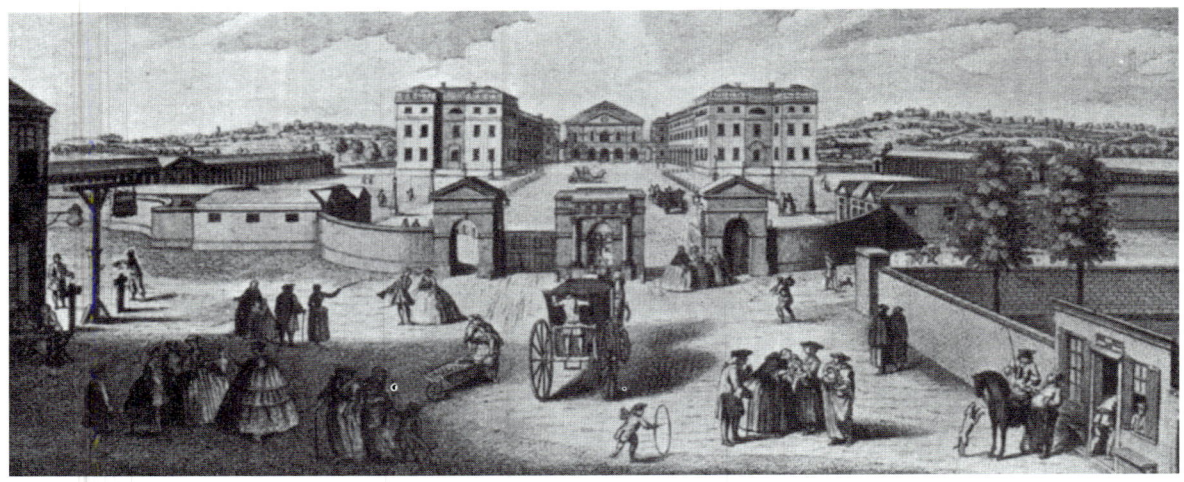

40. *The Foundling Hospital, Guilford Streeet, from a print published in 1753, after a drawing by L.P. Boitard.*

cessful, but his tenacity won in the end. In 1739 a Royal Charter was procured at a gathering which included six dukes, eleven earls, numerous other landowners, City worthies and Hogarth. The project continued to attract famous names for some years, and had the attention of the composer, Handel, who gave benefit concerts at the Hospital and eventually left it the score of his *Messiah*.

The first Foundling Hospital opened in a house in Hatton Garden in March 1741. Of the 136 children received in the first year, 56 died – a rather better survival rate than in central London workhouses. Though Coram's enterprise was generally welcomed, the governors received a visit from the Vestry of St Andrew, Holborn, in whose parish the Hospital stood, complaining that mothers who had had their children refused by the Hospital had often just abandoned them in the locality instead, with the result that the parish had to care for them.

Needing to expand, the Hospital acquired 56 acres of land north of Lambs Conduit Street, an area then almost devoid of buildings and with an uninterrupted view to the Northern Heights. Here a new building, designed in classical style by Theodore Jacobsen, was erected in 1745 in ample grounds, leaving plenty of spare land for future development.

The Hospital was overwhelmed by its success, for far more children were offered than could be taken. In 1756, 1,783 children were admitted and it became clear that parish authorities in London and in the provinces were dumping their own parish children on the institution. A woman who lived three hundred miles from London wrote:

'There is set up in our corporation a new and uncommon trade, namely, the conveying of children to the Foundling Hospital. The person employed in this trade is a woman of notoriously bad character. She undertakes the carrying of these children at so much a head. She has, I am told, made one trip already, and is now set upon her journey with two of her daughters, each with a child on her back.'

In the same era another venture began to tackle the problem of homeless boys hardened by a lifetime of living rough, without skills or education. In May 1758 some gentlemen met at a London coffee house to establish a school for orphan children, in which they could be prepared for apprenticeships. Later that year a house was rented in Hoxton. This was the Orphan Working School which, after a number of moves to larger premises, eventually settled at Maitland Park off Haverstock Hill in September 1847.

An ambitious plan to take in central London orphans was envisaged for Highgate Village. The scheme was proposed by William Blake, a citizen of London (either a draper or a vintner), in a book entitled *Silver Drops, or Serious Things*, published in 1680. Blake bought quite a lot of property in the village including the site of the later Flask tavern, the Banqueting House that stood on the site of St Michael's Church, and Dorchester House, roughly on the site of Witanhurst. In doing this he went bankrupt and

41. The Orphan Working School, Haverstock Hill.

fell out with his family, but at the same time he invited central London parishes to send orphans to the school he proposed to build to the rear of today's Flask. The minutes of St Giles's Vestry record an approach from him in 1682. The Vestry agreed to form a committee to inspect his plans and if found satisfactory to send twenty parish children at a cost of £6 per annum each. It is not clear if the school was ever built, but the fact that there is no further reference in the St Giles records suggests that the plan came to naught; in 1688 the St Giles Vestry considered sending children to another establishment.

St Pancras set up a Female Charity School (*see p.70*) in which girls were taught to be humble and obedient to their superiors and become good housemaids. Despite the undoubted rigour of the regime here, and the inevitable placement into the drudge of domestic service, the girls probably had a better fate than those shipped off by St Pancras Vestry as 'apprentices' to mill owners. In 1805 an agent for these mills, a Mr Gorton, answered an advertisement placed by the Vestry, and obtained 25 children from St Pancras Workhouse, together with premiums paid by the Vestry, for work in mills. Of these, 15 were nine years old, while another six were only eight. Gorton was aided and abetted in this by the parish beadle. In 1817, 19 children were shipped off to Hounslow Flax Mills. In 1851 the *Morning Chronicle* reported that St Pancras Vestry had arranged to supply children to the cap-

tain of a brig going to the Bermudas – the Vestry supplied each child with a bible, prayer book, a brush and comb and 2s 6d.

Burial Grounds

The reputation of St Pancras was not helped by the management of its burial ground. This was under the care of the Church Lands Trustees and any improvements or enlargements were their responsibility. Prints of the 18th century show Old St Pancras Church surrounded by a picturesque burial ground about the same size as any village graveyard still to be found in the countryside. But it had become woefully inadequate. In 1689, when extant burial records begin, there were 43 burials. In 1720 there were 130, of which many were 'foreigners' – people from outside the parish. The burial ground was enlarged in 1726 by the acquisition of a small piece of land to the south. In his *Book for a Rainy Day*, the antiquary, John Thomas Smith, relates how he and other pupils, about 1777, used to go on sketching parties to St Pancras churchyard, from which there was an uninterrupted view of Whitefield's Chapel in Tottenham Court Road and of Montagu House (now superseded by the British Museum). In 1789 the sexton reported that the burial ground was so crowded that he hardly knew where to inter the dead, especially the poor. It was still a rural scene in 1814 when the Vestry asked the vicar to desist from allowing a cow belonging to him from grazing in the churchyard and a year later it was reported that the vicar charged the sexton two guineas a year for allowing him the same privilege.

There was another side to this rurality. In the *New Monthly Magazine* in 1815, the churchyard was reported as dilapidated:

'… the state of this churchyard is most discreditable to the parish to which it belongs, and disgusting to the eyes of all who view it. Monuments and gravestones are in the same ruinous condition, fallen or falling in all directions; foot and other stones nearly covered with clay, bones of all descriptions and fragments of coffins are spread over the ground…'

Three years after this the Vestry opened a 'bonehouse' in the churchyard in which to store bones dug up when new bodies were interred.

This did not solve the problem. A local resident, writing in *The Times* in 1850, noted that the burial ground consisted of four acres, and that because of its strong tradition of being a resting place for Roman Catholics, was more than usually popular for burials. However, he noted, during the last twenty years over 26,000 bodies had been interred in a churchyard much of which had been used for centuries. He then goes on, in grisly detail, to describe large pits, disinterments and graves only two feet below ground level.

St Pancras Vestry had failed to do what other vestries had done many years earlier and buy new ground in the nearby fields, or else purchase land outside of the parish. St Giles parish, faced with a similar problem, but rather earlier, bought land for a new burial ground right next to that of St Pancras. It was badly needed, judging by contemporary reports of the churchyard. Pennant in his *Account of London* (1793) describes the St Giles burial ground at St Giles High Street:

'I have, in the churchyard … seen with horror a great square pit with many rows of coffins piled one upon the other, all exposed to sight and smell; some of the piles were incomplete, expecting the mortality of the night.'

An expert on burial grounds, Dr George Walker, who practised in the Drury Lane area, noted of St Giles churchyard:

'Here in this place of "Christian burial", you may see human heads, covered with hair; and here, in this "consecrated ground", are human bones with flesh still adhering to them.'

The first remedy in St Giles was to import soil and so raise the level of the ground to provide more burial space, but in the end the vestry was obliged to buy land outside the parish. The plot it bought, only just smaller than the St Pancras burial ground adjacent, was consecrated in 1803. But by the middle of the 19th century the situation in the new St Giles ground was, if anything, worse than in the St Pancras ground. Between 1843 and 1845, 10,000 bodies were interred there, and it was reported that during a cholera outbreak as many as 3,000 bodies were placed there in six months.

Five other parishes acquired land in St Pancras for burial grounds. St Andrew, Holborn bought about three acres off Gray's Inn Road in 1747; land was bought for the two Holborn parishes of St George the Martyr and St George, Bloomsbury in 1713, before the latter had even been built. St James's, Piccadilly bought a plot to the east of Hampstead Road and also built a handsome chapel there, consecrated in 1793. Finally, St Martin-in-the-Fields bought nearly four acres to the east of Camden High Street in 1805, just as Camden Town was developing, and there built almshouses as well.

All these burial grounds are now public gardens, some with quite distinguished monuments. St Martin's has one for Charles Dibdin, the composer. In the St Giles ground, the sculptor, John Flaxman, and the architect, Sir John Soane (his house in Lincoln's Inn Fields was just inside St Giles parish), are buried. In the St Pancras burial ground (though it is no longer possible for the casual visitor to determine which was St Giles and which was St Pancras), a host of famous people were originally laid to rest. They included William Godwin and Mary Wollstonecraft, Jonathan Wild the notorious fence and informer portrayed in John Gay's *Beggar's Opera*, many of the local Rhodes family whose descendant, Cecil Rhodes, put up their memorial, Captain John Mills, who survived the Black Hole of Calcutta, and the Corsican hero, Paoli, whose remains were later removed to Corsica.

Hampstead has managed to keep its old churchyard *as a churchyard* – probably the only unspoilt one in central London. The burial ground adjacent to the church has certainly been used since medieval times, and when that was full an extension on the other side of Church Row was opened in 1812. The two grounds contain many well-known people, including Constable, John Harrison (recently famous again for his device that first measured longitude with any precision), Norman Shaw the architect, Hugh Gaitskell, George and Gerald du Maurier, Beerbohm Tree and Dr Cyril Joad.

Private Cemeteries
The deterioration of parish burial grounds ensured an enthusiastic response to the private cemeteries opened in the 1830s in the London suburbs. The first were Kensal Green in 1833 and Norwood in 1837. Highgate Cemetery was opened in 1839 and was immediately popular for its landscaping, site and general convenience to the middle classes of north London and the City. It was owned by the London Cemetery Company, which later built Nunhead. The architect was Stephen Geary who is also credited with having built the first gin palace in London, but who is also noted in the minutes of St Pancras Vestry in 1853 as proposing a petition to Parlia-

ment prohibiting the sale of drink on Sundays. He also designed the truly awful monument and statue of George IV at Battle Bridge, which though of short duration, brought about the change of name to the area to King's Cross.

Though Geary laid out Highgate Cemetery, his assistant, James Bunning, seems to have done much of the rest of the work. The style of the cemetery was essentially Romantic and far removed from the squalor of local churchyards and their reputation for body snatchers. In these private cemeteries the marking of death became more sophisticated and expensive; tombstones and memorials became more elaborate and the wording on them indicates a resurgent belief in the hereafter. At first the residents of Highgate did not welcome this 'great garden of sleep', but once tickets were issued so that they could walk the avenues of trees, shrubs and flowers, it was regarded as a local amenity.

42. *Highgate Cemetery as depicted in the Penny Magazine, December 1839. Shown is the Egyptian entrance to the catacombs.*

The first part of the cemetery, on the west side of Swains Lane, was opened on the grounds of Ashurst House, a mansion in South Grove owned by a former Lord Mayor of London, which is now replaced by St Michael's church. Two chapels, one for anglicans the other for nonconformists, are at the entrance. After the eastern cemetery was formed in 1854, a tunnel was constructed beneath Swains Lane through which bodies could be conveyed direct from the chapel via a hydraulic lift.

A cheap grave cost £2. 10s. 0d – well beyond the means of a working class family, and a brick grave accommodating twelve coffins, about £21. The cemetery thus contains numerous familiar middle-class names such as Charles Cruft, George Eliot, Radclyffe Hall, Frederick Lilywhite, Carl Rosa, Christina and Gabriel Rossetti, Herbert Spencer and Mrs Henry Wood. But there was also the famous pugilist, Tom Sayers, whose funeral here was paid for by his many admirers. And there is of course Karl Marx – his grave has been a place of pilgrimage for many years. In 1918 the Russian Communist Party petitioned the Home Office to remove his remains to Russia, but this was energetically opposed by the British Communist Party which insisted that Marx belonged to international Communism and not to Russia: he was German, anyway.

The Metropolitan Interment Act of 1852 (substantially drafted by the Vestry Clerk of St Pancras) at last enabled London authorities to establish cemeteries. It was an irony that St Pancras, so long known for dragging its feet when it came to its teeming population, should be the first authority in London to adequately cater for its dead. The Vestry bought 88 acres of Horse Shoe Farm on Finchley Common and the first interment was in 1854; 25 years later another 94 acres were added. It was and is a vast cemetery, sufficiently large for St Pancras to have sold some of it to Islington. Its early character emulated the ostentatious nature of Highgate Cemetery. There are many interesting monuments there, including a very large Ionic temple belonging to the Mond family, who made their money out of alkali production and whose company became an integral part of ICI. Also buried here is Henry Croft (d.1930), reputed to be the first Pearly King, and George Fortescue who departed this life 'at the British Museum as Keeper of the Printed Book Department' in 1912.

Hampstead Cemetery in Fortune Green Road was opened by the Vestry in 1876. It is said that

43. Hampstead Cemetery, 1876.

once thirty gardeners kept the Cemetery in trim, but today it relies heavily on the Friends of Hampstead Cemetery for some of its care. Erected here were some bizarre tombs and monuments until 1934 regulations restricted their size. The most magnificent is the Bianchi monument erected in the 1930s by an Italian restaurateur for his opera-singer wife. Nearby, a stone organ complete with stool and music, commemorates Charles Barritt.

Once the burial grounds of the various Holborn parishes were closed in the 1850s, Holborn burials (or at least those relating to families who did not have the money to use Highgate Cemetery) were often at Brookwood Cemetery near Woking. A special train left Waterloo station each day with appropriate facilities for coffins and mourners. Even after the formation of Holborn borough in 1900, no more convenient official arrangement was made.

[1] The assets of the Hampstead Wells and Campden Trust in 1998 were £12 million. See Christopher Wade, *For the poor of Hampstead, for ever*, p.116 (1998).

[2] Now in the possession of the Camden Local Studies and Archives Centre, Holborn Library, Theobalds Road, WC1.

[3] Thomas J. Barratt in his *Annals of Hampstead*, Vol. 1, pp.134-136 (1912), gives details of some cases of witch hunts in Hampstead in the 17th century.

[4] For discussion as to its site, see John Richardson, *Kentish Town Past*, p.21 (1997).

[5] Anon. *An Account of Several Workhouses*, (1st edn 1725, 2nd edn 1732) quoted in Geoffrey Harris, 'The Humanity of Hampstead Workhouse' in *Camden History Review* 4 (1976)

[6] Much of the above information is taken from Geoffrey Harris's article as above.

[7] John Parton, Some Account of ... St Giles in the Fields, pp.315-316 (1822).

[8] Walter G. Bell, *The Great Plague in London 1665*, p.103 (rev. edn 1951).

[9] Aidan Flood, *The Irish in Camden*, 1990.

CHAPTER SEVEN

London stirs itself

Bloomsbury Square

Two of the most important developments in the expansion of London occurred in Camden. The first was the building of Bloomsbury Square and the second was the construction of the New Road – today's Euston Road is part of that.

Bloomsbury Square was the first true London square, a prototype for dozens in the capital from Hackney to Fulham. Squares are for many the quintessence of London's architecture and with some exceptions these oases have resisted developments of a more intensive nature. Their acceptability ensured that London and provincial developments would revolve around the *vertical* house, each floor for a different purpose, each

44. *Inigo Jones.*

scaled up or down in room height to suit the social status of activity.

Bloomsbury Square had been preceded in the 1630s by Covent Garden's piazza and by Lincoln's Inn Fields. Covent Garden itself was a revolution in a capital which had grown up in a haphazard way and which had, even after the destruction of the Great Fire, resumed most of its old topographical habits. But Covent Garden, modelled by Inigo Jones (1573-1652) on the piazza at Leghorn in Italy, was an open (and then empty) square dominated by a Tuscan church, a place for the community to meet, to have recreation, perhaps to trade a little, and to be seen. Those who occupied the grand apartments that surrounded it lived cheek-by-jowl with the world at large. From their windows they could view their peers or social superiors, but just as likely they would see beggars, tradesmen, carters, sweepers, criminals, prostitutes and cabmen. However Jones, in introducing this concept to London, had not divined in the affluent English an incipient wish to separate themselves from the lower classes in exclusive developments.

As we have seen (*p.16*), in the 1630s William Newton obtained permission to build houses around three sides of Lincoln's Inn Fields. Here also Inigo Jones made a contribution with a plan for a grand square, of which only the western side was built – Lindsey House (nos 59-60) is its only survivor, though now covered with stucco. Despite the popularity of Lincoln's Inn Fields amongst occupiers, the Fields themselves remained open to the public. They were even the scene in 1683 of the execution of William Russell, for conspiracy in the Rye House Plot. But they were also dangerous enough for John Gay to issue a poetic warning in 1716:

> Where Lincoln's Inn, wide space, is rail'd around,
> Cross not with venturous step; there oft is found
> The lurking thief, who, while the daylight shone,
> Made the walls echo with his begging tone,

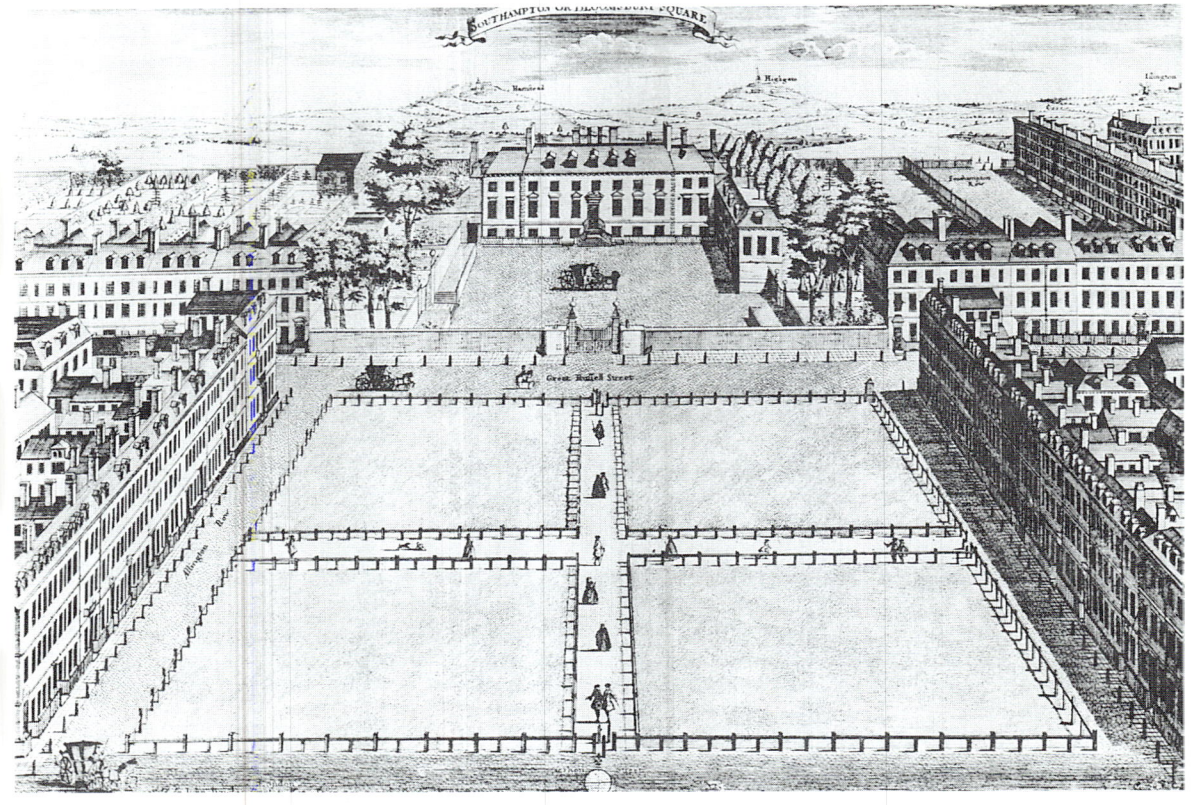

45. Bloomsbury Square, with Southampton, later Bedford, House on the northern side.

That crutch, which later compassion moved,
shall wound
    Thy bleeding head, and fell thee to the
ground.
    Though thou art tempted by the linkman's
call,
    Yet trust him not along the lonely wall,
    In the mid way he'll quench the flaming
brand
    And share the booty with the pilfering band.

The first 'closed' square was Bloomsbury – at
first called Southampton Square in honour of its
developer and landowner, the 4th Earl of Southampton. In at least two ways it did *not* resemble
many of its subsequent imitators: on one side
was originally the set piece of Southampton's
own mansion; secondly, the houses were not
particularly uniform in size or style or built as
an architectural whole. Another feature distinguished it from most later squares: it had a
hinterland of specially built houses for tradesmen and artisans, and a market to serve them

all (hence today's Barter Street), so that it was,
as John Evelyn remarked, 'a little town'. Given
that at the time of its creation, *c.*1661, the square
was almost surrounded by fields, it was indeed
a singular entity. When, some years later, Lord
St Albans developed St James's Square, he too
included a market in the neighbourhood.

Southampton's method of development was to
be followed frequently. Instead of shouldering
the expense of it, he let out plots of land to
speculators who themselves, within a framework,
invested in the erection of houses on reasonably
long leases. But eventually, the freehold of those
houses reverted profitably to the landowner.

Bloomsbury Square was successful, not only
because of its healthier situation away from the
City, but from its exclusiveness, which was
enforced by bars and gates, and it matched the
aspirations of those getting rich during the 17th
century. The destruction of much of the City in
the fire of 1666, inevitably consolidated its success.

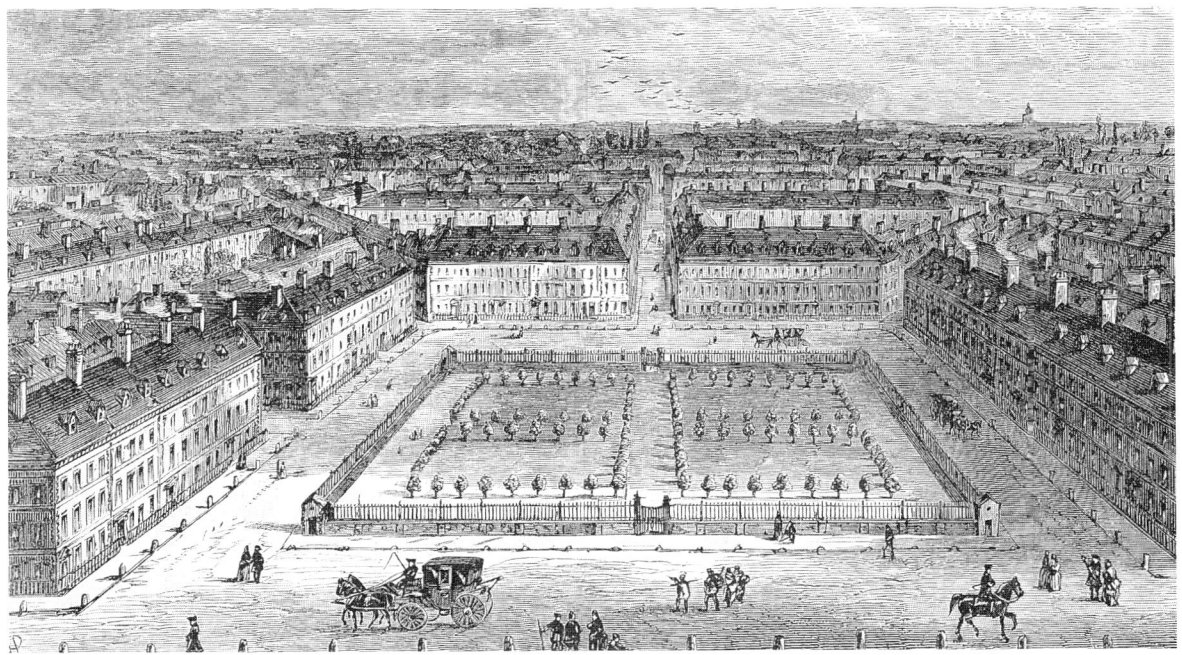

46. Red Lion Square in 1780.

Red Lion Square

While Southampton's development had three sides of the square standing in obeisance to his mansion on the north, a more egalitarian square was constructed from 1684 just to the east. This was the project of a man who could be regarded as the first real London property speculator. Red Lion Square was built by Dr Nicholas Barbon (c.1640-98), an innovator who generally kept one step ahead of his creditors. He was active in the rebuilding of London after the Fire and at the same time pioneered fire insurance amongst a population bruised by that event. In 1681 he is noted as having purchased 'the Red Lyon fields, near Graies Inn Walks, to build on'. The scheme got off to a bad start when his workmen were attacked by 'gentlemen' of Gray's Inn who did not want buildings so near their chambers. His method of development was described by his contemporary, Roger North:

'He was the inventor of this new method of building by casting of ground into streets and small houses, and to augment their number with as little front as possible, and selling the ground to workmen by so much per foot front, and what he could not sell build himself.'

John Summerson points out that he 'grasped the advantages accruing from standardization and mass-production in housing'. He rarely dealt in small ventures and tried as far as possible to fund his developments on credit rather than by loans. He demolished Essex House and York House, mansions on the Strand backing on to the Thames, and on their grounds built streets. He built in the Temple precinct. And after Red Lion Square he moved on to the adjoining Harpur and Rugby estates on Theobalds Road.

Harpur and Rugby

The Harpur Estate stretched from today's Boswell Street at the western end of Theobalds Road to the east side of today's Emerald Street. It also contained an oblong of land to the south of Theobalds Road that includes the western side of Bedford Row. It had been formed by Sir William Harpur, Lord Mayor of London in 1561. He was mayor at the time of the oft-quoted occasion when City of London dignitaries rode out to Paddington and the Tyburn in September 1562 to inspect the City's water conduit heads there and 'after dinner they hunted the fox, and there was a goodly cry for a mile, and after the hounds killed the fox at the end of S. Giles'. He bought his Holborn estate in 1564 with the intention of helping to endow a free school in his native Bedford. The endowment and the school were administered by the Corporation of Bedford – hence Bedford Row and the confusion for the unwary of a 'Bedford Estate' so near the larger Bedford family estate in Bloomsbury. Harpur joined a Tudor trend of supporting schools rather than charities. Other Camden examples are Sir Roger Cholmeley (Highgate School, 1565), Sir Andrew Judd (Tonbridge School, 1572, based on an estate in King's Cross) and Lawrence Sheriff (Rugby School, 1567, based on land adjoining the Harpur estate).

Barbon took on a lease of the Harpur estate at the end of 1687, but it is difficult to know just how much of it he developed before he died in 1698, but the conclusion of the former GLC's Architectural Department was that he left it in an embryonic state but with plans that dictated its character. Nos. 36-43 Bedford Row are said to be Barbon houses, though with small amendments.

Ever on the move, Barbon also took a lease on the estate bequeathed by Lawrence Sheriff to Rugby School. The Rugby estate is directly north of the Harpur, and includes Great Ormond Street, developed from the 1680s and Rugby and Millman Streets, from the 1690s.

Seven Dials

While Barbon developed the Harpur and Rugby estates, a less successful venture was begun in the south of St Giles's parish. This was Seven Dials, consisting of tightly packed properties on seven roads radiating from an ornamental pillar. The original plan had only six roads and, indeed, the original pillar erected at the conjunction of the roads had six dials on it – this, minus dials (which are outside the local library), may still be seen in Weybridge, where it was re-erected. Sir Thomas Neale (d.1699?), whose scheme it was, was Master of the Royal Mint and also had other, no doubt profitable, sinecures such as the furnishing of the king's lodgings, the provision of cards and dice, and the settling of any disputes which arose at card tables or bowling greens; he was also responsible for licensing or suppressing gaming houses and in 1694 organised a national lottery based on the security of a new Salt Tax.

The location of Seven Dials, so near the rookery of St Giles and to the growing vegetable market at Covent Garden, determined its character. John Gay, writing in 1716, mentions narrow alleys

47. *The old Seven Dials pillar re-erected, without its dials, at Weybridge.*

and winding courts, and the area was renowned for its ballad singers and printers, the best known of the latter being James Catnach. In the 19th century it was notorious for its gin shops, sellers of old clothes and furniture, and its pickpockets. Dickens described it in *Sketches by Boz*:

'The stranger who finds himself in the Dials for the first time ... at the entrance of seven obscure passages, uncertain which to take, will see enough around him to keep his curiosity and attention awake for no inconsiderable time. From the irregular square into which he has plunged, the streets and courts dart in all directions, until they are lost in the unwholesome vapour which hangs over the housetops, and renders the dirty perspective uncertain and confined; and lounging at every corner, as if they came there to take a few gasps of such fresh air as has found its way so far, but is too much exhausted already to be enabled to force itself into the narrow alleys around, are groups of people, whose appearance and dwellings would fill any mind but a regular Londoner's with astonishment ... In addition to the numerous groups who are idling about the ginshops, and squabbling in the centre of the road, every post in the open space has its occupant who leans against it for hours with listless perseverance.'

It was, once the creation New Oxford Street had forced Irish families out of the St Giles rookery, an Irish area. Henry Mayhew who investigated it in detail for his *London Labour and the London Poor* (c.1861), noted that there was hardly an English tradesman there – they were all Irish. One man reported to Mayhew that a Roman Catholic of his acquaintance, who knew he was dying, declined to ask the priest to come to his lodgings in Seven Dials because they were so filthy – five men lived and worked in the same room as he. 'In many houses in Monmouth Street there is a system of sub-letting among the journeymen. In one room lodged a man and his wife [a laundress], four children and two single young men. The woman was actually delivered [of a baby] in this room whilst the men kept at their work – they never lost an hour's work.'

Seven Dials was later to house much of the expansion of Covent Garden market and rebuilding took the form of warehouses which today suit the shops, restaurants and studios of a niche shopping area.

Queen Square

Development spread northwards. Within Camden, Queen Square was developed as from 1706. It was at first fashionable, but as the wealthy were attracted to more affluent parts of London, artists and intellectuals moved in. Fanny Burney and her father, Dr Charles Burney, were here in 1771-72, when they were able without obstruction to look up to the heights of Hampstead and Highgate, as the Square had still not been built on its northern side. Most of the original houses were demolished during the 19th century as the Square assumed its present mix of hospitals and institutions.

The Bloomsbury Squares

If Bloomsbury Square is the earliest London square, then Bedford Square is the most complete In 1776, the Bedford family was still ensconced at Bedford (formerly Southampton) House, overlooking Bloomsbury Square. As they wished to protect their rear view of the northern heights, the development of their fields to the east of Gower Street was inhibited. But from the 1790s theirs became an unrealistic ambition since they could not prevent development north of the New Road, and in any case, the location of Bedford House was not now of ducal status. The family moved out of its own estate into the West End and authorised the demolition of Bedford House. From then the full development of the Bloomsbury estate was begun.

The Bedford Square project was carried through not by a Duke of Bedford, for then the new Duke was an infant, but by his mother and by Robert Palmer, agent for the estate. He it was who managed the enterprise at a period of feverish building activity in London and – fortunately for us – at a high point of architectural innovation. The design of Bedford Square appears to have been mostly the work of Thomas Leverton.[2] Each range has a central stuccoed house, accompanied either side by brick-fronted houses decorated with Coade stone features. The Square at first attracted aristocratic occupants, but in the 19th century it was popular with professional people such as architects and writers, and as it became too expensive for residential use, it was colonised by organisations, such as the Architectural Association and by publishers.

The Estate wanted further expansion and fortunately a remarkable builder-architect was to hand in James Burton. He built Russell Square as from 1800, with the gardens laid out by Humphry Repton, and at the same time, once Bedford House had gone, built the houses on the north side of Bloomsbury Square. Beyond the Bedford Estate, he also developed the streets and squares on the Foundling and Skinner Estates south of the Euston Road – Burton Street was named after him as was Burton Crescent before its change of name to Cartwright Gardens. He also began Tavistock Square in 1803, though it was finished much later by Thomas Cubitt. For nearly twenty years Burton created much of what we think of today as Bloomsbury; he then left London and unwisely sank most of his money in the creation of St Leonards-on-Sea, where he died in 1837 as the Victorian era began.

The New Road

John Rocque's great map of London and its immediate environs of *c.*1746 was drawn ten years before Parliament gave authority to build 'the New Road from Paddington to Islington'. His map shows the Camden area almost entirely rural. Built-up London ends at Queen Square and one can imagine the rector of St George the Martyr in 1747, Dr William Stukeley, walking across pleasant fields to his country house at Kentish Town, a village visible from his church. The openness of the area is illustrated in the opposition to the New Road, albeit exaggerated, of the Duke of Bedford. He did not wish to see the road from the rear windows of Bedford House in Bloomsbury Square, or have the effects of dust kicked up by horses on it. More likely, anticipating development along the road, he did not want his view spoilt.

The origins of the New Road project remain obscure. Petitioners to Parliament in 1755 consisted not only of inhabitants of parishes in Westminster and St Marylebone, but of various gentlemen from provincial counties. These latter gentlemen were presumably graziers and farmers tired of the awful scramble to get their cattle into Smithfield. How all these people were got together, and what held them together, is a subject for research. The anticipated benefits from the road were several. One was genuine and others were thrown in, in the hope that the Bill would attract the support of otherwise apathetic Members of Parliament. The real benefit was that residents of Holborn, Bloomsbury and St Giles would not have the enormous traffic of animals treading through their neighbourhoods on their way to Smithfield. The already unpleasant area near St Giles' church was made worse by herds pushing their way through the narrow streets. Local residents complained of 'oxen frequently running wild about the streets alarming and doing mischief in the neighbourhood'. The petitioners also claimed, rather less convincingly, that the road would be useful for moving troops in times of emergency.

The Act stipulated that the road was to be 40 feet wide and that no buildings, other than toll houses, were to be erected within 50 feet of the roadway. Hence, the houses that eventually lined it had long front gardens. Oddly, the Act did not permit the paving of the road since it was to be used primarily for moving animals. This restriction made possible a quick opening of the road – in September 1756.

Some development in Camden, as noted below, inevitably followed it. In St Marylebone it was important to the prosperity of the Portman Estate, and in Islington the planned suburb of Pentonville relied on it in the 1770s. Originally, the road ended at the Angel, Islington from whence cattle went down St John Street to Smithfield. The New Road was however, also seen as a route to business in the City and five years later the City Road was constructed to continue it to Moorgate.

The New Road had a lasting effect on the development of north London. Not only was it the first by-pass, but more importantly, a hundred years later, it acted as a barrier to railway companies – the government insisted that no railway line coming from the north and west should go beyond it. The by-pass became a *cordon sanitaire* with significant consequences for transport and 19th-century development. Unfortunately for Camden, that rural, unpaved road, suitable for herds of cattle, would eventually bring the blight of filthy and noisy railway lands.

Somers Town and Fitzroy Square

Somers Town was begun in 1784 when the landowner, Lord Somers, leased part of his Brill Farm land to Jacob Leroux, a Huguenot. Leroux proposed a pleasant suburb north of the New Road and also an unusual building, three storeys high, shaped as a circle of 32 houses, each two adjoining houses with a joint façade, so that there were 16 angles in all. This building, called The Polygon, was later enclosed by the now demolished Clarendon Square. The writer, William Godwin (1756-1836) occupied a house in Chalton Street before taking an apartment in The Polygon when he married Mary Wollstonecraft in 1797. She died here the following year, after giving birth to the future Mary Shelley, the creator of Frankenstein. Mr Leroux set to work at quite the wrong time if he was aiming to entice middle class residents, for there were many developments much nearer to London which merited their attention. Instead, work came to a stop and, as a local resident writing to the *Gentleman's Magazine* in 1813 described it, 'many carcasses of houses were sold for less than the value of building materials.' Fortunately for many of the house owners, there was an influx of French refugees who settled in this ready-made affordable suburb. The French population was large enough for the Abbé Carron to establish the Roman Catholic church of St Aloysius in Phoenix

48. The 16-sided Polygon in Clarendon Square, Somers Town.

Road, itself a successor to a chapel in Chalton Street. Carron, according to the 1813 writer, presided over four schools.

By c.1801 the Leroux estate consisted chiefly of the Polygon, two parallel streets running towards the New Road, today's Chalton and Ossulston Streets, and Phoenix Road crossing them to the north. East of these the Skinners' Company, whose estate straddled the New Road, had developed the land now occupied by the British Library and St Pancras station with properties built to an even higher density than in Somers Town proper.

As Leroux was trying to make something out of Somers Town, Lord Southampton began developing Fitzroy Square with some panache. The eastern and southern sides were begun in the 1790s, designed by the Adam brothers (who had a financial interest in the scheme), though it was not until the 1820s, when property speculation had recovered, that the north and west sides were built. Oddly, although Fitzroy Square was expected to benefit from its nearness to the New Road, it was the last part of the Southampton Estate south of the Road to be constructed. The grandeur of its architecture indicates that Lord Southampton hoped to attract aristocracy and upper middle class tenants into an area already grid-built around with fairly humdrum premises. But the Square's location, in an unfashionable part of town and quite hidden from view by second-class developments, was discouraging. At any rate its tenants tended to be arty or middle-class, sometimes both, but by the end of the 19th century it was distinctly seedy.

Camden Town

In the 1790s any London landowner who needed money was examining the potential of his fields. There were many mistakes and developments were often stalled, abandoned or else reduced in quality as the hope of a better class of occupier faded. One such development was Camden Town, built with bricks from local clay, as from 1791. As a recent study shows[1], the west side of Camden High Street, then a virtually deserted road leading to both Hampstead and Kentish Town, was the first to be built up, and so the area might well have been called Southampton or Fitzroy Town from the owner of the land on that side of the road. The east side belonged to the 1st Earl of Camden, Charles Pratt (1714-94), a famous Lord Chief Justice. In 1788, when he obtained an Act to develop his lands here, it was called the 'Kentish Town Act', but such was the impact of his proposed grid plan and the initial buildings along the main road, each with a wider frontage than the rather mean premises on the Southampton side, that the area was called 'Camden Town' by 1791, the same year that construction began. It is known as such in an advertisement which enticed the embryo Royal Veterinary College to take a plot in the hinterland where there was room to stable horses, and a water supply (the Fleet) for them to use.

Camden Town, and therefore Camden, derive their names in a convoluted way from a 16th-century headmaster of Westminster School, William Camden. He retired to Chislehurst, where his house was called Camden Place. In the 18th-century it was the country house of Charles Pratt, 1st Lord Camden, noted above. Other Pratt family and estate names dot the Camden area – Bayham, Brecknock, Jeffreys, Murray and Rochester. Camden died in 1794 before much of his scheme, farmed out through speculators, had been constructed. The c.1801 map of the parish shows little more than buildings along the High Street (save what became the Bowman site), and roads laid out eastwards towards St Pancras Way; Royal College Street did not then exist. The early promise did not materialise, and development proceeded slowly. Even a local church, the usual sign that an area was established, was not built until the Camden

Chapel, designed by the Inwoods senior and junior, opened in 1824. A writer in 1874 noted that many builders had bought plots of land in Camden Town at the beginning of the century, but so small was the demand for houses there, that they were unable to finish what they had begun. When the much grander houses of Camden Square and the streets around it were built as from the 1860s, they were called 'Camden New Town' to distinguish it from those roads near the High Street which by then had fallen on to very hard times.

The Regent's Park

In 1538 Henry VIII obliged the Prebendary of St Paul's Cathedral to exchange Rugmere manor for some property near Faversham – as always with Henry, an unequal bargain. The little manor consisted of about 275 acres in the west part of St Pancras parish (some of it extended into St Marylebone), including what became Chalk Farm Tavern (probably the old manor house), the Camden Goods Yard, Regent's Park Road, Gloucester, Cumberland, Chester and Cambridge Terraces in the Outer Circle, part of the Zoological Gardens, Albany Street and Cumberland

Market. Some of that land later found its way into the ownership of the Southampton family, but much of the rest was utilised first as part of King Henry's Marylebone hunting ground, and as from 1811, as part of Regent's Park and its service hinterland. In all, 145 acres of St Pancras parish were enclosed within the park.

When the old hunting ground, by then farmland and called Marylebone Fields, was considered for transformation, the New Road (Marylebone Road) had encouraged building development to its south. It would have been logical, once the farming leases ended in 1811, for the Crown to have developed Marylebone Fields in much the same way, but fortunately for London, the decisive voice at the time was the Prince Regent, the future George IV. He wanted a much grander scheme than a grid plan of houses. His vision, and that of his architect John Nash, was for a triumphal road leading from his own extravagant Carlton House in Pall Mall, through undistinguished property north of Piccadilly, to emerge at a magnificent new park of villas on his Marylebone farm land. In any case, it was reasoned, it would be difficult to sell expensive houses in the park unless there was better access

49. Albany Street in c.1905, showing Christchurch and Christchurch School.

62

to them from the West End. As a consequence, Regent Street and Langham Place were built.

Readers are referred to Dr Ann Saunders' book[3] for an account of how the park, its villas and terraces came to be built, and of their subsequent history, for we are here dealing only with that part of the Crown Estate within the old St Pancras parish. The four terraces on the Outer Circle within St Pancras were built between 1825 and 1827. Simultaneously the Colosseum was built on the site of today's Cambridge Gate. This roughly circular building behind a classical portico, was designed by the young Decimus Burton (he also designed The Holme in Regent's Park). It was built to house the giant panorama concocted by land surveyor Thomas Hornor who, from a vertiginous perch on the dome of St Paul's which he climbed to each morning, sketched the swathes of London beneath him. These sketches, enlarged and painted by artists at the Colosseum, were shown to an admiring public in January 1829, but the venture, already racked with financial problems, soon lost its curiosity value and was always a doubtful financial asset. The building was demolished in 1875.

Panoramas were static, whereas dioramas which could utilise moving lights, changing views and sound effects, were not. Around the corner from the Colosseum was The Diorama in St Andrew's Place. This was designed by James Morgan and Augustus Charles Pugin and opened in October 1823. It had a circular auditorium which could seat 200 people, and which could be rotated through 73 degrees so that the audience had a view of a series of special effects and illusions. In 1854 the building was converted to a Baptist chapel and over the years it has been much altered, though the façade remains today.

Another stylistic intrusion in this east side of the Outer Circle was the Gothic St Katharine's Chapel just south of Gloucester Gate. Its origins lay with St Katharine's Hospital (almshouses), founded by Queen Matilda in the 12th century, just outside the City wall near the Tower of London. The Hospital and its precinct were demolished in 1826 to make way for St Katharine's Dock and moved to a compensatory site, still on Crown territory, in Regent's Park, where a group of almshouses accompany a chapel, all designed by Ambrose Poynter in 1829. During the 1st World War the chapel was given to her fellow Danes by Queen Alexandra and is nowadays the principal Danish church in London.

John Nash himself developed Park Villages East and West, in the north-eastern extremity of the Crown estate. These two groups of delightful villas in various architectural styles were by Nash and James Pennethorne and built between 1823 and 1834. They look, at first glance, as if the architects were enjoying themselves, and no doubt they were. Unfortunately, one side of Park Village East was demolished in 1906 when the LNWR railway cutting was enlarged.

The streets on Crown Estate land east of Albany Street were intended for the most part to be service areas to the terraces and villas in the Park, but the Cumberland Market on a spur of the Regent's Canal just north of Robert Street, was also viewed as a London entrepot – the Hay Market south of Piccadilly Circus was moved here in 1830. Other facilities included a vast ice well which took in ice shipped from Norway and towed up the canal from London Docks. The Cumberland Market was never particularly successful and was even less so once railways began to carry freight in any quantity.

Other interesting buildings of this period are the Ophthalmic Hospital and the Regent's Park Barracks (1820-21) in Albany Street. The Ophthalmic Hospital (on the east side of the street on a site now covered by Rothay flats) was founded in 1818 to treat soldiers who had been infected with eye diseases, particularly trachoma, during service in Egypt – the beginnings of Moorfields Eye Hospital were similar. The building was designed free of charge by Nash and opened in 1818, but by 1821 it was the workshop of Sir Goldsworthy Gurney who pioneered the use of steam carriages. He astounded everyone by going to Bath and back at an average speed of 15mph. Around 1900 the old hospital was a depot for buses and after damage in the last war was demolished in 1967.

[1] See Marian Kamlish, 'Before Camden Town 1745-1795', Camden History Review (1998).
[2] Andrew Byrne, Bedford Square, p.23 (1990).
[3] Ann Saunders, Regent's Park from 1086 to the Present (2nd edn 1981)

CHAPTER EIGHT
In Pursuit of Knowledge

The British Museum

London is now so packed with museums, art galleries and libraries that it is difficult to imagine it bereft of them. But such was the case in 1753 when Sir Hans Sloane died at his Chelsea home leaving a vast collection of books, manuscripts, drawings, natural history specimens and coins. In his will he directed that these be offered to the nation at the knock-down price of £20,000. An unusually sympathetic House of Commons accepted the offer and at the same time decided to house it with another collection already in public ownership, that of Sir Robert Cotton (1571-1631), then languishing in inaccessible premises in Westminster. Cotton's collection included thousands of manuscripts, cartularies and state papers, coins, the Lindisfarne Gospels and two copies of Magna Carta. The manuscript collection of Robert Harley, 1st Earl of Oxford (1661-

1724) and his son, the 2nd Earl, was also up for sale, and this the government bought for £10,000. To these treasures was added the old Royal Library, dating from Tudor times, which brought with it the automatic right to a copy of each book registered at Stationers' Hall (then a necessary requirement of publishers). This has translated in modern times to the right to each book published.

But where to put these collections? Buckingham House, which later became Buckingham Palace, was seriously considered, but the choice was made of Montagu House in Great Russell Street, the next-door neighbour, so to speak, of the Duke of Bedford's mansion in Bloomsbury Square. This decision eventually determined the nature of the neighbourhoods surrounding these two houses. A sum of money was raised from an unusually corrupt national lottery, the

50. *The garden front of Montagu House, Great Russell Street, the home of the British Museum; a print published in 1813.*

house was bought for £10,000, and trustees were appointed who made access to the general public as difficult as possible. The British Museum was inaugurated on 15 January 1759, when only eight readers turned up. The Museum opened for three hours a day to general visitors of whom the Principal Librarian approved, and who had written in advance stating the day and time of their visit. These rules applied until 1808 and only in 1879 was free and general access instituted. In its earliest days, people visiting the museum – usually less than sixty per day – were accompanied round by staff.

The first Montagu House was built for the 1st Duke of Montagu in 1675. The architect was Robert Hooke, who had been active in the rebuilding of London after the Fire of 1666. John Evelyn described it as 'Mr Montague's new palace neere Bloomsbury', but this fine house was unfortunately burnt down eleven years later. Montagu next hired a French architect, Puget, whose house, in the style of a French hôtel, was the one bought as a home for the nation's neglected treasures. It also had $7^1/_2$ acres of garden, much of which was taken up by subsequent rebuilding and expansion. At that time, before development of the Bedford Estate to the rear had begun, the north side of the house had rural views. Thomas Gray, who used the Reading Room from its inception, wrote in a letter to a friend that from his own lodgings (in what became Southampton Row) he could see Highgate and Hampstead, and in the Museum he would 'pass four hours in the day in the stillness & solitude of the reading room, wch is uninterrupted by any thing except by Dr Stukeley the Antiquary, who comes there to talk nonsense...'

It is calculated that the collections of Sloane, Cotton and Harley, which formed the basis for the new museum, took up over a mile of shelving, and there was as well an enormous number of natural exhibits in the Sloane collection for display. Colonial expansion and wars, particularly the Napoleonic wars, brought a flood of antiquities to the Museum, such as the Rosetta Stone, the Portland Vase and, of course, the Elgin Marbles which a parsimonious government felt obliged to buy from the unfortunate Lord Elgin. It was the gift of George IV of his father's magnificent library, amounting to over 65,000 volumes, which made inevitable the erection of a purpose-built museum. At first the architect chosen, Robert Smirke, built a quadrangle of buildings behind Montagu House, which included the King's Library. Construction of these continued until 1838 and in 1842, with the demolition of the old house, the grand classical front that we see today was commenced. This was still not enough and by 1857 Sydney Smirke had built his famous round Reading Room on the site of the old quadrangle.

Sir John Soane

As we have seen, the British Museum evolved from the collections of private individuals rich enough to amass them. Another bequest to the public – until recently not well enough known – was that of the architect, Sir John Soane (1753-1837). The son of a Berkshire bricklayer, Soane came to London to study architecture in 1768, and was apprenticed to the eminent George Dance the Younger and then to Henry Holland. He married the niece of architect George Wyatt and with a legacy on Wyatt's death, the couple were able to buy 12 Lincoln's Inn Fields, which he then demolished and replaced with a house of his own design in 1792. Soane had developed a prosperous practice – he was appointed architect to build the new Bank of England in 1788; by then he had pupils of his own working at the back of the house. It was during this period that he began to assemble his comprehensive collection of architectural and archaeological specimens, but he also enjoyed and bought paintings and drawings. In 1800 he acquired Pitshanger Manor in Ealing, which gave him more room to display his treasures and to entertain, but this was still not enough, for in 1808 he bought next door 13 Lincoln's Inn Fields which, some years later he again demolished and rebuilt. Once he had given up Pitshanger in 1810, he bought the adjoining no. 14 as well, and rebuilt this too.

When he died in 1837 the house and its contents were made open to the public, one of the most satisfying museums in London.

The University of London

At the beginning of the 19th century London was almost alone in European capitals in not possessing a university. Moreover, young men who were Dissenters, Roman Catholics, Jews or non-believers were not permitted to attend the universities of Oxford and Cambridge. The cause to institute a university which would have no theological base or bias was not altogether popular, and when University College in Gower Street was established, it was nicknamed the 'Godless College' by its opponents.

Daniel Defoe in the 1720s had espoused the merits of a university of colleges spread around London, but it was the Scots poet, Thomas Campbell, who appears to have set the project in motion. Impressed by Bonn University, he proposed a 'great London university' for 'effectively and multifariously teaching, examining, exercising and rewarding with honours, in the liberal arts and sciences, the youth of our middling rich people'. He was supported by Henry Brougham and George Birkbeck, both of whom had been active in the development of mechanics' institutes and the founding of the Society for the Diffusion of Useful Knowledge. By 1826 a limited liability company was formed to issue shares and to create a university. It opened in 1828 at the top of Gower Street, in a Greek revival style that only served to confirm the worst fears of those who called it 'Godless', designed by William Wilkins. This was accomplished only two years after the first formal meeting convened to establish it.

There was immediate reaction from the opposition. The Duke of Wellington chaired a meeting which included three archbishops, seven bishops and some nobility, to found another college in London which would 'immure the minds of youth with a knowledge of the doctrines and duties of Christianity...' This was to be King's College in the Strand. The aim of University College to grant degrees was challenged by Oxford and Cambridge, and the intention to include medical schools was opposed by the medical profession. To resolve what became an embarrassing and unnecessary dilemma, a Whig government established a body called the University of London, which could issue degrees to students at both the new colleges. In time this federal arrangement has been extended to include numerous educational institutions, many of them in Bloomsbury where large tracts of the old Bedford estate have either been converted or replaced.

A spirit of inquiry

In the 1820s science became popular. The mechanics' institutes in particular embraced it, and in the 1840s institutions were formed whose aim was to spread knowledge of the humanities *and* science. The spirit of inquiry affected all classes of society, so that alongside the mechanics' institutes there were organisations for the middle classes, usually called Literary & Scientific Institutions. One of the earliest in Camden

51. *Mr and Mrs H. Holt, librarians at the Highgate Literary and Scientific Institution, in 1895.*

was the Russell Institution in Coram Street (the site of today's Witley Court). Its building was erected in 1804 by the developer, James Burton, as assembly rooms, but these lasted only three seasons. In 1808 the building was taken over by investors who formed the Institution soon afterwards. Early members included Samuel Romilly and Henry Hallam, and later ones were Thackeray, Dickens and John Leech. According to Samuel Palmer's *St Pancras* (1870), it comprised a large library for reference and lending, a theatre or lecture room, a news room, a magazine room, a committee room and a residence for the secretary.

These facilities were also included in the Highgate Literary & Scientific Institution, founded in 1839, and still today the hub of Highgate Village. It is one of only twelve similar organisations in the country founded in that era, that still survives. The Institution began at a meeting convened by Harry Chester at the Gatehouse Tavern. Chester was one of the Highgate elite. His father had lived at the Old Hall in South Grove and he himself lived nearby at South Grove House (now superseded by a block of flats of the same name). Professionally, he was a Clerk to the Privy Council Education Committee, and education for the masses was indeed a passionate interest of his. He advocated more cheerful school rooms and also facilities for children to learn crafts and agriculture. In 1850 his influence secured a large grant to build a National School in North Road, Highgate, today's St Michael's School.

The Institution, although theoretically open to working class people, did not attract them. The original members 'were people with private means, professional men and local shopkeepers'. No doubt some of them belonged also to the Highgate Book Society, founded in 1822, at whose monthly dinners books bought by their subscription were circulated and lent. The Society's subscribers over the years included Dr Gillman, with whom Coleridge lodged, and Captain Peter Heywood who, when young, had played an involuntary part in the mutiny on the *Bounty*.

The first premises of the Institution were in a house in Southwood Lane, but in 1840 a move was made to the stabling and outbuildings of Church House in South Grove, then occupied by Leopold Neumegen, who ran a school for Jewish boys in the main house. The Institution has had several critical periods in its history. One was in the 1870s, when it almost closed, and another in the lacklustre 1950s when it was obliged to sell the adjoining Church House at a very low price.

At 36 Whitfield Street in Fitzrovia was an organisation simply called the Literary & Scientific Institution. This was founded a year later than the Highgate organisation by followers of Robert Owen, who therefore determined its secular and political nature. Its members were radicals, and the building was a meeting place for the National Secular Society. Chartists gathered here for a mass meeting in 1848 after the big Chartist demonstrations in London, and were addressed by Feargus O'Connor. This Institution closed in 1858.

The short-lived Camden Literary & Scientific Institution was formed and went out of existence before the Highgate Institution had even begun.[2] In June 1835 seven gentlemen met in a house in Camden Road opposite the present Sainsbury's, to form a committee that would found an Institution. Unable to afford the expense of its own building, the Institution rented rooms at 40 Camden High Street and commenced a series of lectures which it threw open to the St Pancras Institution based in Edward Street off Hamp-

52. *The Hampstead Subscription Library at Stanfield House in Hampstad High Street.*

stead Road, an organisation about which little is known. The Camden Institution opened its rooms from 9am to 10pm, but it was always short of funds, books and natural history specimens. In 1836 it began to hold lectures, previously at the Castle Tavern in Kentish Town, in the premises of the Commissioners for Paving and Lighting the Camden Estate in Pratt Street, just behind Camden Chapel. The minute books of the Institution show a steady decline in members and funds until in 1839, when only 13 members had renewed their subscription, it was closed down and its possessions auctioned.

The spirit of scientific enquiry in Hampstead did not result in a dedicated local society until 1899, when the Hampstead Scientific Society was formed, but the intention to encompass it is indicated in the original name of the Hampstead Subscription Library. The Hampstead Public Library of General Literature and Elementary Science was established in 1833 at 65 Flask Walk. John Constable, then living in Well Walk, was a founder member as was the poet, Joanna Baillie. It moved twice in its erratic early history before settling in 1884 at the former house of the artist. Clarkson Stanfield, nos. 85-88 Hampstead High Street. Membership was decidedly low church and progressive. It included a good number of local Unitarians, and also radical publishers such as Charles Knight, a man closely associated with efforts to extend literacy to the masses. Several established publishers, such as Bell, John Murray and T.N. Longman, donated books. Other members represented essential Hampstead society. Typical was the chairman, Charles Holford, after whose family Holford Road is named. His family was established in Hampstead in the 18th century, and at one time occupied the 16th-century house in Holly Hill that was demolished for the University College preparatory school. It was Charles Holford who helped buy Romney's house on Holly Bush Hill to establish Assembly Rooms for dinners, social gatherings and balls; he was prominent in the Hampstead Volunteers formed originally in 1799 and revived in 1803 with the threat of invasion from France. A successful business man, Holford was chairman of the New River Company, and also an enthusiastic astronomer, going so far as to build an observatory at his house overlooking the Heath, which was a regular meeting place for scientific specialists.[3]

The Hampstead Subscription Library did not close its doors until 1966, well into the era of good public libraries.

The Royal Veterinary College

Quite another field of knowledge was the specialty of the Royal Veterinary College in Camden Town. The first veterinary college in Europe had been established in 1762 in Lyons, but not until 1791 did a committee chaired by Granville Penn, grandson of William Penn, set in motion a scheme for a similar college in England. As their first principal they appointed a M. Vial de St Bel, from the Lyons establishment, whose main interest was horses. The College was established in May that year and the committee began looking for a site to house it. M. St Bel urged them not to choose marshy or low ground, because of the putrid vapours exhaled. Why the committee took on the low-lying acres next to the Fleet river as it entered the notorious bog called Pancras Wash is not known, but perhaps the land was cheap. The Bloomsbury developer, James Burton, prepared the plans for the College buildings and despite some turmoil because St Bel was found to be unsatisfactory, the first patient, a horse, was admitted on 1 January 1793, its treatment watched by 14 pupils.

St Bel was superseded by Edward Coleman, who was to be in charge for nearly 46 years. A memoir by a student who was there in 1828 recalls that the college was built in quadrangle form, in the middle of which was a lawn and a place for exercising horses; to the rear was a garden which bordered the Fleet and nearby was the Elephant & Castle pub whose landlord would not 'allow more than a proper quantity of either ale, wine or spirits' to be drunk by the students.

As it happened, the purely chance location of the College here was fortuitous because once the railways had come in force to the area, with thousands of horses in their care, the presence of the College was of great benefit.

Some early schools

By the early 19th century parts of Camden were popular locations for the sort of schools and academies kept by impecunious clergymen and spinster ladies. Their stories and quaint advertisements, and the images of them that have come down to us, loom large in local histories, possibly a consequence of their rarity and the usual attractiveness of their buildings as compared with modern educational buildings. Private schools of this type flourished up to and beyond the 1870 Education Act under which the State made a serious start on the education of younger children. Though their proprietors may have seen a hazy writing on the wall, state intervention was not immediately troublesome, for the parents of *their* pupils were not likely to send them to state schools in which the working classes were predominant. The main casualties of state competition and the state's more demanding requirements of conditions and quality in schools, were those run by the National Society on behalf of the Church of England, or the less well-funded British Schools whose pupils came from non-conformist families. In any case, as the Education Act had been introduced by a Liberal government, the British Schools, being non-conformist, were happy to hand over their role to the new Board Schools, while the National Schools resisted the relatively religion-free curriculum of the London School Board.

Quickly ousted were Dame Schools and Ragged Schools. The Field Lane Ragged School, one of the best known in the Holborn area, soon found itself under the management of the London School Board. It closed other than for 'Christian training', but the Field Lane Foundation revived as it acquired a new role in 1871 when it was made responsible for two Industrial Schools. These were eventually relocated to Hampstead – the boys to Hillfield Road off Fortune Green Road, and the girls to 9 and 9a Church Row.

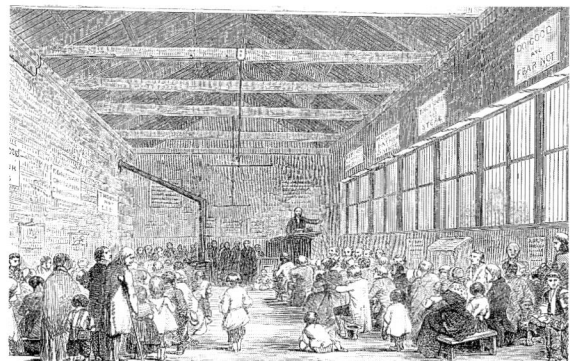

53. Preaching in a Ragged School, Gray's Inn Road. From the Illustrated London News 7 August, 1858.

Before the organised provision of National and British schools, there were parochial or free schools for the poorer clases. One of the earliest may have been in Holborn. The rector of St Andrew's, Gilbert Worthington, possibly set up a grammar school in the 1440s, for it was he who, together with other City rectors, petitioned the Commons to be allowed to establish grammar schools in their own parishes. In their petition they complained that 'where there is a great number of learners and few teachers, and all the learners be compelled to go to the same few teachers and to some others, the masters were rich in money and the learners poor in cunning'. The petitioners were successful but no record survives to confirm that a school was established in Holborn.

Chronologically, the next 'Camden' school was Highgate School, though just over the border in what was then Hornsey. As we have seen (*p.39*), the school and its chapel were founded in 1565 by Highgate resident Sir Roger Cholmeley and it was probably functioning by 1571, when the school rules were formulated. The intention was to educate forty poor children from Highgate, Holloway, Hornsey, Finchley and Kentish Town virtually free of charge. The regime there was not untypical of the period – the boys had to be present at seven in the morning, so that they could be on their knees for morning prayers. They were taught until 11am and then from 1pm to 5pm or 6pm, depending on the time of year. From this unpromising beginning developed a famous public school. Similar enterprises all over the country, begun with private bequests, can be found but few have flourished so well as Highgate. Most others became National schools and were later subsumed into the state educa-

54. The parish school of St George the Martyr off Theobalds Road.

tion system, usually as church schools. An example of this is in St Giles-in-the-Fields, where William Shelton (after whom Shelton Street in Covent Garden is named) left his worldly goods in 1672 to continue a school he had founded for 50 poor children in the neighbourhood of Parker Street. The Shelton Charity School eventually became a part of the state system. Other schools were from the outset the responsibility of the local vestries, such as the Bloomsbury Parochial Schools, founded in Museum Street in 1705 on the initiative and expense of a vicar of St Giles, for 25 girls to be trained as servants, and 80 boys. In St Andrew's parish, a chapel in Hatton Garden was converted in 1721 to use by a parochial school which had previously been in Brooke's Market. Figurines of blue-dressed charity school children (similar to those that are on the front of St Andrew's church) still adorn the façade of their old building. In the parish of St George the

Martyr, a school for 20 boys and 20 girls was established in the vestry of the church in 1708. This today is a primary Church of England School in John's Mews.

Hampstead's parochial school had unusual origins. It was founded by a local society of gentlemen called the Philo-Investigists. Barratt in his *Annals* (1912) describes them as 'certain well-disposed Hampstead gentlemen, grown weary of the eternal wrangle which pervaded ordinary intercourse'. The Hampstead Museum at Burgh House and the Local Studies and Archives Centre in Holborn have examples of the medallions they had cast for themselves, replete with masonic-like symbols: these are also to be found on the gravestone of founding member, Thomas Mitchell, in Hampstead churchyard. Members were to be temperate and, at least at club meetings, only discuss 'topics that tend to improve the understanding and mend the heart'. If they disagreed with another's opinion, they were encouraged to 'lay it down with temper and precision, using no pun, jest or witticism'. More practically, these worthy gentlemen founded a Sunday School in *c*.1787 at a time when the Sunday School movement was being popularised by its founder, Robert Raikes. The patron of the school was the prime minister, Spencer Perceval, who lived at Belsize House. From this institution developed Hampstead Parochial School which eventually was centred on Hollybush Vale, where it remains today.

St Pancras did not have a parochial school in the usual sense. In 1775 the churchwardens reported that there had recently been collections at the Percy Chapel in Charlotte Street on behalf of the charity children of St Giles and St George Bloomsbury. Probably annoyed that money from St Pancras parishioners was being spent outside the area, they suggested that St Pancras too should have a school for which money could be raised. In other words, it was to be supported by public donation rather than charged to the rates. In 1776 the St Pancras Female Charity School was established at 12 Windmill Street in premises previously used by the French Charity School. It was, needless to say, an instrument of repression as well as education, for the purpose was to produce domestic servants and apprentices. There was, after all, nothing else to do with poor children of 'unfortunate parents' who had had no 'opportunity of being instructed in the principles of Christianity, to the gross ignorance of which all vices, idleness, and debauchery are

chiefly owing'. The girls were, as Samuel Wiswould observed in his 1865 book on St Pancras charities, 'brought up with proper ideas of humility and obedience to their superiors, and trained in all such necessary qualifications as are most likely to render them beneficial to the community, by becoming honest and useful domestic servants.' Originally, six girls were taught there but there were 65 by the time they moved in 1790 to a new building erected in Hampstead Road, just north of St James's Chapel. It came replete with a 'handsome' board room in which the Vestry met until 1829, when Vestry rooms were taken in Gordon Street. The School was rebuilt in 1904 and later moved to 14 Highgate West Hill where it is now part of the St Pancras Foundation. Its old building in Hampstead Road is now used for offices.

Academies

Typical of the sort of minor academy which took boys early in the 19th century was the one that Charles Dickens attended – Wellington House Academy, in Hampstead Road, just south of Mornington Crescent on a site now taken by the railway. He was a pupil here when his family were living in Johnson Street (now Cranleigh Street), Somers Town. He and a schoolfriend went back to look at the school in 1851, to find that the railway had by then (because of track widening) taken away the playground, sliced away the schoolroom, and pared off a corner of the house. In *Household Words* Dickens describes the Master, the usher, the Latin master, the dancing master, the French master and a serving man named Phil.

Of a classier nature was the Southampton House Academy, whose premises still overlook Highgate Road just past the railway bridge, though on modern conversion the word 'Academy' has been erased from the wall plaque. The railway long ago took away much of its rear playground. This school was functioning in 1828, when the headmaster let it be known that 'His first wish for his pupils is that they should have the fear of God.' He believed that 'from this springs a self control and diligence ... such as nothing else can give.' For their 24 guineas a term the boys got a lot of physical exercise, English, penmanship, history and geography. Opposite Southampton House was a 'French Academy kept by a Gentleman of the name of Jollie' who, on the breaking out of the French Revolution in the year 1789 introduced 'manual

55. The playground of the Southampton House Academy in Highgate Road. Most of the playground was taken when the Tottenham and Hampstead Junction Railway was built. Drawn by E.R.E. Pease.

exercise' and had his pupils regularly drilled and 'dressed in Uniform … according to French nationality'. M. Jollie was gone by 1805, the year of Trafalgar.

Also in this stretch of Highgate Road was the Gordon House Academy, on the corner of to-day's Gordon House Road. It is shown on James King's wonderful panorama of Kentish Town drawn so as to represent the village in about the year 1800. He notes that it was an 'old establish'd Academy kept by Mr Cooper, who died suddenly of Apoplexy in the year 1788 whilst sitting at his Desk giving Lessons to his pupils; among the number was the Artist of this Sketch. His Successor was A. Mensal, esqre, from Aberdeen, who married the widow.'

The large houses of Highgate and Hampstead were particularly suitable for schools. In part of the Old Hall, South Grove, Elizabeth Tutchin was running a school in 1710 'where young gentlewomen may be soberly Educated, and taught all sorts of Learning fit for young Gentlewomen', and at the end of the century Diana Kearton and Harriet Sheldon managed a girls' school at Lauderdale House, which was succeeded by a boys' school. Dr Benjamin Duncan was in charge of an unusual establishment at Elm Court, next door to Lauderdale House, based

on Pestalozzian principles. His curriculum included astronomy, biology and chemistry, as well as architecture, surveying, logic and elocution. His pupils were free of rote learning, corporal punishment and fagging, which was some consolation for not being allowed to go home at Christmas as Duncan found 'vacations to be very prejudicial to the interests of young gentlemen'.

Another unusual school in Highgate Village was a Jewish Academy, probably the only one in the country other than an establishment in Brighton. It was run from 1802 by Hyman Hurwitz, a friend of Coleridge, at Church House in South Grove. His successor, Leopold Neumegen, eventually went bankrupt and the school also went to Brighton.

At 46 Highgate West Hill was Grove House School, which probably began around 1825. Most of it was given over to boys, but an 1837 advertisement claims that 'Young ladies are liberally boarded and carefully instructed in every department of plain and ornamental education.' When the school closed in 1930 it consisted of accommodation for a number of pupils in the main house, and a schoolroom attached which took three classes without any dividing walls. The daughter of the long serving headmaster,

Alfred Dickinson, recalls that the art master there during her childhood was Francis Barraud, the designer of the HMV dog and record player motif.

The census of 1851 shows 39 private day schools in Hampstead and by 1872, 60 private schools are listed. Two of the best known, partly because of famous pupils or staff, were Henley House in Mortimer Place, and Heath Mount at the top end of Heath Street, on the west side. Henley House, which was in business from the early 1880s, had A.A. Milne as a pupil, with his father the head-master, H.G. Wells teaching science and Alfred Harmsworth, the future newspaper baron, as another pupil. The school provided secondary education, but J.V. Milne, according to his son, sold up in about 1892 convinced by then that only preparatory schools stood much chance of success. Heath Mount School had an older pedigree and, indeed, a classier one. It was founded in 1817 'for the sons of gentlemen', who

included in, more modern times, Evelyn Waugh, Cecil Beaton and Gerald du Maurier. The school moved out in 1934 to Hertfordshire (where it still is), and the building was demolished and re-placed by some neo-Georgian houses.

One of the most influential Camden schools began, not in a large house in Highgate or Hampstead, but in a cramped terrace dwelling at what was then 46 Camden Street. The North London Collegiate School for Girls was founded here by Frances Mary Buss who became a leader in the field of women's education. As Miss Buss asked on Prize Day 1866: 'Why should all the endowments appropriated to the education of the middle and upper classes belong almost exclusively to boys?

Frances Buss came from a family that was interested in education. She was lucky with her parents – a mother who seems to have been a paragon of knowledge, encouragement and comfort, and a father who was a gifted painter.

56. The gymnasium of the North London Collegiate School for Girls, Sandall Road, in 1882.

Her mother, in fact, began her own school in Clarence Road, Kentish Town based on Pestalozzian methods and her announcement in 1845 is in sharp contrast to the other private schools which laid such stress on discipline and Christian inculcation. She would, she said, 'spare no exertion to fulfil her duty to those children whose Parents may confide them to her for the elements of an Intellectual Education'. Her daughter Frances, taught at that school while very young.

The turning point for Frances Buss was her attendance at Queen's College in Harley Street, which was founded in 1848 largely by the efforts of Frederick Denison Maurice (who six years later would also establish the Working Men's College) and the Rev. David Laing, the energetic vicar of the yet unbuilt Holy Trinity church in Hartland Road, Kentish Town. Laing was also secretary of the Governesses' Benevolent Institution, which was to crop up again in the development of Miss Buss's schools. The object of Queen's College was to train women to teach in schools or else to be competent governesses.

Miss Buss's interest lay in the education of girls who came from families neither poor nor rich, who were not sent to National or British Schools because socially those schools were unacceptable, yet whose parents could not afford the better girls' academies or to employ governesses. This section of society may be summed up in the mix that arrived on the first day of her school: their fathers consisted of 'retired gentlemen, surgeons, artists, clerks and the most respectable tradesmen in the neighbourhood'.

By December that year the school had 115 pupils crammed into the house (Frances and her family lived in the basement and attics). It was destined, as the Fleming Report of 1944 noted, 'to become the model of girls' Day Schools throughout the country.' There was no distinction of social class in her school and no remoteness between staff and pupils: 'For the purpose of arresting the pupils' attention and exciting a habit of observation the majority of the lessons are necessarily of a conversational character and set forms of words are used only when certain facts have to be engrafted upon the memory.'

At that time girls were not permitted to go to university, but a scheme was implemented in 1863 whereby a certain number sat Cambridge examinations on a trial basis so that the quality of their education might be assessed. Of the 91 candidates, 29 came from the North London

Collegiate. In 1866, the third year of the experiment, of 126 candidates, only 36 failed. The battle was almost won. Soon after Girton College was opened at Cambridge, one third of the students came from Miss Buss's school, which by then had moved to larger premises at 202 Camden Road.

The move away allowed the indefatigable Miss Buss in 1871 to set up a new school in the Camden Street premises, the Camden School for Girls, for which the fees were lower and whose pupils came not from the professional classes, but often from working class homes. The accommodation was insufficient, just as it had been for the North London, but it was some years before Miss Buss obtained from the Brewers' Company, who administered the William Platt charity in St Pancras, sufficient funds to rehouse both schools. With the aid of the Clothworkers' Company, a site was bought for the North London in Sandall Road, and in 1876, when the Governesses' Benevolent Institution moved out of Prince of Wales Road, its building and commodious site was bought for the Camden School. The building was remodelled, though the initials of the Governesses' Institution are still on the gates of what recently has been a part of the St Richard of Chichester School.

The object of the Governesses' Institution, formed in 1844, was to 'raise the character of Governesses as a class, and thus to improve the tone of Female Education; to assist Governesses in making provision for their old age; and to assist in distress and age those Governesses whose exertions for their parents, or families, have prevented such a provision'. The building in Prince of Wales Road, opened in June 1849, was principally a home for aged governesses fallen on hard times.

Here the Camden School for Girls remained until the North London moved out to Canons in Edgware just before the last war, and then once again took over that school's former premises in Sandall Road.

Another illustrious school for girls began as the St John's Wood High School in Winchester Road, Swiss Cottage in 1876 – in those days what was perceived as St John's Wood extended as far as the lower reaches of Fitzjohns Avenue. It chose the right location, for with the building of the Avenue and its attendant roads, there were more than enough families affluent enough to educate their daughters. Six years later, what became the South Hampstead High School for

Girls, moved to its building in Maresfield Gardens, designed by E.C. Robins.

By the end of the 19th century the nature of educational methods was a contentious issue. One result of this was the establishment in 1897 of the King Alfred School Society which aimed to pursue the theories of Pestalozzi, Froebel and others with similar views on teaching. This led in turn to the opening of the King Alfred 'Co-Educational and Open Air' School at 24 Ellerdale Road, Hampstead in 1898. Usual teaching methods of the day were jettisoned. Pupils sat around tables rather than at desks; there was no religious instruction; the curriculum was for the benefit of the child and not for examining bodies. This school, despite a serious schism amongst its Society members in 1901, still flourishes.

Earlier in the same field, but without the same emphasis on fresh air in the classroom, was William Ellis School. A former marine insurer, Ellis founded ten schools known collectively as Birkbeck Schools in honour of the educationalist, George Birkbeck. The basis of teaching was that pupils should think for themselves and not rely on learning by rote. Only one of his foundations, called at first Gospel Oak Schools and established in Rochford Street, off Lismore Circus, survives today. In 1864 it moved to new buildings in Allcroft Road and went on to its present building in Highgate Road in 1937.

Another successful private school is Hall School in Crossfield Road, Hampstead. The building it occupies was built in 1890 as a girls' school, but was bought by what became the Hall School in 1905. The Hall, formerly Belsize School for Boys, had begun in Buckland Crescent in 1889.

Of Camden's private schools the largest presence today is that of University College School. It opened in December 1830 in a house in Gower Street as a feeder school to University College, then itself newly established. Unfortunately, the first headmaster decamped with the original 58 pupils and set up a school of his own in Kensington. In November 1831 the school reopened, this time within the grounds of the College. Like its parent, it did not have religious instruction or observance and it was, unlike many private schools, a day school only. Furthermore, there was no corporal punishment. It became fashionable, but as time went on and the middle

57. The opening, by King Edward VII, of the University College School in Frognal, in 1907.

74

58. A school room at the Boys' Home, Regent's Park Road.

classes gradually moved out of declining Bloomsbury into the suburbs, the school found it difficult to attract the students it catered for. A junior school was set up in Holly Hill, Hampstead 1891 where it was thought, quite rightly, a better pupil intake might be achieved. The main school followed in 1907 to the present building by Arnold Mitchell, built on a sloping terrain bedevilled by underground streams. The first ten years or so were difficult, but by 1930 the school role had surpassed its target of 500.

An Industrial School

In the 1850s London had five reformatories for destitute boys who had previous criminal convictions. It was the idea of George Bell and George William Bell (they were friends, but not related) to set up a school and home for destitute boys who had no criminal record. This was in 1857, and the inevitable committee of worthies, including the just as inevitable Frederick Denison Maurice, and Thomas Hughes (author of *Tom Brown's Schooldays*) established what was called The Boys' Home for the Maintenance by their own Labour of Destitute Boys not Convicted of Crime. First it rented a house at what was then 44 Euston Road – this opened in February 1858 as an industrial school, the first to be registered

as such. Initially, only two boys were taken, one from a poor home in which he was mistreated by his stepfather, and the other who attended ragged school irregularly and had even been dismissed from a shoe-black brigade for dishonesty. These two boys were sent from refuges but mostly pupils came with personal recommendations from people concerned about the welfare of street children.

The boys learnt woodwork, tailoring, shoemaking and printing, though part of each day was spent on conventional school subjects. When the Midland Railway claimed their premises in Euston Road, the Boys' Home moved in 1865 to the corner of Regent's Park Road and King Henry's Road near Chalk Farm.

It was a school of its time, made superfluous by the state education system, and it closed in 1920. Some parts of its buildings still survive.

[1] *Heart of a London Village: The Highgate Literary and Scientific Institution 1839-1990*, p.13 (1991).
[2] Information on the Camden Literary & Scientific Institution has been taken from Roger Cline, 'A light that failed: The Camden Literary and Scientific Institution 1835-1839' in *Camden History Review* 21 (1997).
[3] Felicity Macqueen, 'The Holfords of Hampstead', *Camden History Review* 6 (1978).

CHAPTER NINE

By Water and by Wheels

The Regent's Canal

In 1801 the Grand Junction Canal, connecting the Midlands and north-west with Paddington, was opened. The choice of Paddington, then just a village on the fringe of London, was influenced by its position at one end of the New Road and its easy access to the City. Here, boats arrived with heavy goods such as stone, timber and coal, while others carried vegetables, straw and animals, saving the expense of herding cattle to London. Other goods intended for export via London docks were usually offloaded on to Thames' boats at Brentford. To cope with this trade the Grand Junction Company created a basin at Paddington with a complex of wharves and warehouses.

With the canal built to Paddington trade with London was easier than before, but it was obvious that if the canal could be extended to the London docks with unloading facilities en route, a great deal more time and money could be saved. An extension was proposed by Thomas Homer but abandoned due to the difficulties of finding a satisfactory route. Homer revived the project about ten years later when it was realised that Marylebone Fields, much of which was farmland leased by the Duke of Portland, was soon to revert to the Crown and be developed as a 'residential park' by John Nash. Homer approached Nash with a scheme to run the canal through what became Regent's Park and the architect welcomed the idea of such an ornamental feature. Nash may also have feared that the alternative was a canal parallel to the New Road, which would have put a physical barrier between the West End and his proposed developments in the Park. Originally, it was planned that the canal should cross the park but after difficulties with the Portman estate it had to be routed around its northern perimeter; from there it went through Camden Town and beneath St Pancras Way and York Way to Islington and Limehouse.

A number of problems occurred once the relatively simple Regent's Park stretch, commenced in October 1812, had been finished. A new type of lock was constructed at Chalk Farm Road where land levels change, but when the Paddington-Camden Town stretch was opened in 1816 the lock did not work very well. So serious was its malfunction that the Regent's Canal Company was forced to abandon it altogether and replace it with the flight of three locks we see today. Camden Town became an entrepôt for the canal, but its real importance was still to come.

South of the later site of the Zoological Gardens a canal spur and basin were formed to provide a north-west London dock and trading place. Part of the spur remains by Prince Albert Road, and another part, filled-in, may be seen by looking south of the wall at Gloucester Gate bridge. The intention was to build three markets at the basin half way down Albany Street for meat, vegetables and hay – the last replacing the Hay Market in the West End.

From Camden Town, the canal ran to St Pancras Way, from which it went through land occupied by William Agar, a lawyer who lived in a large house called Elm Lodge on the site of the old St Pancras manor house (*p.20*). The construction of the canal through his land was resolutely opposed by Agar, and he provoked litigation until 1832 at great cost to the canal company, long after the canal had opened fully in 1820.

South of the Agar estate the Imperial Gas Company built six large gasholders as from 1824 – the canal was ideal for conveying coal either from the Midlands or else up from the docks to where it had been brought by sea. None of the early gasholders survives, but the tanks of three of the present telescopic structures are of 1864 vintage and will probably be incorporated in any redevelopment of the King's Cross Lands.

Buses on the New Road

The inauguration of the first omnibus service is noted in the diary of a young resident of Kilburn in 1829.[1] John Pocock, a 15-year-old son of a land speculator who was in severe financial troubles, was used to walking everywhere. His diary entry for 30 November that year has therefore a hint of indulgence about it: 'Rode home in a Paddington omnibus.' This may be set against numerous other entries in his fascinating account of life in Kilburn and London generally, which show him walking very long distances in a day on various errands and visits. At the end of August 1828, for example, he writes:

'Left Bishopsgate early, went first to Bromley in Kent, 10 miles from his house, then across the fields to Beckenham – afterwards to the pretty little town of Sydenham – next Croydon – through shady Camberwell to Brixton where we had tea with the Underwoods and recounted our day's adventure. On coming back we found we had walked 25 miles 'for pleasure'. What would your milksop cockney apprentices say to this?'

Less energetic people than young Pocock, but still unable to afford the ownership of horse or carriage, or even the hire of one, were ideal customers for the new omnibus. Its pioneer in London was George Shillibeer, who announced in 1829 that having admired the omnibus introduced in Paris he had commenced running one himself:

'...from PADDINGTON to the BANK. The superiority of this Carriage over the ordinary Stage Coaches, for comfort and safety, must be obvious, all the Passengers being inside, and the Fare charged from Paddington to the Bank being One Shilling, and from Islington to the Bank or Paddington, only sixpence.'

The New Road, no longer a rural London by-pass, thus became a commuter route from the west of London to the City. At first, especially on the insistence of the hackney cab drivers, omnibuses were not allowed into the centre of London, but soon there were numerous companies operating on main roads outside the centre in a desperate, and sometimes dangerous, rivalry. Unscrupulous tactics were employed, such as parking in the middle of the road when setting down passengers so that a rival company should not overtake them and secure the passengers at the next stop.

The coming of the railways

The cost of building the Regent's Canal went well beyond the initial budget and some seventeen years later the recovery of its expenditure was threatened by the coming of the railways.

This is, however, a retrospective view, since at first the nearest railway, the London & Birmingham (later called the London & North Western), was of great benefit to the canal. When planning their line, the proprietors of the railway saw their business primarily as a freight carrying operation and at first resisted the idea of having an expensive passenger terminus near the centre of London. Instead they intended it to be at Chalk Farm, but by 1834 the railway's engineer, Robert Stephenson, had persuaded the directors that an extension should be made to Euston Square on the New Road. The propinquity of canal and railway at Chalk Farm had obvious advantages, and interchange facilities were developed where rail and water met, so that goods were easily transferred. The success of this collaboration is borne out by the presence of Pickford's, the largest carrier of rail and canal goods, who opened a transhipment depot at Camden Town, designed by William Cubitt, between the canal and Oval Road, in 1841.

Oddly, Euston Station was built not very far from the very first display of a passenger carrying train. In 1809, Richard Trevithick, an early pioneer of railway locomotion, set up a small, circular track in Euston Square and members of the public paid a fee to ride on this. Trevithick, however, became discouraged in his attempts at railway locomotion and went on to other things.

The land on which Euston station and its immediate railway approach was built was previously occupied by William Rhodes, an ancestor of the colonialist Cecil Rhodes. One of the engineers of the railway company left it on record that Rhodes always endeavoured to keep 1000 cows on this farm.[2] The decision to extend the line to Euston brought technical problems, the main one being that the railway had to cross below or above the Regent's Canal. Stephenson chose to go *over* it but then, because of the terrain, the track had to go *under* Hampstead Road near Mornington Crescent to reach the terminus. The consequence was a steep incline between Euston and the bridge over the canal, which was too much for the early engines to manage. These engines were puny affairs compared with their successors, as indeed were the open carriages (*ill.61*). The solution to this difficulty initially was a continuous cable which pulled the trains up from Euston to Chalk Farm goods yard at 20mph. The cable was powered by a stationary winding engine linked to two very tall chimneys which let out the smoke from the furnaces which

powered it. Both the chimneys and the mouth of the tunnel that was constructed beneath the gardens of Adelaide and King Henry's Roads in Hampstead, were great tourist attractions for a time. The cable system was used until July 1844.

When the Act to build the railway was procured the intention was to have four tracks into Euston, shared with the Great Western Railway, which was then in the process of construction and needing a London terminus itself. However, the relationship between the two railway companies turned sour and Brunel for the GWR refused to abandon his broad gauge tracks. Fortunately for both companies, the GWR relocated its terminus to Paddington where it too had a canal connection, allowing both companies the expansion they later needed. The London & Birmingham did little to encourage short haul passenger traffic – the first station north of

59. *The two chimneys at Chalk Farm which ventilated the engine powering the continuous cable to Euston and back.*

60. *Construction of the London & Birmingham Railway at Camden Town in 1837, looking south. St Pancras New Church is in the distance. Watercolour by R.B. Schnebbelie.*

61. Euston Station in 1837, a coloured engraving by T.T. Bury

London was at Harrow. The first section of the line was opened from Euston to Boxmoor on 20 July 1837, and the full service to Birmingham began in September 1838. By that time the company had built the extraordinary *propylaeum*, (the famous Doric Arch, designed by Philip Hardwick), in front of a nondescript train shed. It was, John Britton said in 1839, as a specimen of Greek architecture, not only 'upon a grander scale than anything of the kind yet attempted in this country, but also free from any adulteration of the style by the admixture of features, which, however well they may be designed in themselves, almost invariably detract more or less from classicality of design.' This wonderful entrance to the station was wantonly demolished by British Rail in 1962.

As the possibilities (and profits) of passenger rail traffic became apparent the company realised that its Euston terminus needed to be of a distinctive nature, a symbol of the new age of railways, but still in a recognisably classical tradition. The result was a magnificent Great Hall designed by the 24-year-old P.C. Hardwick

(son of Philip) in 1849, with a spectacular ceiling and a grand staircase that led to the Shareholders' Room. However, as in so many buildings built with such pomp, the offices in which the actual mechanics of the station were carried out were wholly inadequate. The Company also underestimated the amount of parcel traffic that would be engendered. In 1838, about 27,000 parcels a month were handled, and three years later this had risen to 52,000; furthermore, the 22 acres at Chalk Farm purchased to handle the goods traffic of the London & Birmingham and the Great Western, was hardly adequate for the L&B.[3] The station shed was always overcrowded and unsuited for its traffic. R.D. Blackmore, author *of Lorna Doone*, denounced it as 'a railway terminus, miserably lighted, a disgrace to any style of architecture, teeming with insolence, pretence, dirt, discomfort, fuss and confusion'.

One innovation at Euston was the building of two hotels, specifically to cater for railway travellers – a new age indeed had arrived. These were on either side of the station facing Euston Road.

62. A watercolour of the Doric Arch in front of Euston Station.

Also at Chalk Farm the company constructed the Roundhouse, originally for train servicing and repair, designed by Robert Dockray. It was an ingenious building. The little engines would enter from the west for maintenance, then ride on a turntable that transferred them to any one of the 23 bays around the building. Beneath the bays were inspection and cleaning pits and a warren of tunnels which connected with other tunnels beneath the goods yard, used by men and hundreds of horses. It is a wonder that this building has survived into modern times and is now listed, since it soon had to cope with larger engines and compete with similar facilities elsewhere. The Roundhouse soon became a warehouse and was most notably used as a bonded store by the firm of Gilbey's, wine importers and gin distillers, which by 1914 occupied about 20 acres locally – every day a whole trainload of alcohol left Camden for the docks. In 1856 Gilbey had been wine importers, eventually operating from the old Pantheon building in Oxford Street (now the site of a Marks and Spencer), but in 1872 they began to distil their own gin and were later to own many whisky producers. Their presence in Camden Town was enormous and led, in 1937, to their commissioning a new headquarters in Jamestown Road, designed by the celebrated architect, Serge Chermeyeff. In 1962, Gilbey's moved out of Camden Town to Harlow.

A map of 1838 shows that there was a plan to construct a railway from the Camden goods yard directly down to the docks. This would have gone either at rooftop level or in a cutting right through the heart of Camden Town and would have transformed the area completely.

The construction of the Great Northern Railway to its terminus at King's Cross posed even more technical problems than at Euston, for the site chosen was much nearer to the canal than

63. Completion of the tunnel near the Great Northern Railway at King's Cross in 1852.

was the case with the London & Birmingham Railway. In fact, the canal was only 200 yards north of the ends of the proposed platforms. The decision by William Cubitt and his son, Joseph, was to construct the line *beneath* the canal, which therefore meant that there was a long incline beyond it, a feature that was to dog the efficiency of the line for many years until it was electrified. There was some delay in building the terminus, which is on the site of the London Fever and Small Pox hospitals (*see p.91*) and so a temporary passenger terminus was built in York Way, which opened in August 1850. The terminus we see today, albeit obstructed by a particularly ugly modern addition, is a simple, yellow brick building, virtually devoid of decoration except for the clock tower, designed by Lewis Cubitt. This opened in October 1852 and at the time was the largest station in Britain. It was not large enough however, for in 1873 platforms for local trains were built to the west of the station.

The railway lines which run out of King's Cross do not, in fact, impinge very much on Camden territory: after the goods yards they go off into Islington. What Camden land the yards took was previously used for unsavoury industries, such as tanning, bone boiling and brick making, and no tears were shed when they were displaced. The goods yards, which have in recent years been the subject of many grand schemes and their consequent opposition, are of a considerable size – at the peak of activity they enclosed about 59 acres.[4] Once again the railway was, at first, of benefit to the Regent's Canal, which ran through the yards. The Granary building, which still survives, had facilities for interchange between canal and railway; coal from Yorkshire, the most important of the goods handled, had an array of facilities such as coal drops from wagons, and transfer machinery to the canal upon which it went to more distant parts of the metropolis. Previously, most of London's coal had come by colliers along the North Sea to the chaos of London docks. What the railways offered was a cheaper and quicker way of moving coal, but it submerged a whole area of St Pancras in dirt and traffic for many years as a result.

Thus, by 1852, when King's Cross station opened, two heavily-used railway lines had been built to finish at the New Road, each accompanied by acres of marshalling and goods yards. The effect of these on local housing and topography was substantial. At Camden goods yard (so-called, but actually on Southampton land),

engines were serviced and tested on its western side near Gloucester Avenue for hours, belching black smoke and smuts over the streets of Chalk Farm. Along Chalk Farm Road a high wall cut the yard off from the locality – for much of its length the wall is over 4ft in width, because it helps to support the raised area of the yard.[5] Local roads took the brunt of numerous delivery vans, just as they did in St Pancras. If this were not enough, even more damage was done by the construction of the Midland Railway down to St Pancras.

The Midland

The Midland Railway came late into London. This 1844 amalgam of three companies centred on Derby at first used London & North Western lines from Rugby down to Euston, but then made an arrangement from 1858 to bring passengers and freight into King's Cross, where it had a large coal depot to the west of the Great Northern's goods yard. But the fast expansion of trade for both companies, particularly in coal, put strains on the relationship and it became essential for the Midland to build its own lines, terminus and goods yard. The Company secured an Act of Parliament in 1863 but by that time there were few empty fields remaining north of the New Road and much ingenuity was needed to bring the line through the available gap in the Northern Heights and then through Kentish and Camden Towns. Not only was this technically difficult but it had to avoid the demolition or undue disturbance of good class housing: if there was any destruction it had to be of sub-standard streets that no-one but the poorer residents would miss. As it happened, a great deal of destruction was necessary. It has been calculated that about 4000 houses were demolished in Somers Town, St Pancras and Camden Town, and 32,000 people displaced to accommodate the new line and terminus. The station, its hotel and goods depot (now the site of the British Library and its potential extension), form a large rectangle of what had been Skinners' Company land that had previously been occupied by streets of very indifferent quality. Just to the north lay the now closed St Pancras burial ground (*see pp.51-52*). The main line was constructed directly across it on arches, but the subterranean branch line that was built simultaneously to link up with the new Metropolitan line, was constructed by the cut and cover method. This involved the disinterment of many bodies in the burial ground in gruesome circumstances much publicised by the press. To the north and east of the burial grounds was a well-known shanty town called Agar Town (*see p.96*) which had to be demolished, again to the general relief of the Vestry and public, but with no compensation or alternative accommodation for the wretched people who had weekly tenancies there. Just to the north of Agar Town and south of the North London line, the Midland squeezed in a goods station. Further north the line was constructed in a tunnel and cutting through the better parts of Camden and Kentish Towns so that it could get to what were then the only available fields they could use for a goods and marshalling yard, west of Highgate Road.

When coming to build the terminus and the lines which approached it the Midland engineer, William Barlow, had the same problem to contend with as those who built Euston and King's Cross – how to cross the canal. Barlow came up with much the best answer. He bridged over the canal and made a virtue of necessity by raising the level of his St Pancras Station so that, as is evident today, it is 17 feet above street level. He built a magnificent station roof, with an unsupported span of 245 feet, one that has been exceeded in that respect only by three others in the United States, but they do not rise as high as the 105ft St Pancras Station. The passenger and train floor acts as a vast tie-beam to pin the two arcs holding up the roof, and from this level hydraulic lifts were built to take whole wagons down to the vast storage areas beneath, where the pillars that hold up the platform level are so placed as to economically encompass barrels of beer from Burton. The station was, and is, a remarkable feat of engineering.

The first passenger train out of St Pancras ran on 1 October 1868, an express to Manchester. It made a stop at Kentish Town and then ran non-stop to Leicester, at that time the longest non-stop railway journey in the world.

In front of its station the Midland Company built one of the most impressive neo-Gothic buildings in the country – the Midland Grand Hotel. A limited competition was held late in 1865 in which 11 notable architects took part. Though the Midland wanted a prestigious hotel, the brief for the contestants was a building of only 150 bedrooms. However, George Gilbert Scott (1811-78) submitted a much grander plan, a building that contained 300 bedrooms. Despite its additional cost and its flagrant diversion from the brief, it appealed to the directors and was accepted, although eventually one storey was lopped off the proposed building.

The first part of the Midland Grand Hotel opened on 5 May 1873 and the remainder in spring 1876, at a total cost, including fittings by Gillow, of about £437,000. It boasts a magnificent staircase with a vaulted ceiling containing panels depicting Victorian values, huge coffee and dining rooms (which have been badly damaged by subsequent occupiers), and a ladies' smoking room. It contained lifts powered by a hydraulic system, it had central heating in some of its public areas, but it did not have bathrooms attached to the rooms: these were, instead, across the corridors. It was regarded at the time as a sumptuous hotel and was very popular until competition diminished its appeal. It also needed an enormous staff, particularly to service the hundreds of coal fires in the building, and as labour became more expensive so the hotel became uneconomic to run. It closed on 19 April 1935, not only a financial liability but dressed in an architectural style then decidedly out of fashion.

The North London and its connections

Apart from these main lines, there were three cross-country lines built through Camden, two of which were later to form what is now usually called the North London Line. The first was opened in 1850. Its cumbersome name – the East and West India Docks & Birmingham Junction Railway – spells out its function, which was to transport freight from the London & Birmingham depot at Chalk Farm to the London docks. In this, its route largely mirrored that of the Regent's Canal. The freight trains on this line had many uses, even serving a large cattle depot behind the south side of Agar Grove built in 1854 to be near the new Cattle Market off York Way.

The line ran at rooftop level – today it may be noted for its bridges, such as those that span Camden Road, Kentish Town Road and Chalk Farm Road. It was joined in 1860 by the Hampstead Junction Railway, which began at a junction for the two just south of Hawley Road in Kentish Town and then drove due north through the Prince of Wales Road area, which had recently been built, to get to Gospel Oak and then ran west by the side of Earl Mansfield's land to Hampstead Heath station and on to Willesden. The third cross route, of 1868, was the Tottenham & Hampstead Junction Railway, which, coming from the east, met the Hampstead Junction Rail-

64. The rural setting of Finchley Road station when first built in 1860.

way at Gospel Oak and also sent a spur down to Kentish Town where it met the main Midland line.

This gathering of lines to the west of Highgate Road was linked with the Midland Railway's goods yard there. Some idea of the complexity of the arrangement may be gathered by visiting the Kentish Town City Farm off Grafton Road, or walking to the end of Carker's Lane, from which it is possible to look down on some of it. The Midland, in acquiring the land, bought up the grounds of Weston's Retreat, a pleasure garden opened in 1863 to the west of Highgate Road; its proprietor, Edward Weston, also ran Weston's Music Hall, in High Holborn, which later became the Holborn Empire (*see p.146*). The Retreat was never much of a diversion. An injunction by the neighbours prevented it from displaying fireworks, balloons, acrobats and playing music, leaving it very little scope other than the many gas lights and conservatories. Mr Weston was probably glad to sell this failing asset to a land-hungry Midland Railway.

In this goods yard the Midland offloaded coal and cattle. The latter could be herded through to the Cattle Market off York Way, or else to a number of slaughterhouses which set up business in West Kentish Town.

The location of the Midland goods yard ensured that the west side of Kentish Town Road / Highgate Road would be semi-industrial in nature and given that much of West Kentish Town had already been built with sub-standard housing it was not surprising that for a century the area was down at heel.

The Hampstead Junction Railway, from Kentish Town to Willesden, had been promoted by the London & North Western to ease congestion on its main line through Hampstead. The Company had baulked at the cost of doubling the number of its lines through its Hampstead tunnel and instead introduced this loop line which is now incorporated into the North London and which, with a few additions, extended to Richmond. It was primarily built for freight – there were few passengers, as illustration 64 of a rural Finchley Road station in 1860 indicates.

The lie of the land and the necessity to placate residents wealthier than those who were inconvenienced in Kentish and Camden Towns led to the building of a number of railway tunnels beneath Hampstead. The first was that of the

London & Birmingham which ran (as it does today) in a cutting parallel with Adelaide Road, and then into a spectacular tunnel at Primrose Hill Road before it emerges at Loudoun Road to run behind Belsize Road. The Midland line, going west from Gospel Oak's Lismore Circus (where it once had a station nearby), was in a tunnel until it reached one of the three stations called Finchley Road, from whence it continued into the sparsely populated West End district. The Hampstead Junction left Hampstead Heath station into a tunnel which similarly ended at Finchley Road where above ground it went on to Willesden.

The concentration of lines (including those of the later Metropolitan line in West Hampstead made housing development there difficult and inelegant. It also created a hinterland which has only recently been developed as a shopping centre west of the Finchley Road.

Tramways

An unsuccessful experiment in the use of horse-drawn trams had taken place in London in 1861-62, but the first permanent lines were authorised in 1869. A Tramways Act was passed the following year which had an important clause prepared and encouraged by William Booth Scott (1822-91) then Chief Surveyor for St Pancras Vestry, who was rather hostile to tramway companies. (Booth Scott developed an estate agency which still survives in the Camden area.) He insisted that local authorities should have the right to buy any tramway within its territory after 21 years. In that same year the London Street Tramways Company, which intended to lay tramways in the Camden area, was formed, but was obliged to promise to introduce cheap fares for workmen before 7am and after 6pm each working day. The first Camden tramway, operated by LSTC from Hampstead Road to Kentish Town station, opened in November 1871. In February 1872 a spur was built along Camden Road to the Brecknock Arms and in April a route from Camden Road to King's Cross was opened. In the tramway mania of the time there were other proposals including one along High Holborn and across the newly opened Holborn Viaduct to the western edge of the City. This was opposed by the City, which also refused to have a route down Farringdon Street and over Blackfriars Bridge to connect with south London lines.

Not much else happened in Camden until 1880,

65. A tunnel for single-deck trams was constructed at the same time as Kingsway in 1905. At first it terminated below ground at the Aldwych, but was extended in 1907 to the Thames Embankment, where trams could go over Blackfriars or Westminster Bridges. In 1929-31, the London County Council deepened the tunnel so as to take double-deck trams (see above). It was closed in 1952, but reopened in 1964 as a traffic underpass connecting Waterloo Bridge and Kingsway.

when the line to Kentish Town was extended along Prince of Wales Road to the Mother Shipton pub (now the Fiddler's Elbow), up Malden Road and Southampton Road, terminating at Rochford Street in Gospel Oak (but in 1901 went on to South End Green using a one-way system we now have for motor traffic). A tram depot was opened in Cressy Road. The opening to the public of Parliament Hill Fields resulted in a new line from Kentish Town to Swains Lane in 1887. In the same year the North Metropolitan Tramways Company opened other lines which touched Holborn, particularly Gray's Inn Road and Clerkenwell Road. By the mid 1890s, when many of the lines were 21 years old, a good number of London tramways were acquired by the LCC which set about the task of electrifying them.

One unusual tramway that served part of Camden was the Highgate Cable Tramway which did what no horse-drawn tram could easily do – go up and down Highgate Hill. The inventor of this, the first cable tramway in Europe, was Andrew Smith Hallidie (1836-1900), whose fa-

66. An advertisement for the Highgate Hill cable tramway.

down. They were in the roadway – one in front of our shop and the other in front of Widdens. The engine house was behind the other side of the High Street from us. The cable cars were used to tow the coal carts, carrying fuel to work the engine up Highgate Hill, and the horses were led up behind to take over at the top. Marriott's corn carts used the same method of getting their loads up the hill. At the terminus there was a single track only and a pointsman was on duty to switch over the tram before it went down. Stopping the trams on the hill was a business. A wooden plug called a scotch was placed behind the rear wheels in case the grippers slipped from the cable.'

The opening of Waterlow Park in 1891 was good news for the Company, but soon afterwards a serious accident closed the line for five years. When it resumed in 1897 there was further trouble and in 1899 a car, full of passengers, went out of control: both driver and conductor were later charged with being drunk on duty. The LCC bought the operation in 1908, electrified and built double tracks all along the route: this necessitated the demolition of part of Fairseat house, which would not have pleased Waterlow if he had been alive.

In the first flush of enthusiasm for Highgate's unusual solution to travelling up a steep hill, many discussions were held in Hampstead to see if the same invention could be used along Rosslyn Hill and Hampstead High Street. In 1882, before Highgate's line was built, it was turned down by Hampstead Vestry and five months after the triumphant opening of the Highgate line, the residents were still unimpressed despite the enthusiasm of George Jealous, editor of the *Hampstead & Highgate Express* for the project.

Apart from the horse-tram line already mentioned that extended to South End Green, Hampstead was otherwise unaffected by the revolution of trams. Poorer residents had to wait until the opening of the Northern Line for cheap travel.

The Underground
The New Road, on which the first omnibus ran, and upon which five main line stations disgorged their passengers, was the route chosen by the promoters of the Metropolitan Line when building the first underground railway from Paddington to Farringdon. The line was constructed by the cut-and-cover method, so that for long periods stretches of the New Road, by then renamed Marylebone, Euston and Pentonville

ther, an engineer, had secured patents for making wire ropes. Father and son emigrated to San Francisco in 1852 and the son devised an underground endless moving cable and a mechanical gripping device which was attached to the underside of tramcars. The first of his tramcars began operations in San Francisco in 1873. In 1881 he formed the Steep Grade Tramway Company, of which a director was William Booth Scott (see above). Its prospectus to raise funds to build a line from the Archway Tavern to Highgate Village was endorsed by Sir Sydney Waterlow, who lived at Fairseat on its route, and the first tramcar travelled with much pomp, ceremony and flag waving on 29 May 1884.

According to Highgate pork butcher, Ewan Attkins:

'There were two great pits for the wheels, one of which wound the chain up and the other

67. King's Cross Underground station in 1868.

Roads, were being excavated.

The stations in Camden opened on 10 January 1863 were King's Cross and Gower Street (now Euston Square), the Company having abandoned plans to open one in Euston Square itself. The promoters (whose shareholders included the City of London and the Great Western Railway) and St Pancras Vestry had numerous legal tussles. The Vestry, for example, wanted the Company to help pay for the upkeep of side streets used more heavily once Euston Road was out of action. Complaints were made at the way soil was dumped at the side of the road, and that old materials had been used for relaying the road once the tunnel beneath was completed. There were, inevitably, complaints from traders who had no passing trade while work was in progress. *The Builder* magazine in 1864 estimated that in the Fleet valley area, much of which was in Camden, 1,000 dwellings housing 12,000 people were demolished during construction though much of it was very sub-standard accommodation. Despite their differences, or perhaps because of them, the St Pancras Vestry was shown the new railway on 30 August 1862, prior to the official opening, in a carriage of their own, on a journey from Farringdon.

There were drawbacks to travelling on this first underground line. The engines were steam driven and therefore vents were made in the road above for the steam to escape. Even so, many people complained that the stations were smoky. Lighting was by a hazardous gas system.

Important though this first stretch was in the history of transport and of Camden, later underground lines were of far more significance in development of the borough. On 13 April 1868 the Metropolitan opened an extension to the then rural Swiss Cottage which was further extended in 1879 to Finchley Road, West Hampstead and Kilburn & Brondesbury. It was not the Metroland beloved of John Betjeman in the 20th century, but the country that it entered after Kilburn was mostly open fields.

The cut-and-cover method of construction caused enormous upheaval. Not only did it usually mean the relocation of sewers, water and gas supplies, but as St Pancras Vestry found, for years the area of contruction caused mess, traffic diversions and temporary loss of trade and rateable value. It was the invention of the Greathead tunnelling machine and the use of electrical power that changed all this. Both these occurred in the construction of the City & South London Railway from Stockwell to King William Street in the City. The Greathead shield, as it was called, proved that tunnelling and the simultaneous installation of a metal tube to contain the railway line was a feasible answer to the challenge of bringing underground railways to London. Electrical traction was also new. Originally, the promoters of the City & South London had planned to haul the trains by a continuous wire rope, but the alarming consequences of a cable snapping, with passengers trapped in badly lit carriages, obliged them to look at electric traction. It was a gamble, but it worked. The line opened in December 1890.

Though the City & South London for various reasons was not a financial success, the advantages of its innovations were not lost on other companies seeking to put lines beneath London. More profitable was the Central London Railway, 'the tuppenny tube', which opened in July 1900 from Shepherds Bush to Bank. This was built using the Greathead tunnelling shield and

69. *Belsize Park station on the Northern line c.1910.*

had the latest in electric traction. It included two stations in the Holborn area – Chancery Lane and British Museum. Holborn station was not built until 1906 and then only on what became known as the Piccadilly line. So, passengers wishing to change from the Central to the Piccadilly, alighted at British Museum station and walked eastwards the 170 yards to Holborn

68. *Brown's Dairy at the junction of Chalk Farm Road and Kentish Town Road, a site now occupied by Camden Town Underground station and a bank.*

station. In 1933 British Museum was closed when a new interchange between Central and Piccadilly lines was opened at Holborn.

The Central and Piccadilly lines confirmed Holborn's ideal commercial location between City and West End, but the most important tube line for the rest of Camden opened on 22 June 1907. What became the Northern line was built from Charing Cross to Golders Green, with a spur at Camden Town to what is now Archway station. In the same year the City & South London Railway, still using its old electric locomotives, was extended to King's Cross and Euston, but it was not until 1924 that it was taken on to meet the Hampstead tube just above Mornington Crescent.

Most of the expansion of the underground railways at the turn of the century was the work of a remarkable American, Charles Tyson Yerkes, a man with a history of less than honest dealings in America, but who had the vision and determination to found what is today the central core of the London underground system. He bought the powers to construct what was called the 'Hampstead tube' and took over the ailing, steam-driven Metropolitan District Railway; he also acquired control of the partly built Bakerloo line and the powers to build what became the Piccadilly line.

It was Yerkes who proposed the extension of the Northern line to the fields of Golders Green – he was soon followed by developers anxious to exploit the potential of new territory served by underground railways. Yerkes also proposed a station at Jack Straw's Castle, but here he was opposed by both the Heath Protection Society and Hampstead Vestry who felt that it would damage the water levels in the area; Yerkes relocated his intermediate station to near the Bull and Bush and despite the protests of the Society laid platforms, but the station itself was never built.

A number of Camden stations, apart from British Museum, have been closed on both overground and underground lines, although some buildings survive. Most familiar is South Kentish Town on the Northern Line (closed 1924). Lesser-known old stations include Camden Road by Sandall Road and Haverstock Hill (actually Rochford Street near Lismore Circus), both Midland Railway and closed in 1916; and Highgate Road by Denyer House where there were two stations for the upper and lower level railways, which closed in 1915 and 1918 respectively.

Mail Underground

Only a month after the Metropolitan line opened for business, another tube railway began operation beneath Camden. This was the Pneumatic Dispatch Railway, which ran from the District Sorting Office in Eversholt Street to Euston Station, 500 yards away. The intention was to relieve congestion of post office vans on the roads. The railway consisted of a tunnel 7 feet in diameter; the cars carrying mail bags were pushed by compressed air, with an air vacuum pulling them from the front. The cars were small but it was possible for a human to travel on it. In fact, when the line was extended to the General Post Office at St Martin-le-Grand in 1865, the Duke of Buckingham did just that to initiate the service. This new route crossed beneath Drummond Street, then down Hampstead Road and Tottenham Court Road where it veered east by St Giles-in-the-Fields church and on to High Holborn.

Some faults developed in the system, but the main problem for the promoters was that the Post Office itself was reluctant to use it, despite the urging of their chairman, the Duke of Buckingham. *The Illustrated London News* in April 1870 noted that 'At present no mail bags are sent to or from St Martin's-le-Grand by the pneumatic tubes', and three years later another report revealed that nothing had changed. The service ceased at the end of October 1874.

The Pneumatic Dispatch Railway was generally forgotten after that and its tunnel used by other utilities. In December 1928 there was a gas explosion in a stretch of the tunnel near St Giles High Street, in which a maintenance worker was killed.

The Post Office did however build its own underground railway, in which Mount Pleasant Sorting office was the hub, but the intended tunnels to Euston and Eversholt Street were not built.

[1] *Travels of a London Schoolboy 1825-1830*, ed. Tom Pocock, (1996).
[2] *Old Euston* (published by *Country Life*), p.10 (1938).
[3] *Ibid*, p.24
[4] Robert Thorne, Stephen Duckworth and Barry Jones, 'King's Cross Goods Yard', *in Change at King's Cross*, p.93 (1990).
[5] Jack Whitehead, *The Growth of Camden Town AD1800-2000*, pp.43-44

CHAPTER TEN

Getting to Grips

Dispensaries

The 19th century saw many reforms in London, which included significant advances in the fields of medicine, public health, education, housing and the provision of open spaces.

Notably, there was an expansion of hospitals, many of which had been founded on modest resources in the 18th century. Some had begun as institutions for the free treatment of the poor. The Royal Free, Charing Cross, Middlesex, University College and Royal Northern hospitals all had their roots in this good intention, while others began as workhouse infirmaries – the Whittington group is an amalgamation of workhouse infirmaries. Specialist hospitals were almost invariably founded by individuals and their friends and it became possible to obtain informed treatment for smallpox, stone, cancer and diseases of eye and ear; in addition there was a growing number of lying-in hospitals for the poorer classes – that in Endell Street, from 1749, is an example. Some hospitals developed from dispensaries, organisations that came into vogue towards the end of the 18th century. These provided free medical treatment for the poor as out-patients, but some of them had a few beds.

The Highgate Dispensary was formed in 1787 when a meeting chaired by Robert Mendham of Bisham House (where Bisham Avenue meets Highgate High Street) established a 'Dispensary at Highgate for the relief of the poor of Highgate, Muswell Hill, Crouch End, Hornsey and Holloway'. The charity was to have the services of 'a medical gentleman, an inhabitant and constant resident of Highgate who is to be both surgeon and apothecary'. To fund the dispensary better-off local residents were invited to subscribe at least one guinea annually and for this they were entitled to nominate one worthy and needy person for free treatment. This was the usual basis of such dispensaries.

As their side of the bargain, the 'patients are to provide all necessary phials etc., they are to behave themselves decently and soberly and are to conform strictly to such rules as are given to them... or they will be immediately dismissed.

70. Dr James Gillman, surgeon and apothecary at Highgate Dispensary. He cared for the poet, Samuel Taylor Coleridge, at his home, first at 14 South Grove, and then at 3 The Grove.

They are to keep their letters of recommendation clean under cover; they are to deliver the same when cured, at the dispensary and are immediately thereupon to return a letter of thanks to the governor who recommended them, on pain of not being admitted to any future benefit...'

There were 61 subscribers the first year, mostly from Highgate, and only 159 patients, of whom one third were seen at home. Even by 1817 the number of patients was only 406.[1] In 1818 the medical officer was James Gillman, then the guardian of the poet, Coleridge, at Moreton House in South Grove. The Dispensary had several addresses, the last of which was 54 Highgate West Hill, until the passing of the National Insurance Act of 1911 made it redundant.

71. A drawing of the proposed dispensary and soup kitchen at New End, Hampstead.

72. Middlesex Hospital in Mortimer Street, c.1848.

Hampstead's dispensary opened much later. The energetic Rev. Thomas Ainger began the Hampstead Self-Supporting Dispensary at 10 New End, next to the workhouse, in 1846. In 1853, as the Hampstead Provident Dispensary, it acquired no. 16 and shared the accommodation with the local soup kitchen, which had begun in c.1844. This institution also ceased to function in 1911.

The records of St Pancras Vestry reveal a Provident Dispensary in Hawley Crescent, a St Pancras & Northern Dispensary at 126 Euston Road, and a Camden Town Dispensary. A better-known establishment was at 62 Great Russell Street. The Bloomsbury Dispensary was founded in 1801 and numbered Edward Jenner amongst its medical staff. The premises were bombed in 1941 and in 1942 it moved to 22 Bloomsbury Street. Though the National Health Service made the Dispensary redundant, it still survives as a charity making grants for preventive health care and holidays for carers of the disabled.

Hospitals

In 1745 Francis Goodge, the landowner, rented nos. 8-10 Windmill Street, off Tottenham Court Road, to the Middlesex Infirmary, an institution set up by private citizens 'for the sick and lame of Soho'. It provided fifteen beds and, by controversially setting aside a third of them for women in labour, it is claimed that it became the first lying-in hospital in England. In 1754 the Hospital acquired some land to the north of Windmill Street (a 'good place for snipe shooting') on a 999-year lease from a Mr Berners, to build a new hospital. It was a plain building which included a maternity department, but though economically run it was constantly short of money and relied entirely on charitable donations and benefit performances. Fortunes improved in 1791 when Samuel Whitbread, the brewer, gave £3000 to endow a ward where cancer patients could be treated until they were 're-lieved by art or released by death'. From 1766 'physician-pupils' walked the wards and paid for the privilege.

The beginnings of both the Royal Free and University College Hospital were in 1828. The Royal Free began with a young surgeon, William Marsden, finding a young woman dying on the steps of St Andrew, Holborn, unable to enter any of the London hospitals because she did not have a letter of recommendation from a subscriber. Marsden determined to found an infirmary to which people were admitted by need and for free. In this he involved the Cordwainers' Company, and under royal patronage rented a house at 16 Greville Street, near Hatton Garden, under the formal name of The London General Institution for the Gratuitous Care of Malignant Diseases, popularly known as the Free Hospital, and thus specialising in cancer. In 1843, over-crowded as all London hospitals were, it moved to a site on the east side of Gray's Inn Road formerly occupied by the barracks of the Light Horse Volunteers. In 1877 it pioneered the admission of women students.

A hospital and a medical school attached to University College had been envisaged by the founders of the College, but due to lack of funds the hospital began as the University Dispensary, treating only out-patients, at what is now 171

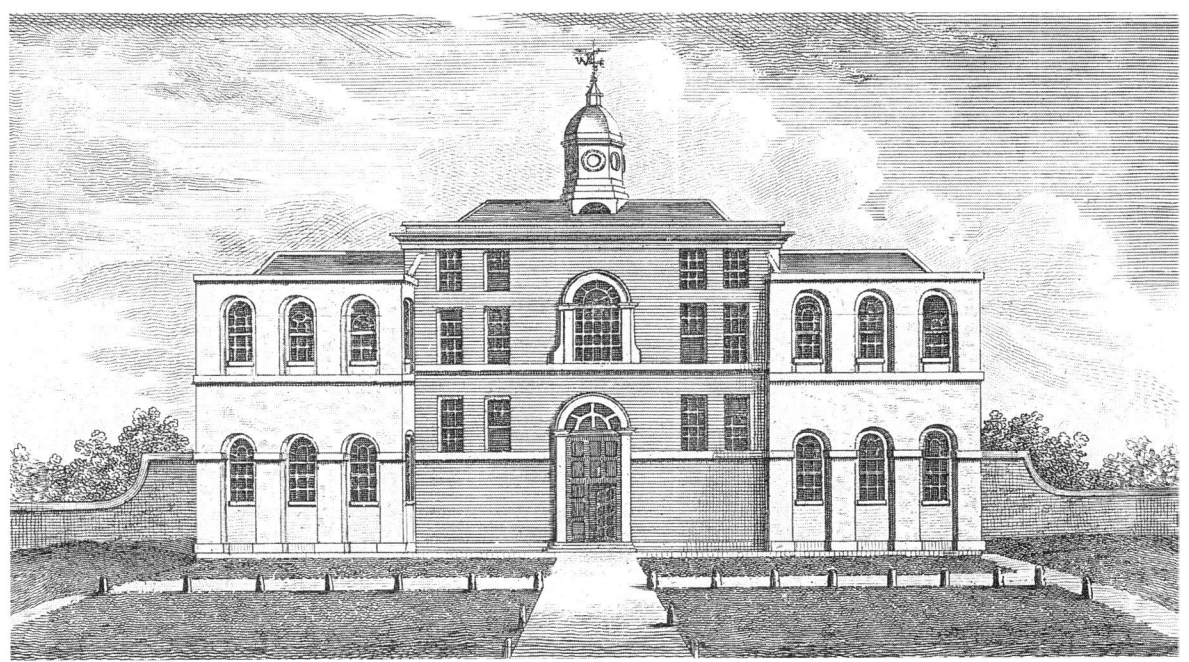

73. The Smallpox Hospital at King's Cross, demolished to make way for King's Cross Station.

Gower Street. In 1834, William Wilkins, architect of the College, built the North London Hospital for £7,600: 'all architectural decorations have for the sake of economy been studiously excluded'. Three years later it was renamed University College Hospital. It was in this building that the first major operation under ether in Europe was made, when Robert Liston amputated a patient's leg, but just as notably John Elliotson pioneered the use of the stethoscope and introduced the use of quinine for malaria in the 1830s. The hospital we see today is the result of extensive rebuilding in 1897 after a gift of £200,000 by John Blundell Maple, of furniture shop fame.

The c.1801 map of St Pancras parish features the 'Small Pock Hospital' and its ample front gardens on the site of King's Cross Station – its siting is confirmation of the general seediness of the area. It moved here from Windmill Street in 1746, a year after the Middlesex had set up in the same street. The handsome building we see on the map and in illustration 73 is the hospital when rebuilt c.1793. Treatment then relied on inoculation, a method popularised in England by Lady Mary Wortley Montagu, who had noticed it being used in Turkey in 1717. Smallpox was

a common and contagious scourge among all classes in the 18th and 19th centuries, and though inoculation was reasonably successful in preventing the disease, it failed to stop one in every six patients from dying once they had caught it. Effective treatment, by vaccination by cowpox, was advocated by Edward Jenner (1749-1823). He had heard, when a boy in the country, that dairymaids who caught cowpox did not catch smallpox. His conclusions, based originally on a small number of successful vaccinations, did not impress some of the medical establishment, but a Parliamentary committee set up to examine the usefulness of his treatment was told by Dr Matthew Baillie that 'it is the most important discovery ever made in medicine.' Jenner spent much of the rest of his life trying to convince his peers and the public that his treatment was effective, and successive governments were pressed to make it widely available. A serious outbreak of smallpox occurred in 1838, particularly in Somers Town, but it also affected St Pancras pauper children housed in an establishment in Tooting.

An Act of Parliament in 1853 made vaccination compulsory, but there was much opposition, leading to petitions for and against. The St Pancras

Vestry minutes record a letter from the parish of St George the Martyr in Holborn in 1859 asking St Pancras to support compulsory vaccination. This indicates that government legislation had not been effective, and then in 1867 St Pancras Vestry printed 1000 handbills urging the virtues of vaccination to an often sceptical public. Matters came to a head in 1871 when a large increase in the disease was recorded. The Medical Officer for St Pancras noted that in the previous two years vaccinations had decreased by 30% and that this was due to gross neglect on the part of the Vestry and the Guardians of the Poor. The hospitals, he said, were full of patients. In December 1870 there had been 20 cases, in January 1871, 110. Temporary accommodation was found near the workhouse, but in March the whole Sanitary Committee resigned because, in its opinion, the Vestry as a whole did not support its efforts to contain the epidemic.

The Smallpox Hospital was displaced from its site at King's Cross c.1850 when the Great Northern Railway built its terminus there, and moved to Highgate Hill to a site now occupied by part of the Whittington Hospital. Some of the early isolation wards still survive there. It was not the first hospital on Highgate Hill. In 1473 a leper refuge was founded by William Pole, a yeoman of the Crown and himself a leper. Revenues were small and the only substantial donation known of is forty shillings bequeathed by Sir Roger Cholmeley, a local resident and founder of Highgate School. By that time leprosy had virtually disappeared and it is likely that the building then became a poorhouse or used for outbreaks of infectious disease. It was closed in 1650.[2]

The Whittington Hospital complex has emerged from three workhouse infirmaries. In 1867, St Pancras Guardians of the Poor purchased land on the south side of Dartmouth Park Hill to build an infirmary for workhouse inmates. This building, with its splendid silhouette of towers, was opened in 1869 and staffed by nurses taught at the Florence Nightingale Training Institute, but in November that year it was taken over by the newly established Central London Sick Asylums Board, a body responsible for providing London's hospital accommodation. In 1883 St Pancras repurchased the building, from which time it developed into a general hospital. The Holborn Union workhouse infirmary, at the apex of Archway Road and Highgate Hill, was built in 1871 and Islington Workhouse Infirmary was

added next to the Smallpox Hospital in 1900. All these buildings, unified as the Whittington in 1949, were designed by Saxon Snell.

It was generally believed – with good reason – that a hospital which treated infectious diseases also unleashed epidemics into the neighbourhood. When it was proposed in 1874 to build such a hospital in Hampstead, reaction was swift, even from St Pancras Vestry whose residents in Southampton Road were concerned. Hampstead residents, especially in the South End Green and St John's Park area, and more specifically, Sir Rowland Hill, the postal pioneer who lived at Hampstead Green, were incensed and stressed the dangers for those on their way to the Heath, then newly won for the public. A local landowner, a Mr Lund, threw up a barrier to prevent patients using Fleet Road (then a private estate road) to get to the hospital.

The proposal for the hospital resulted from emergency action taken by the Metropolitan Asylums Board in 1870, when sheds were built in fields called Bartrams (between today's Royal Free and Lawn Road) to house victims of a severe smallpox epidemic. Soon the fields were covered with huts housing patients from all over north London. As is often the case, the temporary buildings became permanent and although the treatment of smallpox was discontinued at Hampstead, Bartrams became the site of this new threat to Hampstead residents – the North West London Fever Hospital. It did indeed present health risks to the local public, but as Professor F.M.L. Thompson points out in his exhaustive study of property development in the area,[3] the two hospitals also so lowered the perceived tone of the neighbourhood that people who had bought houses in Upper Park Road suffered financially from it. He quotes a letter from a resident in 1893:

'The whole of this road has been greatly lessened in value by the abominable way in which the houses at the north end have been let, viz. in tenements to dirty and objectionable people.'

The Ecclesiastical Commissioners, developers of the area, noted that 'Probably the Smallpox Hospital close by is responsible at any rate in part for the depreciation of the neighbourhood.' The Asylums Board proposals ensured that the development of Fleet Road itself would be very down market, but the area had already lapsed that way judging by the complaints of residents

74. A ward in Hampstead Smallpox Hospital.

about a carpet-beating ground there in 1874. Activity went on from 7am to 8pm, but the owner said residents could have no ground for complaint since the business had been there for twenty years, long before houses had been built. The status of Fleet Road was confirmed by the opening of a tramway to South End Green in 1887. This was the last line to be built for horse trams.

In 1906 the Hampstead General Hospital was built in Pond Street, on the grounds of some large houses, including that of Sir Francis Palgrave (and his son, the compiler of *The Golden Treasury*). In modern times the two hospitals have been demolished and replaced by the Royal Free building whose awful mass spoils many views from the Heath.

Camden is or has been home to numerous specialist hospitals, of which some are mentioned here.

Elizabeth Garrett Anderson, the first woman permitted to qualify in medicine in this country, opened the St Mary's Dispensary for Women and Children in Seymour Place, Marylebone in 1866

with the aim of providing patients with care by members of their own sex. Beds were eventually added for in-patients and after continual growth moved to its own building in Euston Road, designed by J.M. Brydon (1889), where it has remained since, but usually of late under threat of closure.

The Hospital for Sick Children in Great Ormond Street was founded in 1851 at a time when children were rarely admitted to hospitals. A survey in 1843 of all patients in London hospitals showed that only 26 were below the age of ten. No. 49 Great Ormond Street, the former home of physician, Dr William Mead, was rented and no. 48 was added in 1858. In 1877 a new building by E.M. Barry opened with 120 beds, and after the demolition of the original houses, a further new block in 1893 brought the number up to 240. All this was replaced in the 1930s.

The National Temperance Hospital, until recently in Hampstead Road, was not, as often thought, a hospital for people who did not drink alcohol, but was an experiment in treating people without its use – then common in many hospitals. The problem often arose that the staff in hospitals availed themselves of the alcohol as well. A writer in 1883 noted that:

'Sometimes, the matron cannot write and is reported to be very much the reverse of sober, and as a consequence her conduct is irregular and the patients obtain their meals at uncertain intervals. Upon a recent occasion when a visit was made unexpectedly to one of these hospitals, after several times knocking at the door and ringing, the visitor espied the porter emerging from a public house, quite intoxicated and the Matron returned to the hospital after an interval of half an hour in a slightly worse state. It was found that the patients upon this day were entirely left without anybody in the hospital to attend to them...'

The London Temperance Hospital, as it was then called, opened its doors at 112 Gower Street in 1873 to much public criticism, which even suggested that if the experiment failed then the doctors should be charged with manslaughter. In the event the hospital was highly popular and the governors were obliged to open new premises in Hampstead Road in 1881. An odd quirk of the new building was that the operating theatre doubled as a Board Room and therefore had an open fireplace.

Prominent in Hampstead was the North London Hospital for Consumption, housed in a château-like building at Mount Vernon designed in 1880 by Roger Smith. After considerable enlargement it became the National Institute for Medical Research in 1914. It is now being converted into apartments.

Public Health

The improvement of public health, of which new hospitals were only a part, was *the* major challenge for 19th-century reformers in London. It necessitated a radical change in the sewage and drainage systems, the control and notification of infectious diseases, a significant improvement in housing conditions for most of the population, the regulation of cow houses and slaughterhouses, and the efficient disposal of refuse. Just as importantly, it required vestries to take their responsibilities seriously and use the powers permitted them by the Public Health Act of 1848 to appoint Medical Officers of Health.

Both Hampstead and St Pancras appointed a Medical Officer in 1856. Before then Inspectors of Nuisances, the forerunners of Sanitary Inspec-

75. *A large water tank, erected above an archway in St Giles-in-the-Fields, is shown in this engraving in the Illustrated London News of 6 November 1858. It was, the magazine noted, a great improvement in water supply in the area.*

tors, were the only officers employed to investigate public health problems. St Pancras Vestry appointed its man with its usual stinginess and disregard for what needed to be done. A committee noted that a man of good calibre was needed, but decided that the Vestry could not afford a full-time appointment. It therefore recommended that a part-time officer, with a private practice, was the best solution. The Vestry's choice was Dr Hillier of University College Hospital. It was to be an unhappy relationship, recorded over the years in the Vestry minutes. Two years later the Vestry reduced his salary from £400 to £250 (as well as the salaries of medical staff). This set in motion an acrimonious dispute between the officer and the Vestry, although there were Vestry members who disagreed with the decision. Hillier decided to stay but there was rancour thereafter. When he asked for leave of absence in 1863, because he had had no holiday the year before, the Vestry turned him down as there was a smallpox outbreak. Later that year he complained that he did not have a private office nor a lockable drawer in his desk – these were both refused.

It is surprising that Hillier stayed so long, as

his frustration is evident from a report to the Vestry in January 1866. There was, he said, a potential cholera epidemic in St Pancras, which was then the most populous area in the metropolis. The Vestry, he said, did not have a reputation for caring for the health of its population. Because cholera attacks people through their drinking water, improved drainage was wanted. Sewers for districts were not made because the Vestry declined to make them and relied entirely on the residents themselves to pay for them. As a consequence, he cited, the area of Dartmouth Park, already developed, had no sewage system and it went into an open ditch (the Fleet river) east of Grove Terrace. The parish dust collection was poor, he claimed, and there was too much dung left in alleyways and mews. He wanted to see quick interment of the dead. At the moment, he said, the Irish in particular held on to the corpse for days while they collected money for a burial, and in the crowded houses of these poor people, the corpse lay in the room with the living. He urged that the Vestry take advantage of new legislation to erect dwellings for the poor. The Vestry, needless to say, bristled under the attack.

Despite these problems the Vestry still declined to appoint a full-time officer and the row went on. In March, the Sanitary Committee declared its support for Hillier, but the Vestry declined to publicise his proposals for reform or to increase his salary, though they gave him an extra £80 a year for being also 'Examiner of Gas', a responsibility called into being by the high content of ammonia in domestic gas being produced by the Imperial Gas Company.

In April two newly appointed sanitary inspectors reported back on the conditions they found in the Malden Road area. They had investigated 74 houses, which contained 261 families (1052 people), an average of about 14 to a house. 44 of the houses had no WC, and 28 were entirely out of repair.

The number of cowhouses in residential areas was very high in St Pancras. A review conducted in 1857 found that there were 92. Many were too small for animals; in fact, the object of many of the cowkeepers was to keep the animals very warm in restricted premises as this resulted in better cream. In some units pigs were also kept. Disease was rampant and cattle insurance companies considered that town cows were at three times the risk of country cows. There was abundant evidence of meat from diseased cows

76. Ashes from coal fires and from brick making were difficult to dispose of. The scene shows a dust-heap at Somers Town in 1836.

being sold in butchers' shops. The brave Dr Hillier recommended that all cows should be kept outside the metropolis, but acknowledged that this would need legislation.

There was a large pig sty in Highgate Village, at the end of Townsend's Yard where the garden centre is now. This belonged to the Attkins family, pork butchers on the other, Camden, side of the High Street. There were about 80 pigs and the pigman lived in the tumbledown cottage previously occupied by the water carrier (see p34).[4] An old resident of Highgate recalled (in the 1970s) pigs with their throats cut left in brine in Pond Square behind the Attkins shop.[5]

Butchers' shops were not hygienic. There are many pictures of them with carcasses hanging outside their premises in the early 19th century when refrigeration was still primitive. Before the 1920s and the advent of mechanical refrigeration local butchers relied on ice blocks, possibly supplied by Carlo Gatti from his ice well in premises in New Wharf Road on the Regent's Canal (now used by the London Canal Museum). There were numerous butchers at Kentish Town, especially after the opening of the Midland Railway goods yard off Kentish Town Road. Earlier, the aptly-named Giles Silverside, a wholesaler, rented fields on the Christ Church Estate on the east side of Kentish Town Road. Butchers might slaughter their animals at the back of their premises after buying them at the Metropolitan Cattle Market off York Way or direct from the Kentish Town goods yard. 'Home-killed meat' was a proud boast. In St Pancras parish in 1859 there were 104 licensed slaughterhouses and probably more without licence.

Hampstead's relationship with its first Medical Officer of Health was more cordial than in St Pancras. Dr Charles Lord was a qualified surgeon, but had been a Poor Law Medical Officer for some years and was well versed in the deficiencies of public health. He too reported that the parish was severely lacking in sewers and drains. Of course, Hampstead was a much less crowded parish and its houses were generally of a higher standard. Even so, a slum quarter existed between Church Row and the High Street of courts and alleys which was still there after the construction of Fitzjohns Avenue. Travellers in carriages along the Avenue would have found it difficult to reach Hampstead Village through this maze of courtyards and resorted instead to Prince Arthur Road. The extent of the rebuilding in this old slum quarter may be seen in the architecture of the lower part of Heath Street, the upper west side of High Street and many of the buildings inside this apex. This rebuilding was the result of the Hampstead Town Improvements scheme of 1887-89 The area had included Crockett's Court, razed ten years earlier by the Wells & Campden Trust (Wells Buildings are on the site). The 1851 Census revealed 117 people in 18 houses here; they included 20 laundresses whose work at home must have increased the dampness in their already damp and tiny rooms.

Lord was a campaigning Medical Officer.[7] He early advocated cremation instead of burial and in particular inveighed against slaughterhouses, cowhouses, pigsties and the practice of some butchers of keeping sheep in their basements until they were slaughtered. He castigated the habit of bakery assistants of sleeping on their kneading benches, and campaigned for notification of diseases. He was an advocate of vaccination to prevent the spread of smallpox and was a supporter of the infectious diseases hospital at Lawn Road (see above).

Housing Conditions

Until the 1850s local vestries did not have the powers, let alone the inclination, to deal with gross inadequacies in housing conditions. In 1853 the Sanitary Committee of St Pancras recommended that residents be given a pail, brush and a supply of lime wash to purify their dwellings. There were numerous pockets of slums in the parish. One was in Fitzrovia, where it was noted that the 30 houses which made up Fitzroy Market had only 2 lavatories between them.

The most notorious of Camden slums, other than the Rookery of St Giles, was Agar Town,

immortalised as a 'suburban Connemara' by W.M. Thomas in Dickens' *Household Words* in 1851.[8] Agar Town was a short-lease development in one of the least salubrious parts of St Pancras. To its west were the burial grounds of St Pancras and St Giles-in-the-Fields, and St Pancras Workhouse; to the east were noxious industries such as bone boiling, replaced very soon by the goods yards of the Great Northern Railway; and to the south were the Regent's Canal and the gasholders of the Imperial Gas Company. Agar Town derived its name from a lawyer called William Agar, whom we have noticed before (*p76*) for his obdurate opposition to the construction of the canal across his land. His residence c.1800 was Elm Lodge, which he built on the site of the old St Pancras Manor House, just south of today's Agar Grove. He held the manorial estate on lease from the prebendary of St Paul's Cathedral and when he died in 1838 this passed to his widow in trust for their children with the stipulation that she could grant sub-leases of up to 21 years – the maximum by statute that church lands could be leased.[9] Inevitably, only poor class housing was built with such a short leasing period, but in the 1840s cheap housing was needed for a growing number of poor workers in central London. The small plots of Agar Town were taken up by builders to make a quick profit for a minimum outlay.

Steven Denford in a recent publication refutes suggestions that the Agar family neglected their responsibilities in Agar Town, pointing out that the family set aside the £5,000 they had received for permitting what became the North London line to cross the northern part of the estate, for improving Agar Town. Whatever the truth of the matter, or whatever the justification for contemporary and subsequent descriptions of the place, there is no doubt that it was built without amenities such as made-up roads or a sewerage system. The Sanitary Committee reported to the Vestry in 1856 that the roads there 'are in a condition to baffle description – mud lies knee deep. In winter houses will be almost inaccessible and in many cases under water.' In 1859, nearly twenty years after the first houses were built, the inhabitants of Agar Town sent a deputation to the Vestry to complain of the bad condition of the streets and the open sewage ditch there. The Vestry claimed that it had few powers in the matter, since the freehold of the estate was owned by the Ecclesiastical Commissioners and the arrangement was that the Vestry was responsible only for the lighting of the streets. By 1861 the estate had been sold to the Midland Railway.

There were many lurid descriptions of Agar Town. A contemporary, James King, who drew the Panorama of Kentish Town, said of the Elm Lodge estate:

'... all of the poplars had been cut down 'since when ... two-and four-roomed cottages have been built by Working Men at a ground rent, on the road side, payable weekly or monthly. The Leases terminate at the end of 21 years, which have brought together such a variety of Poor to the area known as Agar Town extending to the Gas Works ... as to make it a second Saint Giles, it being very hazardous for any respectable person to pass or repass without insult, or annoyances, as that locality received most of the refuse which the forming of New Oxford Street swept away to improve that previous impure district.'

There are other reports of a substantial Irish population here and that they had arrived, as King suggests above, after the construction of New Oxford Street. Certainly there is a conjunction of dates, but Steven Denford, on searching the 1851 Census, found that those born in Ireland were very much the exception, and that many tenants had quite respectable trades such as clerks and piano makers, and that most of the houses were occupied by single families.[10]

The parish of St Andrew, Holborn had many pockets of bad housing such as Baldwin's Gardens, which had become disreputable in the time that John Strype described it in 1720 as 'a slum frequented by criminals, attracted by its narrow alleys and courts'. Most particularly, north and south of today's Clerkenwell Road where it met Farringdon Road, was regarded as an appalling area and was vividly portrayed by Dickens as the home of Fagin in *Oliver Twist*: In the filthy shops of Field Lane, 'are exposed for sale huge bunches of second hand silk handkerchiefs of all sizes and patterns; for here reside the traders who purchase them from pickpockets'. (This at a time when someone could be transported for stealing handkerchiefs, an item today scarcely regarded as having value.) At that time, Clerkenwell and Farringdon Roads did not exist and the area from Warner Street to the bottom of Saffron Hill was a puzzling concoction of alleyways, courts and mean streets. This was the territory in which the Field Lane Foundation

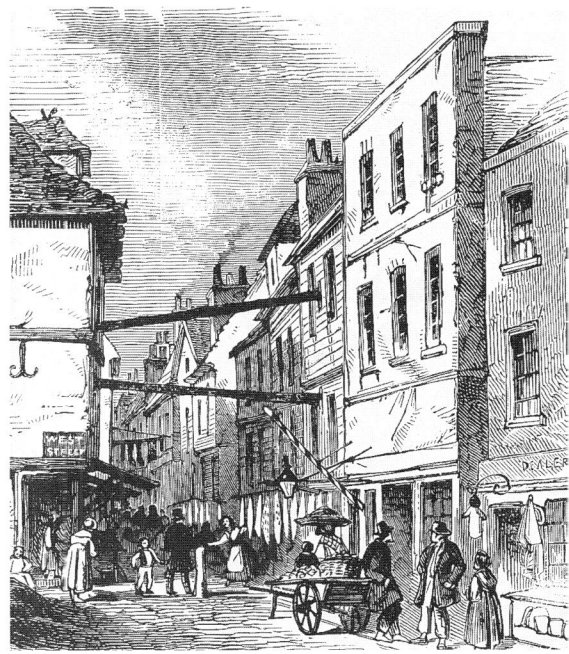

77. Field Lane about 1841.

78 An advertisement in The Times in 1843, which caught the eye of Ashley Cooper (later, the 7th Earl Shaftesbury), who gave the Field Lane mission much-needed support.

RAGGED SCHOOLS.—FIELD-LANE SAB-BATH SCHOOL, 65, West-street, Saffron-hill.—A room has been opened and supported in this wretched neighbourhood for upwards of 12 months, and religious instruction imparted to the poor by a few laymen of the churches of England and Scotland and Protestant Dissenters. Their benevolent endeavours have been greatly blessed : about 50 (adults and children) assemble on the Sundays, likewise on Monday and Thursday evenings. The application for admission far exceeds the room engaged, and the teachers are desirous of taking another adjoining, but are necessitated to APPEAL to the Christian public for pecuniary assistance to carry out their designs. Donations will be thankfully received by the Rev. P. Lorimer, 12, Colebrooke-row, Islington ; W. D. Owen, Esq., 43, Great Coram-street ; Mr. P. M'Donald, Secretary, 30, Great Sutton-street, Clerkenwell ; or by the Treasurer, Mr. S. R. Starey, 7, Ampton-street, Gray's-inn-road. Left-off garments sent to the schools will be carefully distributed.

began in 1841 as a Sabbath School.

Dickens wrote of the Field Lane enterprise: 'It was held in a low-roofed den, in a sickening atmosphere, in the midst of taint and dirt and pestilence; with all the deadly sins let loose, howling and shrieking at the doors.'

Even more colourful is a description in an 1842 report about Gray's Inn Lane (now Road), between Holborn and Clerkenwell Road:

'Grays Inn Lane is not the most salubrious, cleanly, or pleasantly populated thoroughfare in London. It is so narrow that there is but room for two vehicles to pass each other, the shops are small, filthy, and close-smelling – generally devoted to the retail of bad greengrocery, adulterated liquors, vicious newspapers, and cagmag-looking meat.

In the courts running at right angles are apparently deposited all the trucks, costermongers' barrows, and fruit stands of London. You may see them about nine o'clock in the morning pouring out of every alley, driven by sallow woe-begone men, with the unmistakeable Hibernian blue eye cocked nose, and light hair. All day long the wives and other female relatives of these men are either shuffling in and out of the courts or standing listlessly at the entrances – unkempt, slipshod, dirty women clad apparently but in one garment, and even that, in most cases, unfastened and ragged. The faces of these women are worn and macerated by famine and gin, the bones on their necks and hands seem almost protruding through the skin – their eyes are glassy, their whole demeanour utterly listless and uncaring. A visit to the gin-palace or the pawnshop, a thrashing from a drunken husband, the wakening of a neighbour's child – these are all that ever interfere with work, misery, and starvation, except upon certain grand occasions, perhaps one in every two years or so, and then some fell disease – which has been hovering over the entire city, lights upon these courts, and finding everything congenial to his taste – miasma, squalid poverty, want of drainage, and utter absence of pure water – there fixes his head quarters, and there lingers longest.'

Problems were compounded by the large number of Italian immigrants living there who, like the Irish, were desperately poor and regarded (especially as they were Catholics) as very low in the social order. These and their children were beyond even the missionary zeal of the Field Lane Foundation. In 1871, the average number of Italians living in Summers Street, a turning off Eyre Street Hill, was 14 per house. The living conditions of the Italians were to exercise the concern of local vestrymen and councillors for many years. In 1901, the *Daily Mail* printed an article in which the writer claimed to have seen 14 children brought from Italy for cheap employment in London, sleeping in one room. Holborn Council denied the worst aspects of the story but did concede that the area was very insanitary. And in 1904, after a survey of the Warner Street area, the Council said that there was a very high mortality rate and that many houses in the courts could only be ap-

proached through covered arches.

A particularly bad pocket of housing was revealed in Charles Booth's *Life and Labour of the People of London* (1902-03). In Parker Street, between Drury Lane and Kingsway, he said that most of the residents were Irish Catholics and that few of their large families occupied more than one room. The rooms were filthy, prostitution was rife and not a room was free from vermin. One elderly woman he came across spent her whole time shelling peas.

Model Dwellings

Against this background there were some early experiments in social housing in Camden. One pioneer was Thomas Southwood Smith (1788-1861), himself a regular Highgate visitor in that he often stayed at a house called Hillside in Fitzroy Park, occupied by Mary and Margaret Gillies, the latter an accomplished portrait painter. Smith (one of whose grand-daughters was the housing reformer, Octavia Hill), became known for a book which linked endemic fever with bad living conditions. Together with the Rector of Spitalfields, Lord Grosvenor, Charles Gatliff and others, he formed in 1841 the Metropolitan Association for Improving the Dwellings of the Industrious Classes. Its aim was 'The purchase and construction of dwelling-houses, to be let to the poorer classes of persons, so as to remove the evils arising from the construction and arrangement of such dwellings, more especially in densely-populated districts.' More than that, the aim was to attract investors to this project with the prospect of a 5% dividend emanating from the rents. 'Five per cent Philanthropy' had arrived.

It was not until 1847 that the Association's first project opened. Metropolitan Buildings, in Pancras Road, almost opposite Old St Pancras Church and its burial ground, was the first block of flats in London. Designed by William Moffatt, the 5-storey block, containing 110 dwellings, was criticised for its rather bleak appearance and the darkness of its enclosed staircases.[11] But, as *The Times* said in a leader, the rooms 'are so airy, so cheerful and so clean, an Oxford student might find himself at home in any one of the bed rooms and parlours'. Each flat had its own kitchen range, water supply, scullery and wc, and there was a refuse chute and a communal laundry room. Metropolitan Buildings, mainly tenanted by skilled artisans, was generally successful, both for tenants and investors, but its rents were later

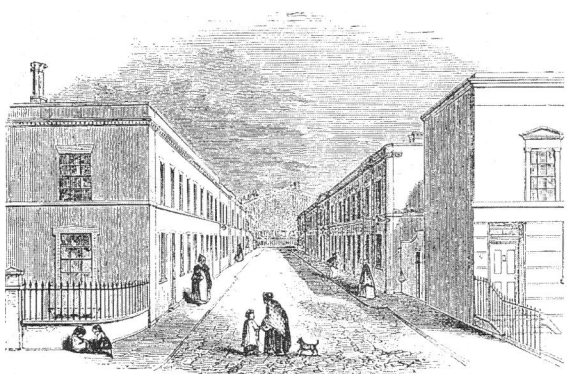

79. Model Dwellings in Pakenham Street, off King's Cross Road, erected by the Society for Improving the Condition of the Labouring Classes in 1845.

undercut by organisations such as Peabody Trust which built to a lower standard and for poorer tenants.[12]

On 17 April 1941 a parachute mine dropped on Metropolitan Buildings, killing 77 and injuring 200. After the war it was demolished and Cecil Rhodes House built in its place.

Southwood Smith was associated with another housing organisation, the Society for Improving the Condition of the Labouring Classes. Its first venture, opened in 1845 (*see ill. 79*), was a group of 23 family dwellings, together with accommodation for 'thirty aged females' in Pakenham Street, off King's Cross Road, designed by Henry Roberts.[13] They took the form of a double row of 2-storey buildings to accommodate 23 families, and a lodging house for 30 women. They were intended to demonstrate just how builders could provide for the poorer classes, with good amenities, but still at a cheap price. But they proved to be an embarrassment to the Society when they were strongly criticised as being congested and a 'hot bed of infection' by *The Builder*. Undeterred, the Society built in 1850 what is now called Parnell House in Streatham Street, south of the British Museum. This handsome block, which is the oldest surviving example of its kind, provides access to flats from balconies overlooking a central courtyard – an innovation at the time. The following year the Society opened Thanksgiving Buildings in Portpool Lane, off Gray's Inn Road, deriving their name from a thanksgiving fund to mark the end of a cholera outbreak. Again the architect was Roberts.

The Society was also particularly active in the Drury Lane area. Despite its glittering connotations, the Lane was part of one of the worst slum areas of London, and a number of artisan housing societies were active in the wholesale demolition of sub-standard dwellings in the second half of the 19th century.[14] The Society took on Wild Court, a teeming alleyway off Drury Lane, and the Central London Dwellings Improvement Co. either improved or rebuilt three courts and part of Parker Street nearby.

'Five per cent philanthropy' did not satisfy investors, as quite often the dividends were substantially below that figure and housing societies began to lower their building standards. For example, the Improved Industrial Dwellings Company (set up by Sir Sydney Waterlow, resident of Fairseat in Highgate High Street and one-time Lord Mayor of London) built Derby Buildings (now Derby Lodge) in Wicklow Street, near King's Cross, with shared water supply and WCs. These were very unpopular and had to be converted to self-contained units within a few years.[15] The Company was responsible for quite a few properties in the King's Cross area – Stanley Buildings in Pancras Road (1865), and Cobden Buildings in King's Cross Road (1863), are good examples. The architect, Matthew Allen, designed these 5-storey blocks with access to balconies from an open spiral staircase. Cobden Buildings survive and far from being thought undesirable, Stanley Buildings were the subject of a conservation battle in the plans to bring the Channel Tunnel Link to St Pancras Station. Their format was adapted by Horace Jones, the City of London architect, to build Corporation Buildings in Farringdon Road, on the site of today's *Guardian* offices. The City, ever slow to build artisan housing, was also obliged to open, after its demolition of poor-class housing while constructing Holborn Viaduct, Viaduct Buildings in 1875. This building, in Saffron Hill, has since been renovated and become St Andrew's House.[15] Waterlow's Company, like most of the societies, catered for the skilled artisan, expressing its belief that their new tenants would vacate premises within the financial reach of poorer people. This might well have happened, but one suspects that the Company did not want the liability of the poorest classes and the hassles of collecting rent from them.

Synonymous with artisan housing are Peabody estates. The Peabody Trust, based on donations of the American millionaire, George Peabody, had over 5,000 dwellings in London by 1885. In

Camden, the Trust's activities were to the south. Large blocks were built between Drury Lane and Wild Street, and around Herbrand Street off Tavistock Place. Peabody buildings have always been regarded as the most austere of the artisans' dwellings and the early regulations, common to other societies, were irksome, such as the injunction against wallpaper and picture hooks in case these should shelter bugs.

One developer specialised in building cheap flats on land related to new roads. James Hartnoll built Cavendish Buildings in Clerkenwell Road (1882), Holsworthy Square (1890), Rosebery Square, Clovelly (now Churston) Mansions (the writers, Katherine Mansfield and John Middleton Murry once lived at what is now no. 19), Dawlish and Tiverton Mansions (1891) and Braunton, Barnstaple and Bideford Mansions (1895-96).[17] The Hartnoll estate is now administered by the St Pancras Housing Association.

Other developments of artisans' dwellings included those reluctantly put up by railway companies whose activities had reduced the available amount of cheap rented accommodation. These included Polygon Buildings in Clarendon Square, on the site of the old Polygon, erected by the Midland in 1896, and Mornington Buildings off Mornington Crescent, put up by the London & North Western Railway in 1905, the Company having been defeated in its attempt to build a similar block at the junction of Regent's Park Road and Gloucester Avenue.

Lodging Houses

One of the most intractable problems was that of lodging houses. There were many in Camden. Most had an ill reputation – vastly overcrowded and extremely insanitary. They housed men who existed on casual work in central London, who walked to work at the docks, markets, building sites or railway constructions. Weighed down by a life of very hard work, impermanent prospects and drink-fed camaraderie until it was time to flop in the mean beds of a cheap lodging house, the men themselves were the least likely to evoke interest in their awful lives.

One who did take an interest was Ashley Cooper (later the 7th Earl Shaftesbury) who campaigned for many such causes, such as ragged schools and artisan housing. It was he who pushed a Bill through Parliament in 1851 to regulate lodging houses. In an impassioned speech he said that he had personally seen five families living in a single room. Unfortunately, the Act put the onus for inspection on to the Police Force which had neither the time nor the expertise. Though the Act made a licence necessary to open a lodging house, it was easily obtained by presenting the signatures of only three residents in the parish as to the respectability of the applicant.

Another pioneer in the field of artisan housing was Lord Iveagh. He interested the first (and last) Lord Rowton in the matter of lodging houses. Rowton decided to form a new organisation to bring about improvement. His first scheme, into which he ploughed £30,000 of his own money, was a very large lodging house providing comfortable beds, affordable food and hygienic surroundings at Vauxhall. It revolutionised such provision. Not only was it, within its own sphere, a respectable address, but it allowed men who had a ticket for a bed that night to come and go as they pleased during the day, instead of being excluded from breakfast to supper. There was central heating and there were clean sheets, a barber's shop and laundry facilities. Of an evening there was the relaxation of the smoking room where there were dominoes and draughts to play, or the library where there was a modest selection of books. Although the men were not allowed to gamble, and were discouraged from drinking, there were no religious homilies or duties thrust upon them.

The Camden Rowton Houses, at Mount Pleasant and Camden Town, were opened in 1896 and 1905 respectively. That at Mount Pleasant was converted into a hotel in the 1980s, and then replaced by a Holiday Inn, surely one of the ugliest modern buildings in Camden. The original building was built in much the same style as what is now known as Arlington House in Camden Town. It had 678 beds, all of which were booked a week after opening, whereas at Camden Town there were 1103 beds in 985 cubicles and 118 'bedrooms'.

Until modern times lodging houses remained, with few exceptions, under the supervision of private individuals or organisations such as Rowton or the Salvation Army. An exception in Camden was Parker House, Parker Street, where an Act of 1886 enabled the demolition of 108 houses and the opening in 1893 of a lodging house for 320 single men in small cubicles. This was under the supervision of the London County Council and is, like Arlington House, now overseen by Camden Council.

Public Baths

Campaigners for better public health in the 19th century included the provision of public baths and washhouses in their objectives. Their enthusiasm was rewarded by the passing of the Baths and Washhouses Act of 1846-47. In the overcrowded conditions endured by the poor, bathing was difficult or impossible, and laundry work unpleasant and arduous. Of the parishes that now make up Camden, St Giles and St George Bloomsbury were the first to take combined advantage of the legislation, with a baths opened in Endell Street, roughly on the site of today's Oasis pool, in 1853.

The Act had in fact been preceded in St Pancras by private enterprise, where the New River Company had built a baths in North Gower Street next to its reservoir on the site of the later Tolmers Square. The building was sniffily noted in *The Builder* in 1845,[18] but it appears not to have opened until August 1847. It described it as a single-storey elongated building containing 22 men's baths, and five vapour baths. There were two swimming baths each 60' x 21', plus women's baths and a room for washing clothes. It was closed in 1860.

St Pancras Vestry first considered adopting the Act in 1849, but it was not until a specially called meeting in 1865 that it budgeted £20,000 to build a baths on the south side of Plender Street, Camden Town, a site now occupied by council housing. This opened in May 1868 with a hospitable ceremony at which 53 bottles of wine were consumed – we know this because a vestryman protested at the extravagance. Nearly a year later we learn that the baths had been used by nearly 146,000 bathers, while the laundry rooms, at first thinly attended, were lately popular, especially with women who were taking in laundry for a living. The average time taken by each woman was $3^1/_2$ hours at a cost of $5^1/_2$ d.

St Pancras opened its second baths in Whitfield Street in 1878 and then a third in West Kentish Town, where the Prince of Wales Road Baths, which still adorns the area, was the first public building erected by the new St Pancras Borough Council in October 1901– this probably explains the relative extravagance of the design, with a liberal use of fashionable terra cotta. It contained four swimming pools, two for each sex, and 129 'slipper' baths. The laundry had fifty washing cubicles, fifty heated drying horses and a mangling and drying room. Illustration 80 suggests that there was either a separate provision for men, or a special time for them to do their laundry. The building was designed by Thomas Aldwinckle, who mainly specialised in public houses.

80. Men doing laundry work at the Prince of Wales Road Baths c.1901.

81. Hampstead Baths and washhouses on Finchley Road, later the site of Sainsbury's.

In Hampstead the early provision of baths and washhouses was left by the Vestry to the Wells & Campden Trust.[15] The charity's first such venture, opened in Palmerston Road in West Hampstead, in 1887. Cold baths cost one penny, warm baths twopence, and the use of laundry facilities was also twopence. In September, a year later, the baths in Flask Walk were opened. They were closed in 1978, but the building still survives, converted into apartments. The Trust made a loss on both ventures. This was made worse by the Vestry opening its own baths on the site of a former skating rink in Finchley Road on 5 June 1888. By 1907 the Trust was negotiating with Hampstead Council for the borough to take over the two old baths and laundries, and this the Council did in 1908. The Finchley Road baths were superseded by the baths at Swiss Cottage, designed by Basil Spence, in 1965, and were destroyed by fire in 1972, when the site was taken by Sainsbury's until 1998.

[1] Minutes Books of Highgate Dispensary at the Highgate Literary and Scientific Institution

[2] VCH Middlesex, vol. 1, p.205.

[3] F.M.L. Thompson, *Hampstead. Building a Borough, 1650-1964.* pp.270-1 (1974).

[4] Reminiscences of Ewart Attkins, held at the Highgate Literary and Scientific Institution

[5] Reminiscences of Edith Walker as above.

[6] See Desmond Whyman, 'Butchers Shops in Kentish Town' in *Camden History Review* 20 (1996), on which much of this paragraph is based.

[7] See Dr Barbara Ely, 'Till Death through Ripe Old Age' in *Camden History Review* 3 (1975).

[8] This description and the article in which it was contained are usually attributed to Charles Dickens, but it has recently been pointed out in an excellent monograph by Steven Denford, *Agar Town: The Life & Death of a Victorian 'Slum'*, published by Camden History Society (1995), that it was in fact written by W. M. Thomas.

[9] *Ibid*, p.14

[10] *Ibid*, p.21

[11] The enclosed staircases were to lead to the whole block being treated as one house and assessed for window tax, making them an expensive feature. The tax was abolished in 1851. See Steven Denford, 'Luxury living for the lower classes' in *Camden History Review* 20 (1996).

[12] See Isobel Watson, 'Five Per Cent Philanthropy' in *Camden History Review* 9 (1981); Steven Denford as above.

[13] An architect patronised by Prince Albert. He went on to design some model dwellings exhibited at the Great Exhibition of 1851, which were later removed to Kennington Park, where today they form a lodge.

[14] It is estimated that by 1885 there were at least 28 philanthropic housing societies functioning in London. See Alan Cox, *Public Housing: A London Archives Guide*, p.7 (1993).

[15] Watson op cit.

[16] *Ibid.*

[17] *Ibid.*

[18] *The Builder*, 8 Nov. 1845, p.534.

[19] Information in this paragraph from Christopher Wade, *For the poor of Hampstead for ever: 300 years of the Hampstead Wells Trust*, pp.70-4 (1998).

CHAPTER ELEVEN
Major Schemes

Hampstead

Some of Hampstead Village is eighteenth century, a mix of outstanding houses and pockets of smaller dwellings carved out of the restricted space between the line of High Street / Branch Hill and the Heath, north of Gayton Road. A number of architectural gems were built early in that century or just before – Fenton House was finished in 1693, and it was joined soon by Old Grove House and New Grove House, Windmill Hill, Upper Terrace, Capo di Monte, Elm Row, Burgh House and Norway House (the last just south of Flask Walk). A walk around the area today will also encounter less grand, but still charming, houses of that period or else their early 19th century replacements. A number of substantial properties were in Frognal to the west of the road to Childs Hill, and in the 1720s Church Row, a speculative development, was built in a reasonably uniform manner either side of the pathway to the old parish church of St Mary.

When expansion on the east side of the High Street became possible during the last half of the 19th century, the band of fields between Gayton Road and the already established Keats Grove / Downshire Hill area was filled in. But it was to the west and south-west of the High Street that the most significant developments occurred.

The exploitation of Belsize Park and the Chalcots estate south of it had, unlike much of expanding London, little to do with the availability of railways: the scenic and social merits of the district were alone sufficient to ensure good-class housing. These two areas were the first in Hampstead to be developed in the great 19th-century expansion of London, and yet the land with the best potential – that which lay west of the church down to Finchley Road and beyond, and with the best views in all directions - was developed later than the fields on Hampstead's lower slopes. This was a consequence of the lord of the manor's long and unsuccessful battle to build on his heath land, for in the process his own building lands were legislatively ensnared *(see pp.109-112)*.

Instead, Eton College led with building on its Chalcots estate followed a few years later by the Dean and Chapter of Westminster Abbey in the development of the Belsize Park area. These two estates were built mainly in solid Victorian terraces, complete with stucco and neo-classical porches, while the lord of the manor's Fitzjohns Avenue area was built in Edwardian and Arts and Crafts styles. It could so easily have been the other way round. If Sir Thomas Maryon Wilson, the lord of the manor, had restricted his first application to Parliament (in 1829) to his *uncontentious* building lands, he would almost certainly have secured the necessary legislation and have begun development. Had he done so a sufficiency of available houses on his estate would have made development on the lesser estates to the south uneconomic for the time being.

Eton College obtained an Act to develop its estate in 1826, but was slow to take advantage of it. This led to even more delay from 1831 when the route of the London & Birmingham Railway had to be taken into consideration and, of course, its proximity deterred potential speculators. There was no reason then why residents of any proposed suburb of villas should benefit from the railway since no local station was planned. And there would be pollution and noise it was feared, despite the assertion of a railway enthusiast that:

> 'The steam engines are prohibited from burning coal – no smoke therefore can issue from the flues. Comparatively little noise is heard when a train of carriages, conveying perhaps 150 persons, is in movement, and the rattling of wheels of an ordinary stage coach conveying a tenth of the number on a turnpike road is to great measure avoided.'

Eton College also owned Primrose Hill there, and a number of overtures were made to use that land – most dramatically for a necropolis, or for a reservoir.

The first part of the College's Chalcots estate, built from the 1840s, was a triangle of villas at the southern end of Haverstock Hill and the new Adelaide Road. Into this small development was inserted St Saviour's church to keep up the status of the area. Progress was slow, as well it might be in such limbo territory, and Adelaide Road did not reach Swiss Cottage until the 1850s, but it did at least join there the increasingly important Finchley Road. This turnpike road was built from the late 1820s with the enthusiastic support of the Eyre Estate in St John's Wood, through whose land it went at its southern end. Beyond St John's Wood the road ran through Hampstead manorial land, which remained undeveloped while the Heath dispute trundled on through Parliament.

The estate of the Dean and Chapter of Westminster lay on *both* sides of Haverstock Hill, north of Englands Lane. It stretched north-west to the present day junction of Akenside Road and Fitzjohns Avenue, and north-east to Parliament Hill. Development was delayed partly by lethargy and partly by existing leasehold arrangements. In 1803, the lessee, the Earl of Chesterfield, sold his interest to four Hampstead men, who divided the estate into eight portions, each of which had a separate sub-lease. The tenure of each lease was dependent on the life spans of three people whose names were written in to each agreement; when one of the lives 'dropped', a new one could be inserted on payment of a fee. This fragmentation and the unpredictability of expiry dates was to cause the Dean & Chapter many problems.

These small estates became 'parks' – then the fashionable word – to contain a sizeable mansion secluded from the road in imitation of a rural retreat. Or else, an original house was utilised, such as Belsize House, at that time occupied by Spencer Perceval, the future Prime Minister.

The first of these parks to be developed from *c.*1852 was on the east side of Haverstock Hill. St John's Park was planned by William Lund, who lived at Haverstock Lodge on the site of Downside Crescent. He began with Lawn Road, Upper Park Road and Parkhill Road, but the quality of the development deteriorated the nearer it got to the dreaded Fleet Road – then unbuilt but projected alongside the uncovered and polluted Fleet river and, as we have seen (*p.92*), near to the temporary fever hospital.

Belsize Park, which contained Belsize House, was begun in 1853 by Charles Palmer. His intention was to develop an exclusive estate with its own square and church, arranged in such a way as to deter through traffic. Exclusive or not (and in the end it was found necessary to have more exits to the proletariat roads around) it has been pointed out by Professor Thompson[1] that although the social class on the Belsize Park estate was higher than on the Eton College estate, it was mainly built for people who did not keep their own carriages, and who used public omnibuses or hired carriages instead. There are very few mews properties on the Belsize estate.

Rosslyn Park was begun at the same time, but no sooner had the developer, Henry Davidson, embarked on Thurlow and Lyndhurst Roads, than a scheme was announced to bring the Hampstead Junction Railway (*see p.82*) beneath his land.

North of the Westminster land was the Greenhill estate, which stretched southwards from the King William IV public house. This was laid out in the 1870s. On it existed some distinguished houses which included Stanfield House, the home of the artist, Clarkson Stanfield, The Rookery, occupied by the Longman publishing family, and the old Vane House which had been partly rebuilt for the Royal Soldiers' Daughters' Home, an institution founded soon after the end of the Crimean war. (Now called the Royal School Hampstead, it is at 65 Rosslyn Hill.)

Other small estates filled out the rest of mid-Victorian Hampstead. Oak Hill Park in Frognal was built in 1856 by Sir Thomas Neave of nearby Branch Hill Lodge; the Carlile House estate off Rosslyn Hill was begun in 1876, when the middle-class houses of Willoughby, Kemplay and Carlingford Roads, and Rudall Crescent were built. In the South End Green area, Thomas Rhodes farmer-turned-developer, built South Hill Park and Gardens to a good standard, and the owner of the adjacent Pickett's Farm built Parliament Hill and Nassington Road which finished abruptly at Parliament Hill itself with the full expectation, as Professor Thompson points out, that the roads would be extended in the not too distant future onwards and upwards.

Camden and Kentish Towns
The history of London is awash with building schemes that ran into financial trouble. Camden Town is a good example. Begun in 1791, it spluttered to a halt in the first decade of the 19th century having progressed only as far as Camden Street, and only then with many blank spaces. It was not until the early 1850s that speculators drew comfort from the increasing

use of the 'New Road to Tottenham' (Camden Road), and supported substantial development focused around Camden Square. Even then an attempt was made to distinguish it from Camden Town proper by calling it 'Camden New Town'.

In Kentish Town most of the east side of the main street was owned by institutions and the other side, where the railway had not already intruded, had been the property of Lord Southampton until 1840. A map of 1849 shows very few houses at all off the main road: along what became Leighton Road there were houses on land owned by the exotically-named Joshua Prole Torriano, and there were some tight-packed streets between Prince of Wales Road and Chalk Farm Road.

The first major estate to be developed in Kentish Town was that of Christ Church, Oxford. These fields, the ownership of which may be traced back, with some gaps, to the 14th century, lay in 31 acres south of today's Kentish Town Underground station – Caversham Road, Gaisford and Islip Streets mark their territory. The estate, bequeathed to the College in 1735, contained a Tudor farmhouse known latterly as 'Morgan's Farmhouse' after the family which occupied it. Morgan found it more economic to send hay to London and bring back horse manure, than to keep animals himself. This agricultural trend, also marked on the Eton College Chalcots estate by the end of the 19th century, was noted in 1795 by Christ Church's agent when he wrote that 'By the tenant's lease the farm is considered a cow farm, and the tenant has covenanted to consume the hay on the premises and spread the dung on the land. The reverse has been the practice and he wishes to sell the hay in London and bring back dung as he is too far from London to sell his milk to advantage.' Morgan moved out in 1831, stating that he 'was perfectly satisfied that to continue in it would be the means of my going to a gaol or a workhouse'. This perennial complaint of farmers, in good times or bad, did not seem to deter his successor, the wholesale butcher, Giles Silverside, who farmed the acres until they were wanted for building purposes. The College built on the street frontage but it was not until the 1860s that the fields were developed. One of the College's problems was that the estate had no exit to Camden Road because Lord Camden's road frontage barred the way. In the end the only exit that could be contrived at that time was via

82. Morgan's Farm, at the junction of today's Kentish Town Road and Caversham Road. An early Tudor farmhouse, which was not demolished until the 1850s.

Torriano Avenue.

The Christ Church development was a mixed one. In 1865 it was noted that tradesmen and clerks in the City were occupants, but that Caversham Road was 'highly respectable and let to solicitors, gentlemen and large tradesmen'. However in Peckwater and Hammond Streets poorer people paid £25-33 per annum and in other properties whole families occupied one or more rooms.

At about the same time, but in different architectural styles, the two small estates south of Christ Church, belonging to the Dartmouth family and to St Bartholomew's hospital, were also constructed.

The Dartmouth family was also busy off Highgate Road, where its land behind Grove Terrace (begun in 1780), was built on. Dartmouth Park Road was a spacious development winding up the hill, but the eastern part of the estate, nearer to Dartmouth Park Hill, was several rungs down the social ladder. Here were built, under the aegis of the Conservative Land Society, Churchill and Ingestre Roads, and Spencer Rise.

The largest estate on this side of Highgate Road was that owned by St John's College, Cambridge. Substantial houses were built in Burghley and Lady Margaret Roads, but such was the surfeit in the early 1860s of this type of housing the College was obliged either to halt construction or else to proceed with cheaper houses.

In the northern extremity of the parish Highgate New Town was built mainly in the 1880s, extending across Dartmouth Park Hill into Islington. On the St Pancras side this followed the break-up of the estate of Highgate worthy, Harry Chester (died 1868). Some of his land had already been sold in the early 1850s to the London Cemetery Company for an extension of its successful cemetery in Swains Lane; other plots now went to the St Pancras Guardians of the Poor for their new infirmary in Dartmouth Park Hill, and most of the rest for the New Town development.

Highgate New Town was an attempt to exploit the cachet of 'Highgate', but it was undermined by its location and building standard. Near to a cemetery and a hospital that contained an infectious diseases unit, it was not best placed to attract good class customers. A report in the *Hampstead & Highgate Express* in January 1890 noted that:

> 'Within the last few years a district of houses erected by a number of builders known as Highgate New town has sprung into existence, part of it is in St Pancras and part in Islington, but the whole district has obtained an unenviable reputation of being hopelessly insanitary. It is known that many houses have no damp courses or foundations and floor boards are laid straight on to the ground.'

The census of 1871 shows a certain amount of overcrowding, but not extraordinary for London – ten or twelve people to a small three-storey house. When the ill-kempt children of the area began attending services at St Anne's church in Highgate West Hill they were accommodated on special benches in front of the congregation but as there were many complaints about the smell and fleas 'the children were turned out'.

One near neighbour unhappy with the quality of Highgate New Town was Baroness Burdett-Coutts, who, excepting the Queen, was the richest woman in the country. Her own house, Holly Lodge, was off Highgate West Hill and her extensive gardens, including a vineyard, extended east and south to Swains Lane. It was she who built nearby Holly Village in 1865, a Gothic fantasy-cum-garden village, designed by Henry Darbishire and constructed by Thomas Cubitt. It has been often claimed – and indeed nowadays a plaque on the gateway says so – that she built this group of houses for either her estate workers or for her Coutts Bank employees. There is no evidence to support this. The census taken six years after building began shows none of the residents (who include a good number of the original occupiers) to be an employee or likely to have been a former one.

On the west side of Kentish Town, the builders who had taken plots of the old Southampton land, seem to have given up hope of a good-class development early. The oppressive presence of railways made it very difficult to entertain anything but artisans' houses with few ameni-

83. The entrance residences to Holly Village.

ties. Karl Marx moved to Grafton Terrace in 1856, where he paid £36 per annum rent – even this stretched the family's resources. The road was not made up and he complained in a letter to his friend Engels, who lived in Regent's Park Road, of the neighbourhood's squalor, which much distressed his wife: 'My wife's nerves are quite ruined by the filth'. An inheritance enabled them to move round the corner to a house in quite a good development on the estate of the Orphan Working School, which had been renamed Maitland Park.

The Southampton lands in the Chalk Farm area had the benefit of Regent's Park and Primrose Hill. Consequently, when Lord Southampton sold them in 1840, development could match these amenities, but quality shaded off down to Gloucester Avenue where the railway lands were.

Spreading west

After the death of Sir Thomas Maryon Wilson in 1869, and the end of the long and acrimonious dispute over the future of Hampstead Heath, the development of the manorial estate west of Heath Street began. Within years development changed completely both sides of Finchley Road. In about 1875. the showpiece Fitzjohns Avenue was laid out in substantial plots and this encouraged renewed attempts to rid Hampstead of the nest of slum courts and alleys that separated Church Row from the High Street. Though Fitzjohn's Avenue was ready for traffic in 1876, it was not until 1888 that it was officially opened to the western extension of Heath Street, which included a newly built Express Dairy building in which butter was made daily.

Fitzjohn's Avenue was an expensive boulevard.

84. House built for Frank Holl, artist, in Arkwright Road.

107

It was built with massive houses with large grounds, many of which survive. No. 61, for example, designed by Norman Shaw, was built 1876-78 for the painter Edwin Long. Hampstead Tower at no. 55, is a baronial fantasy, with 25 rooms, designed by J.T. Wimperis. Not so grand, but very desirable, streets were built between Fitzjohns Avenue and West Heath, such as Redington Road, Templewood Avenue and Oak Hill Park. Mostly built in the Edwardian era, their architecture was strongly influenced by the Arts and Crafts movement, especially those by C.H. Quennell, although one must note the remarkable 1873 Oak Tree House at the end of Redington Gardens by Basil Champneys.

On the other side of Finchley Road, Priory Road marked the western edge of the estate. This road was begun in 1874 and was to provide access to the curving grid of Compayne, Canfield, Greencroft and Aberdare Gardens and Goldhurst Terrace.

West End
In the 1840s, the hamlet of West End, outside the manorial estate, was isolated from the centre of Hampstead, though the sound of the bells at St John's church could be heard summoning the few residents to services. Its isolation was a consequence of the terrain, but as Christopher Wade has pointed out, in actual distance from the parish church, it was nearer than both North End and South End, whose settlements were more integrated into Hampstead village life. Before the opening of Finchley Road, the residents of West End probably had more in common with the village of Kilburn than with Hampstead. The hamlet consisted of a number of large houses, at least two inns, a village green with a pond, and very little else. Even in 1864, with two railways cut across its southern end, this rural scene had hardly changed. The most notable house in the hamlet was Old West End House. This, or an earlier form of it, was the home of the widow of William Beckford (1709-70), famous for his persistence while Lord Mayor of London in presenting a petition to King George III on the subjects of the disbarment of John Wilkes from Parliament and the freedom of the individual, despite the king's reluctance to be harangued. Beckford's impromptu words to the outraged monarch are engraved at the foot of his statue in the Guildhall. Beckford, immensely rich from a mixture of sugar and slaves, left £1 million and an annual income of £100,000, to be

pleasurably spent by his son, the novelist of the same name. About a hundred years after these dramatic events, the Hampstead Junction Railway sliced past her back door and ten years further on the Midland Railway crossed by the front, leaving it isolated and awaiting inevitable demolition. Iverson Road (1879), now leads directly through the site of the house, part of a development by the British Land Company, which was also involved in the building of the Carlile estate off Hampstead High Street (Willoughby Road etc.).

North of the hamlet three substantial houses were built in the first half of the 19th century. Thomas Pell Platt, an oriental scholar, built Childs Hill House on the site of the present Rosecroft Avenue; this was demolished in 1903. John Teil, an East India merchant with tanneries in Kidderpore and Calcutta, built Kidderpore Hall in 1843, which was transformed by Charles Cannon, a dyer; the house was taken by Westfield College in 1890. And Henry Weech Burgess built Burgess Park, which later became the Anglo-French College.

Humdrum development from the 1870s fitted itself around the railway lines, cuttings and marshalling yards that criss-crossed the area. Colonel Percy Cotton's Shoot-up Hill estate was hemmed in by the Midland Railway. Cotton, who also owned the remnants of the Kilburn Priory land, lived at Kingsgate, an enlarged version of the old Shoot-up farm – Kingscroft Road is now on the site. His military career is noted in local street names such as Rondu and Skardu Roads.

[1] F.M.L. Thompson, *Hampstead. Building a Borough, 1650-1964*, 278 (1974).
[2] *Ibid*, p.12. A report of a surveyor in 1796 noted that 'The farm is in general very good land and in a high state of cultivation, which is occasioned in a great measure from its contiguity to London, from whence maure is so easily obtained. The crops of hay it produces annually are very great...'
[3] *Ibid*, p.3

CHAPTER TWELVE
Wide Open Spaces

Saving the Heath

The first major open space in Camden specifically preserved for the public's use was Primrose Hill. After several proposals to build on the land, the Crown acquired it from Eton College in exchange for land at Windsor, and in 1842 it was reserved as a park and regarded as an extension to Regent's Park which, by 1841, had been mostly opened to public use. This was a matter swiftly resolved, in contrast to the battle to save Hampstead Heath, which lasted forty years.

The irascible Sir Thomas Maryon Wilson, lord of Hampstead manor since 1821, was the central figure in the protracted Heath dispute. Though living at Charlton House on the south side of the river, Sir Thomas had already made his presence felt in Hampstead. He had continued his late father's opposition to the construction of what became Finchley Road, a pet scheme of the Eyre estate in St John's Wood to greatly increase the value of the Eyre lands. The elder Sir Thomas did not want his land encroached upon, especially as the original plan was for a turnpike road which began in St John's Wood and crossed Belsize towards Hampstead. In his petition to the House of Commons in 1819, when the Eyre estate first submitted its Bill, he claimed that 'Thefts and depredatory practices by dishonest persons, hedges and fields exposed to continual injury, robberies and destructions by bad, malicious, idle and disorderly persons' would result. Siding with Belsize residents, he said that 'not one in 20 of the gentlemen in Hampstead would have occasion to use it for business or professional pursuits because their business lies in the City or the Inns of Court, not towards Tottenham Court Road.'

Sir Thomas junior was just as strident an objector. When the Eyre estate proposed a new route in 1824 to link with the Great North Road, virtually the same as today's Finchley Road, he claimed that it would provide access from the Portland Town area (a sub-standard quarter near St John's Wood High Street) for lower class people who would destroy his fences. Residents of Frognal were on his side and complained that

85. *Sir Thomas Maryon Wilson, the 7th baronet.*

the road would disturb their privacy. In presenting his petition, Sir Thomas revealed that his father had specifically requested him not to build on his Hampstead estates so as to keep them rural. This important piece of information was not known to his subsequent detractors in the Heath battle, and would have made his case for development of some of his Hampstead property even more difficult to sustain.

Sir Thomas made another mistake: he did not marry and produce a son. As Professor Thompson points out, it was possible, once an eldest son came of age,[1] to jointly break the conditions of Sir Thomas's own father's will, so that the Hampstead building estates could be developed without the need of an Act of Parliament. Without an heir, he was dependent upon Parliamentary favour.

It was when Sir Thomas began to appreciate

109

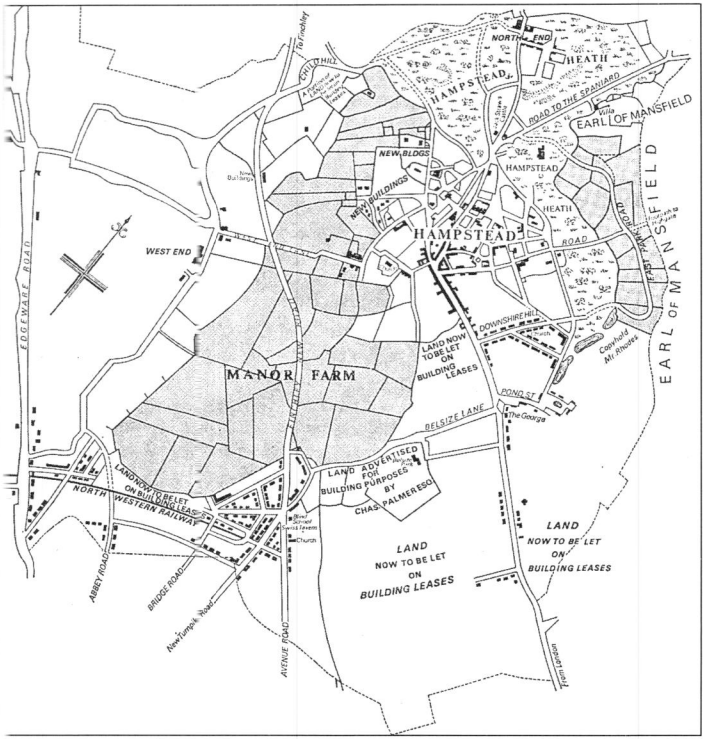

86. Hampstead in 1853. The shaded portions are Maryon-Wilson's 'building' estates.

the increased value of his lands once Finchley Road was built after 1826, that his desire to keep Hampstead unspoiled abated. The story of his unsuccessful attempts to develop them is not only one of technicalities and the rise of local pressure groups, but of a marked change in general public opinion about open spaces: the rights of landowners to build on their estates, hardly questioned before, were put in the balance against the perceived benefits of open spaces to a more urbanised society. However, if Sir Thomas hadn't been so greedy and so insensitive, it could have been an entirely different story.

Sir Thomas inherited manorial rights over three areas of common heathland (*see Ill. 86*). These were East Heath along the east side of East Heath Road up to and encircling the Vale of Health, the Sandy Heath on the north side of Spaniards Road, and the West Heath, to the west of North End Way. Common lands were in a legally grey area when it came to ownership for they were usually open to the manor copyhold tenants, who had rights to graze their animals on them, to collect firewood etc. In theory, any enclosures of the heath had to be agreed by a meeting of the lord and his copyholders. But many such common and waste lands had been enclosed by manorial lords with impunity, despite the opposition of copyholders, and as the pace of development quickened, particularly around London, the pressure to enclose more of them increased.

Sir Thomas was not the first Hampstead lord of the manor to contemplate enclosure of some of his heath land – over the centuries a great deal of it had been built on with the connivance, even encouragement of local copyholders, so that Hampstead Village could be extended. But crucially in the case of Sir Thomas, what remained of Hampstead Heath was not just *another* common on the fringe of London. It had long been used by Londoners for recreation, and not just by local residents. It was appreciated as a metropolitan asset and was known to a wide range of people, from cockneys to fashionable parties to the Wells, and no doubt to Members of Parliament as well.

This London fondness for the Heath was to prove an asset to the copyholders who, perceiving some threat to their rights in Sir Thomas's Bill, were able to persuade many people that the Heath was threatened with buildings. In fact, what Sir Thomas primarily wanted was Parliamentary permission to grant 99-year building leases on his non-Heath lands (the shaded areas in illustration 86), so as to take advantage of the potential of the Finchley Road. There was nothing unusual about this and almost invariably such a Bill would have received Parliamentary approval. But unwisely either he or his advisors tacked on to his Bill a request to make minor adjustments to the present copyhold tenancies, and power to grant building leases on parcels of land that he himself enclosed from the Heath. Hence the initial opposition, for if he had restricted his Bill to include only his private estate then there is little doubt that it would have been granted and Hampstead would have developed in an entirely different way. It should be noted too that part of his building land, known as the East Park Estate, was sandwiched between the East Heath and the open lands of Parliament Hill belonging to Lord Mansfield on the east. These sixty acres were to play an important part in the later story.

Displaying a gift for pressurising influential people that has since been honed to a fine art in Hampstead, the copyholders persuaded Parliament to defeat Sir Thomas's Bill.[2] It is interesting that the value of the Heath to Londoners in general was highlighted at this early stage by, ironically, one of Sir Thomas's own supporters. He said:

'that the Lord of the Manor of Hampstead ought not to be precluded from improving his property with the consent of the copyholders, because the tradesmen of the Metropolis chose to make it a place of recreation for themselves, their wives, children and friends.'

A chastened Sir Thomas returned the next year with another Bill that excluded the heath lands, but by then the public was in no mood to wave a green flag. It was pointed out that if he were allowed to build on the East Park estate, then East Heath itself would be surrounded by houses on three sides, making it ineffectual as a place of recreation. Again Sir Thomas retreated, but he had not learnt his lesson. If he had then abandoned plans for the East Park Estate altogether he would probably have carried the day

and been able to develop his private land to the west without hindrance and with much profit. But when he renewed his efforts in 1843, he had the fixed resolution that the East Park estate was legally his to build on and he was going to do so by hook or by crook. By then the matter was a *cause célèbre* and his Bill was thrown out again, each rejection ensuring that each new effort would be pounced upon. The following year he tried a different tack. If he could obtain permission from Parliament to sell his estate – even that was prohibited by his father's will – he could obtain something approaching a building price for the land and the purchasers would have an automatic right to develop it. Again the residents opposed this clear deviation from the will's intent.

Thwarted in his aim to let out his land or building leases, in 1844 Sir Thomas began what he was legally entitled to do – build on the East Park estate *using his own money*. He planned an ornamental park containing 28 villas; to this end he built a rudimentary road, a wall and a gatekeeper's hut, all of which survive and then, in 1845, commenced building the most visible feature of his scheme, the viaduct across one of the ponds. Fortunately for future generations, this attractive structure proved expensive and time consuming because of landslips and water penetration, and Sir Thomas retired hurt again, with no houses built.

In the 1850s, when Sir Thomas presented his fifth Bill, the residents were led not by unsophisticated copyholders but by articulate professionals such as banker John Gurney Hoare, who lived at The Hill off North End Way, supported by influential residents and the Vestry itself. Their obduracy was severely tested in 1854 when Sir Thomas at last dropped the East Park estate from his Bill, but by then such was the suspicion of the man that it was suggested that if he were granted permission to vary the will once, then it might happen again later if he did apply to build upon the East Park estate. Professor Thompson is here suspicious of the motives of the influential residents.[3] Could it be that they were more concerned to ensure that their mansions by the heath would never lose their view across East Heath? At any rate, Sir Thomas refused to give a pledge not to build on the East Heath estate, and so the fight went on.

The cause was later taken up by the Commons Preservation Society, formed in 1865. But just as the Master of the Rolls declined to give a verdict on the rights of lord and copyholder in the matter of common land, Sir Thomas conveniently died, mourned by few. The Metropolitan Board of Works bought the Heath from Sir Thomas's brother and heir, Sir John, and by 1872 it was formally declared a public property.

The securement of the Heath was not the end of the matter, of course. Sir John was still technically able to build on the East Park estate and, even worse, Earl Mansfield could sell the Parliament Hill estate for building. If Mansfield did that it would make the saving of the East Park estate less of a cause. In 1884 Sir George Shaw-Lefevre, a Liberal MP and a resident of Hampstead, pressed for the public acquisition of both estates. A campaign fund was established with the Baroness Burdett-Coutts of Holly Lodge and Octavia Hill, the grand-daughter of Southwood Smith (*see p.98*), enlisted as fund raisers. St Pancras and Hampstead vestries pledged significant funds – the price per acre was higher than in the case of the heath lands because the estates in question this time were building land. The Metropolitan Board of Works was reluctant to contribute at first. This was mainly because that body consisted of representatives from all over London, many of whom thought that Hampstead was already well endowed with open space. Eventually, a public appeal brought in the money needed, and in 1889 East Park estate and Parliament Hill Fields were added to the Heath.

Some later extensions of the Heath are worth summarising. The Golders Hill estate (part of which is in Camden) was auctioned in 1897 but failed to reach its reserve price and was withdrawn. A second auction in 1898 found local residents prepared and armed to guarantee their own money up to £35,000. But private bidders forced the price beyond that and Thomas Barratt, chairman of Pears Soap, who lived at Bellmoor at the top of East Heath Road, of his own volition bought the estate for £38,000 in anticipation of the public finding the extra money. Golders Hill Park was opened to the public later that year.

What is now called the Heath Extension was part of the old Wyldes Farm estate. In 1889 Henrietta Barnett and her clergyman husband, Samuel, took Heath End House near the Span-

87. A garden party held on Parliament Hill Fields in 1885 to raise funds for the purchase of Parliament Hill and the East Park Estate. The former 201 acres were bought for £200,000 and the latter 60 acres for £94,000

88. Thomas Barratt.

89. Sir Sydney Waterlow.

iards for a weekend retreat from their pastoral work in the East End. Some years later the proposed route of what became the Northern Line included a station at North End near Wyldes Farm which would, inevitably, have brought development to the Wyldes Estate, then still owned by Eton College. Henrietta Barnett organised a Heath Extension Council which obtained an option to buy, but with donations from local authorities very small, it was left to Barratt again, with friends, to buy some of the land, while the rest was bought privately by the Barnetts who built Hampstead Garden Suburb on it.

In 1889 too, Waterlow Park was unexpectedly created when Sir Sydney Waterlow handed over the lease of his house called Fairseat in Highgate High Street to the London County Council. The gift also included the freeholds of Lauderdale House and what was called Andrew Marvell's Cottage, together with the grounds stretching down to Swains Lane. Subsequent efforts to obtain the freehold of Fairseat failed and so Lauderdale House, then regarded as a bit of a liability, was used as public rooms instead. The

loss of Fairseat was fortunate, since it is likely that otherwise Lauderdale House might have been demolished as being superfluous.

The last major campaign was for the acquisition of Kenwood House and its grounds. Campaigners were realistic and set their sights at first on the fields below the main wood and those east of the Millfield Lane extension, rather than on the house itself. These 100 acres were bought, again mainly from public subscription, for £135,000 in 1922. In 1924 a further tranche of 30 acres was bought, which included two ponds. The price for this was £31,000, of which Hampstead Borough subscribed £5,000. Only the house and its adjacent 76 acres remained. The omens were not good, for Lord Mansfield, Kenwood's owner, had sold the contents of the house in 1922 (all through C.B. King, a Hampstead firm of auctioneers) and had already instructed surveyors to draw up plans for a park of 33 villas. The property was saved for the public by Earl Iveagh, former chairman of Guinness, who bought it in 1925 for £107,900 and promptly announced that he would donate it to the public at his death or in ten years' time. On his death in 1927 it was bequeathed to a grateful public.

113

90. Kenwood House in 1788, before the addition of wings on either side.

The smaller spaces

These grand and in many people's opinion, most beautiful of London's open spaces, were welcome, but others were needed in congested parts of Camden. The Holborn area had none, other than the private grounds of Lincoln's Inn, Gray's Inn, and the gated squares such as those on the Bedford estate. No attempt was made to open these up to the public, or as in the case of the borough of Finsbury, to buy up land (as far away as Hornsey Wood, now Finsbury Park) for recreation. The squares of St Pancras were also for residents only, and until modern times the only public open spaces in that part of the borough were the old burial grounds. St Pancras was, in fact, the first local authority in London to lay out burial grounds as public gardens.

The St Pancras burial ground adjacent to Old St Pancras Church was closed in 1855 and that of St Giles-in-the-Fields, adjacent to the north, a year earlier. Thereafter, both grounds were disused and neglected. As we have seen (p.81), worse was to follow when the Midland Railway constructed a cut-and-cover tunnel beneath part of the St Pancras churchyard which necessitated gruesome and insensitive disinterments.

Another problem for St Pancras Vestry in its aim to contrive public gardens, was that the adjacent burial ground of St Giles-in-the-Fields was, in law, extra parochial and, in effect, part of the parish of St Giles. St Pancras eventually acquired control of the ground, but had the foresight to ask Frederick Cansick to copy the inscriptions of visible monuments before setting to work removing most of them. St Pancras Gardens, which include the remaining parts of both burial grounds, were opened in June 1877.

The St Giles ground was not the only extra-parochial territory in St Pancras (*see p.52*). The parishes of St George the Martyr, St George Bloomsbury, St Andrew Holborn, St James Piccadilly and St Martin-in-the-Fields, all had burial grounds in St Pancras. That for the two St George's was between the Foundling estate and the southern range of Regent Square. Those interred here included Jacobites who were hanged, drawn and quartered in 1746. In buying and converting these grounds the Vestry was assisted by the Kyrle Society, whose aim was to provide these oases of greenery in London. St George's Gardens opened in 1884.

The other Holborn burial ground in St Pancras, for the parish of St Andrew, was to the east of Gray's Inn Road at its junction with Wren Street. It had been opened in 1754 and it is quite possible that the poet, Thomas Chatterton, who commit-

91. Pond Square, Highgate in 1860.

ted suicide in 1770 at the age of 18 in Brooke Street, Holborn, was buried in this ground, though as he was a pauper no monument was erected. The ground was closed in the 1850s, but it was not until 1885 that St Pancras was able to lay it out as a public garden.

The burial ground of St James Piccadilly was behind St James's Chapel and the later National Temperance Hospital on Hampstead Road. The land was bought some time after 1788 and the chapel, a prominent landmark in the road, was consecrated in 1793. At its largest the ground consisted of four acres, in which it is estimated that 50,000 interments took place. The public gardens, down to three acres, were opened in August 1887.

The burial ground for St Martin-in-the-Fields off Pratt Street, Camden Town, was opened in 1805, and the associated almshouses built in 1817. There were riots in 1855 when the churchwardens of St Martin's proposed to build houses on part of the ground already used for interments. By then the cemetery had closed. In 1887 St Pancras took over its management and conversion to public gardens, which opened in 1889. At the ceremony that year the monument to local resident Charles Dibdin, the ballad composer, was unveiled by the Kentish Town Music Appreciation Society. In 1828, when Charing Cross Road was widened, a slice of the St Martin-in-the-Fields churchyard was emptied of bodies and these were re-interred in Camden Town. It is contended by some that the remains of Nell Gwyn were removed to Camden Town in the process.

In Highgate, Pond Square has been a public space that can be traced back to the 14th century. It used to have two ponds, but when they became a nuisance, they were drained in 1844. Nowadays they are covered by depressing asphalt. Directly south of the Square used to be a public bowling green, noted in Cantelowes Court Rolls

115

92. The Grange in Kilburn High Road was built in 1833 by Samuel Ware, architect to the Duke of Portland. After the death of the last owner, Ada Peters (wealthy enough to have four coaches and a footman) in 1910, the house was sold, but the grounds were bought in 1911 by Hampstead and Willesden councils together with aid from the LCC and the Middlesex County Council. These were made into Kilburn Grange Park.

as being for the residents for all time, but the landlord of the Flask was permitted in 1730 to dig it up provided he reinstated it in nine years. He never did.

West End Green was keenly fought for. In 1875 John Culverhouse had a lease on the Green from the lord of the manor. He put hoardings around it so as to begin development, but local residents tore them down. After a period of dispute, the Green was put up for sale at £850, of which Hampstead Vestry agreed to pay half if the Metropolitan Board of Works put up the rest. The Vestry later reneged on its promise and the manor sold the Green to a private purchaser who put up some more hoardings, this time of a more substantial nature. On a wet night in July 1882 some 200 men converged on the Green armed with axes, crowbars and a large can of oil. They outnumbered the solitary policeman on guard, tore down the hoardings and set fire to them. In the end the Green was bought by the Vestry with the aid of a public subscription.

Hampstead Vestry did not perform well either in the matter of Fortune Green. In 1888 the lessee, again Mr Culverhouse, was offered £1200 by a property company. The company withdrew after public opposition, and the public then went on to evict some gypsies who had settled on the Green. In 1898, with the reluctant help of Hampstead Vestry, the LCC and local residents secured the Green for public use thereafter.

[1] F.M.L. Thompson, *Hampstead: Building a Borough 1650-1964* pp.132-33 (1974).
[2] For extended accounts of the Heath battle see either Thompson's book above, or Alan Farmer, *Hampstead Heath* (1984).
[3] Thompson op. cit, p.179.

93. Gipsies on Fortune Green, c.1887.

CHAPTER THIRTEEN
Famous Names

There have been distinct periods when Camden residents have been important in the history of visual arts. Constable, Romney, John Linnell and William Blake, all prominent in the first quarter of the 19th century, are synonymous with Hampstead. But it is true to say that though the scenic beauties of the Heath and its horizons attracted many people with easels at that time, very few of them were of innovative calibre. In fact, Hampstead's most productive period, in that there was a concentration of creative activity, was in the 20th century when artists of the quality of Henry Moore, Barbara Hepworth, Mark Gertler, Ben Nicholson, David Bomberg, Oskar Kokoschka, Piet Mondrian and Naum Gabo were expanding frontiers.

Fitzrovia was home for about 125 years to numerous artists. There were three important periods. Charlotte Street was the first street to be popular – by the end of the 18th century to about the end of the 1830s. Major artists of the day, either living in the street or renting studios there, included George Morland, Richard Westall, Richard Wilson, Joseph Farington, and John Constable. Then from about the 1840s, Newman Street was preferred. Artists such as Dante Rossetti, Luke Fildes, James Sant, Thomas Stothard, Ford Madox Brown, George du Maurier and Whistler occupied or rented studios in the street.

In the 20th century it was the turn of Fitzroy Street. Working artists included Roger Fry, Spencer Gore, Duncan Grant, Vanessa Bell, Augustus John, William Coldstream, Paul Nash and Walter Sickert. Sickert was pre-eminent in the Fitzroy Street Group, which rented a floor at no 19, and later in the formation of the Camden Town Group whose members included Gore, Wyndham Lewis, John Rothenstein, Harold Gilman and Augustus John. It was an exciting time in the London art world, made even more so by the first showing by Roger Fry of Post-Impressionists such as Gaugin, Van Gogh and Cézanne. When members of the Fitzroy Group formed the Camden Town Group in 1911 it was resolved that it should number no more than

94. John Constable.

sixteen and contain no women. Most of the painters, such as Gore, Sickert, Robert Bevan and Charles Ginner dealt with urban life; but new members such as Jacob Epstein broadened its spectrum. Sickert (1860-1942) was very familiar with Camden Town – he painted many pictures of local scenes, especially of the old Bedford Theatre, and he lived locally at Mornington Crescent and Hampstead Road. Possibly unnerving to him was a statue of his first wife's father, Richard Cobden, unveiled in 1868, in front of Mornington Crescent station. In 1913 the Camden and Fitzroy groups merged, to form the London Group, but it was immediately beset by personal differences and in 1914 both Sickert and Pissarro resigned.

Some Studios

Hidden behind Fitzroy Road in Chalk Farm is a group of twelve studios which were begun in 1877. They were built and designed by Alfred Healey, a local builder and property owner with offices in Princess Road. An unusual feature of Primrose Hill Studios was that they were provided with a lodge whose keeper and wife supervised the cleaning and even provided main meals. This arrangement continued until the 1940s. The best known occupants have been Arthur Rackham, the illustrator, and Henry Wood, the conductor.

Three notable sets of studios have existed in Camden Town. The oldest, and the least known, was in Camden Road on the site of Sainsbury's store. It consisted of six studios which were occupied from at least 1876 by artists whose names did not achieve posterity. They were demolished to make way for the ABC Bakery building in c.1905.

The better-known Camden Town Studios were in Camden Street, but again they housed no artist of note today. The nine studios were demolished when the borough council redeveloped the area in the 1960s. New studios were built there to replace them together with an exhibition hall, the largest door of which was too small to allow larger paintings through. Of this period, the sculptor, Peter Peri, is the best known artist. In Cliff Road, off Camden Park Road, are some studios built after the last war, still mostly used by artists. Naum Gabo (1890-1977), the Russian constructivist had one which was afterwards used by the sculptor, the late Ghisha Koenig.

The Steele's Road studios, built in 1876 off Haverstock Hill, boasted the Vorticist painter, C.R.W. Nevinson (1889-1946), as an occupant. He was a member of a long-standing Hampstead family. A large number of artists used studios in the Parkhill Road area, off the other side of Haverstock Hill. Henry Moore (1898-1986) lived at 11a until it was bombed and he moved briefly to the Mall Studios (see below). Barbara Hepworth (1903-75) and her husband Ben Nicholson (1894-1982) also stayed here, and further along, at 60, the Dutch painter, Piet Mondrian (1872-1944), lived until he too was bombed out.

Between Parkhill Road and St Dominic's Priory leads a pathway to the Mall Studios. These look like a group of converted stables, but were purpose-built as studios in 1872 by Thomas Batterbury, who was also responsible for the Steele's Road studios. Originally, they were non-residential and early artists such as Robert Macbeth (1848-1910) and James Linton (1840-1916) lived nearby in Parkhill Road. In 1879 George Clausen (1852-1944) was the occupant of no. 4. In 1927, two sculptors, Barbara Hepworth and her first husband, John Skeaping, lived at no. 7 with their son. This relationship foundered when Ben Nicholson moved into the studios: he and Hepworth later married. Herbert Read, the art critic, lived at no. 3, and he was able to say in retrospect that the studios were 'a spontaneous association of men and women drawn together by common sympathies ... and there was a prevailing good temper, an atmosphere in which art could grow.'[1]

Contemporary with the Mall Studios group was another which had Richard Carline (1896-1980) at 47 Downshire Hill as its main influence. Stanley Spencer (1891-1959), at one time a resident at the Vale of Health Hotel, married Hilda, Carline's sister. Nearby, at no. 21, Roland Penrose (1900-84) lived – he and Paul Nash were responsible for staging the first international Surrealist exhibition in London. Like those of the Mall Studios, the Downshire Hill artists were politically left, and Carline was chairman of the Artists' International Association. Artist Fred Uhlman and his wife Diana eventually took over the Carline house and helped the work of the Artists' Refugee Committee, which aided artists hounded out by Hitler. One of these was John Heartfield (1891-1968), founder of the Dadaist movement, who came to stay with the Uhlmans for two weeks but stayed five years.

Writers

Two well-known writers are associated with a small white cottage opposite the Load of Hay pub on Haverstock Hill. Sir Charles Sedley (?1639-1701), a Restoration wit, settled down here after a rumbustious life, but was in ill health and died here in 1701. Eleven years later the cottage was taken by Sir Richard Steele (1672-1729), then editor of *The Spectator*, but very much in need of a retreat from his political enemies and creditors. This did not prevent him from attending meetings of the Kit-Cat Club, which often met at the Upper Flask Inn at the top of Heath Street near East Heath Road, in the early part of the 18th century. The purpose of the Club was to espouse the Hanoverian succession and when that was achieved the Club withered. Other illustrious members who one may imagine gath-

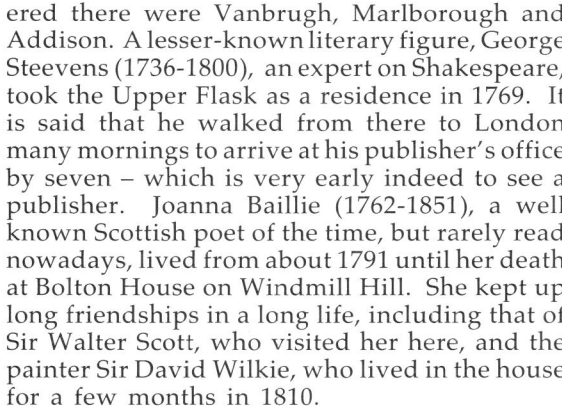

95. John Keats, painting by Joseph Severn.

96. Charles Dickens, photograph by Fradelle & Young.

ered there were Vanbrugh, Marlborough and Addison. A lesser-known literary figure, George Steevens (1736-1800), an expert on Shakespeare, took the Upper Flask as a residence in 1769. It is said that he walked from there to London many mornings to arrive at his publisher's office by seven – which is very early indeed to see a publisher. Joanna Baillie (1762-1851), a well known Scottish poet of the time, but rarely read nowadays, lived from about 1791 until her death at Bolton House on Windmill Hill. She kept up long friendships in a long life, including that of Sir Walter Scott, who visited her here, and the painter Sir David Wilkie, who lived in the house for a few months in 1810.

The most famous literary figure associated with Hampstead is John Keats (1795-1821). Though his residence was brief, it was here that he wrote most of his poetry before he died at the age of 25. In December 1816, Keats went to pay his respects to Leigh Hunt (1784-1859) for his enthusiastic review of one of his poems. Hunt, poet, writer and journalist, who lived in the Vale of Health, was to be a close friend of Keats in his last years. By 1817 Keats was lodging with his brothers in the house of the local postman in Well Walk, roughly on the site of the Wells Tavern. He was befriended too by Charles Armitage

Brown who had just moved into one of a pair of villas called Wentworth Place, built in Albion Grove (the present Keats House in Keats Grove). After the death of his brother Tom in Well Walk, Keats moved into Brown's house, where he paid £5 a month for his board. He spent Christmas Day 1816 at the home of the Brawne family (on the corner of Downshire and Rosslyn Hills, for he had become emotionally attached to Fanny Brawne. When the other villa which made up Wentworth Place became vacant, the Brawne family moved in. It was during this period that Keats wrote some of his best poetry, including *Ode to a Nightingale*, in the garden of the house. In 1819 Keats became very ill indeed and in 1820, when Brown had let the house, he moved in with Leigh Hunt, then ensconced with his numerous children and wife in a small house in Mortimer Terrace, that odd cul-de-sac off Highgate Road near Gordon House Road. By August that year Keats was back in Wentworth Place to be nursed by Fanny Brawne and her mother, and in September left Hampstead for good in the hope of a respite in an Italian climate. He died in Rome in February 1821.

The best-known literary figure in St Pancras was Charles Dickens (1812-70). In a long series of moves around London, he resided in several

97. *George Bernard Shaw, St Pancras vestryman and borough councillor, later Freeman of the Borough.*

parts of Camden. The Dickens family came to live in Camden Town in 1822, when Dickens was aged ten and at a time of domestic distress and disarray. They took on what was then 16 Bayham Street, a house identified as being on the site of today's 141. When he described this part of his life to his biographer and friend, John Forster, Dickens remembered it with much unhappiness. His father was in serious financial difficulties and was soon to be in Marshalsea prison for debt. In this small house the parents, their five children and a servant squeezed. Dickens himself occupied a garret room overlooking the backs of Camden High Street. He thought, in retrospect, that Bayham street was awful, but it does seem that his memory was clouded by the family crisis and the overcrowding in his house. A contemporary resident said that Bayham Street was like a village; there were twenty or thirty newly-built houses, whose occupants included their builder. Other residents included an engraver, a retired merchant and a former linendraper. One writer has said that Dickens based the Cratchit house in *A Christmas Carol* on his house in Bayham Street. However, when Dickens lived there, the house was less than a hundred yards from fields.

In 1824, while his family lived at the prison with his father, Dickens lodged in the northern part of today's College Place. Gradually the family fortunes revived and they moved to a house at what was then 29 Johnson Street (now Cranleigh Street), off Eversholt Street. Dickens was soon at school at Wellington House Academy in Hampstead Road, just south of Mornington Crescent, whose grounds were later taken for a widening of the LNWR line. Other addresses in Camden in which Dickens lived included The Polygon in Somers Town, Fitzroy Street, Tavistock House in Tavistock Square and, of course, 48 Doughty Street where the Dickens Museum opened after it was bought by the Dickens Fellowship in 1924. Dickens moved here in 1837 with his wife, child, brother and Kate his sister-in-law, who died here to the intense distress of the writer.

George Bernard Shaw (1856-1950) not only lived in St Pancras – in Osnaburgh Street and Fitzroy Square in the 1880s and 1890s – but was on St Pancras Vestry and the first St Pancras Council. When Shaw came to London aged 20 he was to be found regularly attending meetings of the misleadingly called Hampstead Historic Society and the Fabians. The former was founded by Charlotte Wilson c.1884 and met at her home in the old Wyldes farmhouse to discuss politics, free love and social reform. Some of its members also belonged to the newly-formed Fabian Society. Other frequent attenders at one or both were Olive Schreiner, Havelock Ellis and Sidney Webb. Wilson's group also discussed *Das Kapital* without much unison of views. Shaw described their discussions of the work, before an English translation was available:

'A young Russian lady used to read out 'Capital' in French to us until we began to quarrel which usually occurred before she had gone on long enough to feel seriously fatigued. The first chapters were of extraordinary efficacy in getting us by the ears ... The controversy raged at Hampstead until Bax shook the dust of the heath off his boots, and the Historic Club, having had enough of impassioned disputes as to whether the value of Mrs Wilson's vases was fixed by the labour socially necessary to produce them, by their cost of production on the margin of cultivation, or by the final utility of the existing stock of vases, insisted on passing to the later chapters and dropping the subject.[3]

Shaw's first appearance as a St Pancras vestryman, at the old Vestry Hall in Pancras Road near Old St Pancras Church, was in May 1897. He was an Independent, though thought of as a Socialist. One of his causes was to promote an insurance company for local authorities, in which he succeeded, and another was the provision of free lavatories, especially for women.

H.G. Wells was very much a Camden person. He stayed with his aunt at 46 Fitzroy Road, near Primrose Hill, when he was working as a schoolmaster at Henley House School in Kilburn. It was on Primrose Hill that the invaders in *War of the Worlds* expired. Wells's complicated love-life revolved around the Mornington Crescent area where at one time he lived with his wife, although with his mistress, Catherine Robbins, around the corner. He also lived at Church Row, Hampstead for a time.

Three famous poets lived in Chalk Farm. The late Ted Hughes (1930-99) and his wife Sylvia Plath (1932-63) were at 3 Chalcot Square, before they separated and she moved to 23 Fitzroy Road, which had once been occupied by W.B. Yeats. In Delancey Street, Camden Town, Dylan Thomas (1914-53) lived at no. 54, and had the use of a caravan in the back garden.

Alfred Harmsworth (1865-1922), who was a pupil at Henley House (see above), became a newspaper and magazine owner whose influence is still felt in today's publications. Harmsworth (who became Lord Northcliffe) and his brother (ennobled to Lord Rothermere), were residents of West Hampstead before their flair for popular journalism made them wealthy. Alfred lived in Sherriff Road, Iverson Road, West End Lane and Pandora Road before moving on to more affluent surroundings.

More cerebral writer residents of Camden have included Aldous Huxley (1894-1963) in Bracknell Gardens, Hampstead Hill Gardens and Pond Street; Professor Cyril Joad (1891-1953) in the Vale of Health and East Heath Road; and Edith Sitwell (1887-1964) and others of the Sitwell ménage at the Greenhill flats in Prince Arthur Road and in Keats Grove.

Other Camden writers have included Stella Gibbons (1902-89), author of *Cold Comfort Farm*, whose addresses include early homes at Malden Crescent and the Vale of Health; for most of her life she was at 19 Oakeshott Avenue on the Holly Lodge Estate. The peripatetic George Orwell (1903-50) lived, when he was very strapped for cash, above a bookshop at the junction of Pond Street and South End Green in Hampstead in 1934-35. His reactions to Hampstead are recorded in *Keep the Aspidistra Flying*. But he also lived in Parliament Hill, Mortimer Crescent and Lawford Road in Kentish Town where his landlord complained that Orwell kept him awake at night with the noise of typing.

The poet, John Betjeman (1906-84), grew up at 31 Highgate West Hill, where he developed a crush on a young lady with the unlikely name of Peggy Purey-Cust, the daughter of a retired rear-admiral who lived further up the road. In retrospect, Betjeman wrote an evocative poem called *Parliament Hill Fields*, which records a tram ride from Kentish Town to the terminus at Swains Lane.

> Till the tram went over thirty, sighting terminus again,
> Past municipal lawn tennis and the bobble-hanging plane;
> Soft the light suburban evening caught out ashlar-speckled spire,
> Eighteen-sixty Early English, as the mighty elms retire
> Either side of Brookfield Mansions flashing fine french-window fire.[2]

Agatha Christie (1890-1976) lived at the Isokon flats in Lawn Road, John Galsworthy (1867-1933) at Grove Lodge in Admiral's Walk, George du Maurier (1834-96) in Church Row and Hampstead Grove, Kate Greenaway (1846-1901) in Frognal, Evelyn Waugh (1903-66) at Hillfield Road, and D. H. Lawrence (1885-1930) at numerous Hampstead addresses,.

Highgate's literary lion is Samuel Taylor Coleridge (1772-1834). In ill health and addicted to opium, he moved into the care of Dr James Gillman at Moreton House in South Grove in 1816 and then with him to 3 The Grove in 1823. It seems unlikely that Coleridge was ever released from his addiction. In 1816 he acknowledged the problem in a letter to Gillman:

> 'I have full belief that your anxiety need not be extended beyond the first week, and for the first week I shall not, I must not, be permitted to leave the house, except with you. Delicately or indelicately this must be done, and both your servants and the assistants must receive absolute commands from you. '

Though some have claimed that Coleridge conquered the habit, others, including Thomas de Quincey, himself an addict, said that he never did. Coleridge died at Highgate and was originally interred in the burial ground of Highgate Chapel and then reinterred at St Michael's church

98. Samuel Taylor Coleridge.

opposite Gillman's house. This house in The Grove was also the residence of the writer and playwright, J.B. Priestley (1894-1984), in 1933-39.

Writers and artists drifted in and out of what is called the Bloomsbury Group. This network of friends and relatives revolved around Virginia Stephen and her sister Vanessa who moved into Gordon Square after the death of their father, Sir Leslie Stephen. Vanessa married Clive Bell and Virginia, Leonard Woolf. The extended Bloomsbury set included Lytton Strachey, Dora Carrington, Roger Fry, Duncan Grant, Geoffrey Keynes, E.M. Forster, Desmond MacCarthy, Arthur Waley and Aldous Huxley. In a memoir, Clive Bell complained that the term 'Bloomsbury Group' implied 'a point of view, a period, a gang of conspirators or an infectious disease.' There was, he said, 'beyond mutual liking ... precious little in common'. Certainly 'Bloomsbury' has at times been used perjoratively as a reaction to this most written-about network of friends, but there is no doubt, especially if one includes other artists and writers associated with it, such as David Cecil, Wyndham Lewis, Christopher Isherwood, Vita Sackville-West and Hugh Walpole, that its artistic legacy has been enormous.

Luminaries of the theatre, where they have lived in Camden, have preferred the cachet of Hampstead. Mrs Patrick Campbell (1865-1940)

lived at Pitt House, North End Avenue, Fay Compton (1894-1978) was in Well Walk, Donald Wolfit (1902-68) in Wildwood Grove, Lillie Langtry in Alexandra Road and Sarah Siddons (1755-1831) at Capo di Monte in Windmill Hill; in recent times there have been Peter Sellers and Peter Cook. In Highgate, houses in The Grove have sheltered Gladys Cooper, Robert Donat, John Drinkwater and Christopher Hassall.

Notable musical residents have included the late Yehudi Menuhin at 2 The Grove in Highgate, Sir Thomas Beecham (1879-1961) in East Heath Road, Sir Arnold Bax (1883-1953) in Haverstock Hill, Sir Edward Elgar (1857-1934) in Netherhall Gardens, Dennis Brain and Kathleen Ferrier in Frognal, Dame Clara Butt in Harley Road, Delius and Sir Henry Wood in Elsworthy Road, Elisabeth Lutyens in King Henry's Road and Adelina Patti in Primrose Hill Road.

Camden has been particularly rich in politicians. Prime ministers include Spencer Perceval (1762-1812) at Belsize House, Herbert Asquith (1852-1928) at Keats Grove and Maresfield Gardens, Ramsay MacDonald (1866-1937) in Howitt Road and Frognal; would-be prime minister Hugh Gaitskell (1906-63) was at Frognal End when he died. Other notable politicians and theorists include Annie Besant in Mortimer Crescent, Henry Hyndman in Well Walk, Beatrice and Sidney Webb in Netherhall Gardens, Edith Summerskill in Millfield Lane, and Krishna Menon, the Indian politician and St Pancras borough councillor in Camden Square. Most famous of all was Karl Marx (1818-73). In 1856, the penurious Marx family, then living in Dean Street, Soho, received a £150 inheritance and on the strength of it moved up to what was a fairly isolated road in the largely unbuilt West Kentish Town. They lived in the house now numbered 46 Grafton Terrace. Here, as Jenny Marx recalled, they 'slept in our own beds for the first time, sat on our own chairs and even had a parlour with second-hand furniture'. They paid £36 a year rent, but even so they were financially stretched. He wrote to his friend Engels that 'Today I am actually worse off than I was five years ago when I was wallowing in the very quintessence of filth.' In 1864 they were saved once again by inheritances and moved to 1 Modena Villas, subsequently renumbered 1 Maitland Park Road, a house built on the estate of the Orphan Working School. It was while he lived at this house that 'Charles' Marx was nominated by St Pancras Vestry as an unpaid

99. Karl Marx.

100. The then 22 Theobalds Road, Holborn, the birthplace of Benjamin Disraeli, prime minister.

constable, but he was never appointed. The first volume of *Das Kapital* appeared in 1873, and in 1875 he is noted in the Vestry minutes as appealing against the rate assessment of a third house, 41 Maitland Park Road. It was there that he died in 1883. The house has since been demolished and 101-107 Maitland Park Road are now on the site, complete with a plaque recording his residence.

There have also been some residents whose contributions to the way we live have been remarkable. The pioneer of television, John Logie Baird (1888-1946), lived in Lawn Road; Lord Leverhulme (1851-1925), mass producer of soap (initially), was at Inverforth House in North End Way; Marie Stopes (1880-1958), pioneer of birth control, was in Denning Road and Well Walk; Richard D'Oyly Carte (1844-1901), impresario of Gilbert & Sullivan operas, lived in a small cottage opposite the Swains Lane bus terminus, before moving to 2 Dartmouth Park Road; Henry Durant (1902-82), the populariser of opinion polls (the Gallup in his case), lived in Brookfield Mansions; Sir Rowland Hill (1795-1879), pioneer of the modern postal system, lived at several addresses in Hampstead near Pond Street; and the famous and very rich Victorian philanthropist, Baroness Burdett-Coutts (1814-1906), had an out-of-town residence, Holly Lodge, whose grounds were later built over with mock-Tudor houses. Sigmund Freud (1856-1939) came as a refugee to 39 Elsworthy Road in 1938, before moving to 20 Maresfield Gardens, where he died the following year. His daughter, Anna, carried on his work, and opened her Child Therapy Clinic in 1952. The house is now the Freud Museum.

We should not forget the numerous architects who have lived in Camden. Among them were George Gilbert Scott (1811-78) in Admiral's House, Admiral's Walk, just before he set to work on the Midland Grand Hotel at St Pancras; Sir James Pennethorne (1801-71), who designed the Public Record Office in Chancery Lane and was responsible for the construction of a number of new streets, such as New Oxford Street and Endell Street – he lived in Elm Court, just north of Lauderdale House in Highgate; Henry Flitcroft (1697-1769), designer of the present St Giles-in-the-Fields church, who lived in Frognal in the 1740s and 1750s; R. Norman Shaw (1831-1912), the most influential architect of his time, lived in Ellerdale Road; and Erno Goldfinger (1902-87), who built the small row of Modern Movement houses in Willow Road in 1938, to the disquiet of local residents and the later approbation of architectural students.

1 For fuller description of the Mall Studios see Gwen Barnard, 'A Nest of Gentle Artists' in *Camden History Review* 8 (1980).
2 From 'Parliament Hill Fields' in Betjeman's *Collected Poems* (1958).
3 Quoted in Phillip Venning, *Wyldes, A New History*, 13 (1977).

CHAPTER FOURTEEN
Trading Places

With some exceptions industrial firms in Camden have been small scale affairs. Notable among the larger companies have been piano makers. As late as 1911, 125 firms involved in piano making were spread over Camden and Islington. In addition, a glance at a street directory of the period will reveal numerous individuals manufacturing small parts of the instrument.

The first time the piano was heard in public was probably at Covent Garden Theatre in May 1767. The first notice of it being used as a solo instrument in public was in June 1768, when it was played by J.C. Bach, the 18th child of the famous composer, who lived for much of his life in London and was buried in St Pancras churchyard. The first adequate composer for the piano was Muzio Clementi, whose name was used for a piano making firm in c.1806 established at 195 Tottenham Court Road. That area of London was already well known for its cabinet makers, and early piano makers utilised their skills.

Clementi's company was eventually taken over by the Collard family which in 1847 moved to Oval Road, Camden Town, where it could off-load timber from the canal, brought up from London docks, or alternatively export pianos to home

101. The Brinsmead piano factory in Kentish Town.

and abroad. Here in 1850 Collards built a circular factory, which in December 1851 burnt to the ground, and was replaced a year later by the present 22-sided building of 5 floors, with a hoist shaft in the centre; this was designed by Thomas and William Piper.[1] Within this construction, mass production was possible as pianos in different states of assembly were hoisted up or down floors. Another company, run by John Brinsmead, began as cabinet makers in Windmill Street, but in 1841 his piano factory, a vast affair, was built in Grafton Road, Kentish Town. By 1904 he was producing a piano every working hour at prices ranging from 33 to 300 guineas, and at the height of his prosperity he had 300 employees.

Gunther and Horwood, piano makers, occupied premises behind 12 Camden High Street (the southern end) which were later temporarily used by Collard & Collard after the fire of 1851. At 44 Fitzroy Road was the Hopkinson piano factory. This imposing building, erected 1867 to the design of J.T. Christopher, survives, but only because a spirited local campaign in 1975 saved it and seven adjoining houses from Camden's demolition.

Another piano firm near the canal was Chappell's, at the junction of Belmont Street and Chalk Farm Road, and further along the water was Zewadski in Wrotham Road, off Pancras Way, which specialised in organs. The great organ builder, Henry Willis, occupied the Rotunda building at the top end of Royal College Street, a site lately taken by St Richard of Chichester school. This building was erected in 1824 in which to paint the giant panoramic views that were used in Burford's Panorama off Leicester Square.

Piano making was a seasonal affair. Charles Booth in *his Life and Labour of the People of London* (1903) noted that the standard working week was 54-56 hours in winter and 48 in summer, but this was often increased.

The furniture men

Though cabinet makers-turned-piano makers mostly moved north to be nearer the Regent's Canal, the making of good quality furniture remained resolutely around Tottenham Court Road to where, in the 18th century, it had migrated from the St Martin's Lane area. An early settler was Peter Langlois, a renowned ormolu craftsman, who was at Stephen Street by 1763, where his clients included the Duke of Bedford and

102. *Ambrose Heal.*

Horace Walpole. The variety of furniture specialists may be judged in the large volume by Sir Ambrose Heal depicting tradesmen's cards in the 18th century. Heal himself was a descendant of John Harris Heal whose upholstery business in Rathbone Place was the origin of what became the most prestigious furniture shop in London.

Kelly's Directory of 1863 shows 110 addresses in the Fitzrovia area devoted to aspects of furniture making, but gradually as prosperity and Victorian fashion demanded an excess of furniture, so those who had the space to produce it by machine and on a conveyor belt system using relatively unskilled labour – located mainly in Shoreditch and Bethnal Green – became the principal suppliers of the large furniture shops that became a feature of Tottenham Court Road.

John Harris Heal moved his upholstery business to Tottenham Court Road in 1818 and on his death his widow, Fanny, enlarged the business with property acquisitions nearby. It was Heal's great grandson, Ambrose (1872-1959) who made the store famous, having it rebuilt in 1917 by Smith and Brewer, demolishing at the same time the old Capper farmhouse behind, which had been used by the Heal family as residential space. Contemporary furniture, relying for its attractiveness on the wood itself, vastly different from elaborate Victorian design, was encouraged and the store continued to be dominant in its field until recent times when its extended building was shared with Habitat.

John Maple's business was established at 145 Tottenham Court Road in 1841 and he subsequently acquired the adjoining 146 and 147 (then, as now, the numbering of Tottenham Court Road goes up one side and down the other). Eventually the three shops were rebuilt with a unified façade, but this early progress was marred in 1857 when reconstruction work at 148, owned by another company, brought down the wall between it and 147, causing the collapse of 146 as well. Many of Maple's staff slept in the upper floors – six of them were killed in the incident. One who survived was the young Horace Regnart who rose to become general manager of the business, a St Pancras alderman and a noted supporter of the St Pancras Almshouses. He was also strongly criticised, as we shall see, in an official enquiry into sweated labour used by the business. By 1870, when Maple's son Blundell had joined the business, the shop was well-known and by 1885 it had expanded to take up an island site formerly occupied by over 200 houses.

Blundell Maple was then in charge of the business with Horace Regnart as his general manager. In very competitive trading conditions there is no doubt that the buying power of the store encouraged the exploitation of poorly paid workmen in the East End where much of the furniture was made. Strong accusations were made against the company in 1888 when an enquiry into the use of sweated labour heard details of the Maple working and paying practices. The enquiry also revealed some interesting facts about Maple's turnover – in 1887, it was testified, Maples made over 24,000 mattresses, and palliases, over 15,000 bedsteads and nearly 3,000 bedroom suites.

Other local stores selling large quantities of furniture were Shoolbred's and Oetzmann's, both at the cheaper end of the market. James Shoolbred began in Bloomsbury in 1820, but moved to a site just south of Maple's which his sons expanded to fill the block. Shoolbred's, it is contended, was the first shop to take a full-page

103. A skilled and traditional industry: the carton-Pierre ornament factory of George Jackson, at 49 Rathbone Place, in 1908.

advertisement in *The Times*. Oetzmann's had a large shop at the lower end of Hampstead Road and a cabinet factory in Camden High Street opposite the Cobden statue, which had previously been occupied by the North London Collegiate School for Boys.

In Camden Town, Bowman Brothers reigned supreme. Thomas and Robert Bowman, sons of a Lakeland farmer, established an upholstery business at 108 Camden High Street in 1864. It was Thomas who made the firm's fortune by selling mass produced mahogany furniture, then as much in vogue as pine is today. He rebuilt the shops he had as one building in 1893, and added more in the 20th century.

The last half of the 19th century were hard years for shop assistants and market stallholders, who were expected to work virtually all their waking hours. There was an active movement to enforce a closure at 5 o'clock on Thursdays in the 1870s, and an attempt to persuade retailers to close at 8pm on days other than Saturdays when trading could go on very late. Archibald Taylor, a Highgate resident who worked as a shoemaker in Junction Road, recalled that his shop would be shut at midnight on Saturdays. When John Sainsbury and his wife opened their second shop in Queen's Crescent in 1876 (their first was in Drury Lane in 1869), they employed a man whose job was to be there very early in the morning so that when the trading whistle was blown he could grab a place in the market outside to give Sainsbury a presence there as well. This market usually closed at midnight on Saturdays. V.S. Pritchett in his book, *A Cab at the Door*, recalled that his parents worked at Daniels (see below), the drapers-cum-department store in Kentish Town. Here, the hours were 8 to 8 on weekdays and until 11 on Saturday nights. As if the hours were not long enough, in Highgate the tradesmen were obliged to call at the homes of the more affluent for orders and then had their boys deliver them. Often, when bills were paid, the lady of the house in question might be of sufficient status to remain in her carriage while the shop owner came out to collect his money.

In Kentish Town the principal store was C & A Daniels in Kentish Town Road. This began with one drapery shop in 1865 at a time when excessive drapes and voluminous dresses were in vogue and umpteen seamstresses competed for work. Daniels expanded into shop after shop, and the time came between the wars for a complete rebuilding as a unified store. But this did not quite go to plan. They bought the site of the old Kentish Town Chapel (which they already occupied – Owl bookshop is in part of it today) in 1926, intending to rebuild this terrace together with the group of properties they already owned to the north. Unfortunately, they were unable to purchase an old property which lay between the two terraces and were obliged instead to build only part of their new store to the north – this still exists in form at 217-223, while having the rest of the store in the undeveloped terrace to the south. The shop that was in the way (which Daniels declined to buy much later because the price was more than they wanted to pay) is still there, called Bluston's.

The development of department stores often increased the workload of the staff because they lived above the shop and felt obliged to be on call. Staff numbers were very high. Jones Brothers in Holloway Road, for example, a store much used by Highgate and Camden Town residents, had between 500 and 600 staff, 50 horses and 35 carts or vans. Their catalogue of 1895 had 1400 pages and over 3000 illustrations. Living above the store meant that staff had little privacy or independence. In 1907 the shop assistants of Kentish Town went on strike for the abolition of the live-in system.

The oddest department store was Gamage's in Holborn where the browser could find all sorts of job lots on sale. Albert Walter Gamage began at one shop, no 128, in 1878 selling hosiery. He tried to sell everything cheaper than his rivals and aroused the same enmity as William Whiteley did in Queensway, but the business grew so that virtually the whole of the façade from Leather Lane to Hatton Garden was eventually taken by his store. He did particularly well with bicycles and motoring goods. It is said, and this may be apocryphal, that when Gamage died in 1930 he lay in state in the motoring department of the store, with staff forming a guard of honour.

The Kilburn area was served by the B.B. Evans store at 142-162 Kilburn High Road. Benjamin Beardmore Evans had begun, again as a draper, in 1897; so well did he do that in 1905 he turned eight adjoining properties into a large store which, in 1910, was destroyed by fire. Rebuilt, it remained prosperous until after the last war, but closed in 1971.

John Barnes was a late addition. It came in 1900 and was regarded as very *avant garde*. The *Hampstead and Highgate Express* reported breathlessly on its pneumatic money change system, which only three other shops in the West End had, and on its staff accommodation and stables at the rear in Canfield Place. In contrast to the businesses noted above which spread themselves into adjacent properties over the years, John Barnes was built as one store, superseding a terrace of properties. Modern though it might have been, it was replaced in 1936 by the stylish building we see today (now divided into Habitat and Waitrose) designed by T.P. Bennett, a Highgate resident responsible also for the admirable Saville Theatre in Shaftesbury Avenue (now a cinema) and the not-so-admirable dinky houses opposite his own house in North Road, Highgate. John Barnes himself did not live to see his first shop open – he was drowned at sea shortly before. In 1926 it was bought by Selfridge's and just before the last war was sold on to the John Lewis Partnership. It was, without doubt, a novelty in north London. Wendy Trewin, recalling the 1936 version of the store in her younger days, remembers that it had a Kosher counter and the grocery department had such exotic items as tins of lichees and passion fruit.[2]

These few large stores aside, most businesses were single shop enterprises until the end of the

104. *The Attkins' pork butcher's shop in Highgate High Street. It was rebuilt in 1892.*

105. *The stationer's shop of Frank Bishop in Kentish Town Road.*

19th century, as the detailed photographs made before the construction of the Northern Line show.[3] A good number of them lasted well into modern times: some Hampstead people, or at least those that are middle-aged, still yearn for Forster's the up-market grocers with an aura of ground coffee, Fowler's and Skinner's, both ironmongers, Stamp's the chemist, Gaze's the haberdashery and clothing store, and Knowles-Brown the jewellers who moved to the High Street in 1898; in Highgate, people can remember Mudd's the butchers, but would have to be quite old to remember Attkins the pork butcher in the High Street, founded at a time when butchers' shops had their own specialities and when the terms 'high class butcher', 'family butcher' and 'cash butcher' conveyed trade nuances. The Attkins business in Highgate Village dated back to about 1809; not only did it have a shop, but also its own pig sties at the end of Townsend's Yard.

Two Victorian businesses, typical of the old single shops, lasted until fairly recently. Bishop & Hamilton, bookshop and stationer, opposite Kentish Town station, was begun c.1894 by Frank Bishop. He sold out in 1914 to his young assistant, Hamilton, who remained in charge until he retired in 1979. William Flint began his ironmonger's shop in Fortess Road in 1855. His grandson, also William Flint, retired in 1984 aged 71, having worked in the old shop for 55 years. In an article in the *Camden History Review*[4] his description of trade over the years is a valuable commentary on his specialty which gradually changed from ironmongery to tools. He relied to a large extent on the employees of local old-established builders who needed new tools; but gradually those firms, such as Smerdon's and Potter's, died out or were relocated outside the area. Mr Flint liked people to know exactly what

they wanted and one can imagine that he bit his tongue on many occasions when his customers were do-it-yourself enthusiasts. Frank Romany's shop in Camden High Street, established after the 1st World War, went through a similar transition from being a regular shop for workmen to one geared to the general public. Ben Eley remembers being taken there in his youth so that his father could buy four small wooden wheels for a toy he was making. He recalls the way all the walls were covered, in an orderly fashion, by merchandise. One panel was entirely composed of wooden wheels in different sizes and when they returned to the counter to order four of number 17 wheels, the assistant found them within seconds.[5]

In his recollection of the distinct and recognisable smells of each type of shop, Mr Eley brings to life the atmosphere of early 20th century shopping. And Ena Baker[6] too remembered the smell of corner shops, a mixture of paraffin, pickles and bacon. She also recalled the amount of music in the streets – barrel organs, German bands (before the 1st World War) and other itinerant musicians. The roads were of cobblestones, the lighting was gas, there was the smell of horses and the noise of solid rimmed wheels on the cobbles. There were also aspects of life that would repel the present generation. There were itinerant sellers of fly papers who, to demonstrate their efficiency, wound them round their hats so that by the end of the day they would look grotesque; cats-meat sellers called each day and if you were out, pushed a skewer of horsemeat through the letter box; horses that grew old were not retired, but just died in their tracks in the streets. Ice cream came round in carts but Ms Baker's mother refused to buy it as it was made by Italians and she thought they kept it under their beds overnight. Shopping for perishable foods, in the absence of refrigeration, was done at the last moment: the Sunday joint was bought on Saturday night when the butchers were open until very late.

Playing cards, hats and loaves

An unusual industry in Camden Town was the production of playing cards. The firm of Goodall was established in Soho in 1820; in the early 1830s it moved to three houses in Royal College Street whose gardens ran down to the river Fleet. Here they built a small factory which by the middle of the century housed high-speed presses. By 1862 Goodall's and their rivals, de la Rue, produced two thirds of all playing cards sold in England, and 50 years on Goodall's sold over 2 million packs a year, more than all other British manufacturers put together. They built a new factory which at one time employed 1000 people, but in 1922 were merged with de la Rue. The Post Office now has a parcels office on the site.

At the top end of Royal College Street at the junction with Kentish Town Road stood Dunn's hat storeroom. In fact it stocked men's clothes of all sorts, but they were best known for their hats and caps in an age when every man wore something on his head. The building, opened in 1895 by George Arthur Dunn, was a central distribution depot from which items were despatched to over 100 branches. The business, prosperous until after the last war, hardly attempted to keep up with new fashions and its ageing customer base diminished. The depot at Kentish Town closed in 1984.

The ABC (Aerated Bread Company) built a large bakery in Camden Road c.1905. The company became one of the largest mass-produced bakeries in the country, and also spawned a chain of tea shops which hoped to rival those of the Lyons company, but they never did. Their Camden Road premises were demolished in 1986 to make way for the Sainsbury supermarket.

Cigarettes and cameras

In 1924 London Transport was anxious to close Mornington Crescent station on the Northern Line, a move opposed by St Pancras Council. But the station probably owes its retention to the erection of a bizarre building nearby employing a lot of people – the Carreras tobacco factory. A developer bought up the garden rights of the

106. The refurbished Carreras building in 1999.

houses in the Crescent and by November 1928 a modern cigarette factory in fashionable Egyptian style was on the garden (other buildings of the time included the Carlton Cinema in Essex Road, Islington, and the Hoover Building in Perivale). The Carreras name derived from a Spanish maker of cigarettes in Soho who, legend had it, owned a black cat which sunned itself in his window. The Carreras business was bought out by Bernhard Baron who had founded the Rothman cigarette company, and it was he who commissioned this vast building at Mornington Crescent, complete with Egyptian motifs and two black cats in memory of Senor Carreras – the cat gained even more fame from the Black Cat brand of cigarettes. This handsome and innovative building, designed by M.E. and O.H. Collins, was ruthlessly stripped of its quirky finery once Carreras had moved out in 1960, in the hope that 'Greater London House', as it was then called, would appeal as offices. It was left to its new Taiwanese owners to restore the building to its former glory in 1999.

At the top end of Bayham Street was Ernest Moy & Co. This engineering firm specialised in film cameras (they worked with William Friese-Greene the cinema pioneer), but they made much else besides. Harold Bastie, a descendant of one of the founders of the firm, was a mayor of St Pancras.

Old ratepayers

Almost certainly the oldest ratepayer in Camden is Leverton's, the funeral undertakers, nowadays one of the few 'independents' of any size. It was the company's independent status and track record, if one may use that term in relation to funeral undertakers, that led in recent times to the transfer of royal custom in such matters to Leverton's, away from Kenyon's, a firm which had been swallowed up by an American conglomerate. Because of this it was Leverton's who conducted the most remarkable funeral of modern times, that of Diana, Princess of Wales: memorable for the unflappable cortege driver, slowly proceeding along the motorway with flowers falling upon his windscreen – he came from Kentish Town.

John Leverton established the firm in 1789 at the age of 26. He made coffins and also undertook carpentry and building. His first workshop was in Henry Street (now demolished) off Hampstead Road and he appears to have had a house in Stanhope Street. Appropriately, his own tombstone – he was interred in the burial ground attached to St James's Chapel in Hampstead Road – is still (neatly relettered by his descendants) in the public gardens which have superseded the burial ground. The move of the firm to its most familiar home, Eversholt Street, came in December 1888. The site of that is now covered by the Crowndale Centre, but Leverton's are just a few doors away to the south. Stanley Leverton, who

died in 1963 aged 80, recalled that during his time the funerals of children of two years and under outnumbered those of adults by about three to one.

The firm of Lawford, building merchants, began in Camden in 1840. John Eeles Lawford set up shop in Euston Road as a slate merchant and after a few years took up a yard in Royal College Street conveniently by the Regent's Canal. It was John Eeles junior who expanded the firm into Willesden, Edgware, Finchley and Highgate. He was also a prominent St Pancras vestryman, elected and re-elected eight times, but he must have made some enemies on the way for when in 1877 the vestry proposed a tribute to him on his death – usually a formality – a vote was demanded and carried 28-2.

The Markets

Street markets were a marked feature of Camden shopping in the 19th century. They appeared in streets by custom, rather than by right but were usually condoned by the authorities. At one time, an unofficial but flourishing market occupied much of Camden High Street on Fridays and Saturdays – its remnants are in Plender

107. Chalton Street and market stalls in 1927.

J. SAINSBURY, Provision Merchant,

Office & Warehouses, ALLCROFT ROAD, KENTISH TOWN.

Branch Establishments:—159, 151 & 94, QUEEN'S CRESCENT, HAVERSTOCK HILL; 173, DRURY LANE, HOLBORN; and 68, WATNEY STREET, COMMERCIAL ROAD, E.

J. SAINSBURY has now removed his Wholesale Business from 173, Drury Lane, to more extensive premises situate in Allcroft Road, Kentish Town, and has made the necessary alterations to carry on a larger retail trade at the above address; he therefore begs his customers to understand that the same quality goods are sold as those so much admired by his wholesale customers, and as he is a large Importer of all kinds of provisions, is enabled to offer them at first cost.

108. John Sainsbury was an early occupier of a shop and market stall in Queen's Crescent, Kentish Town. As he grew more prosperous he opened offices, warehouses and bacon stoves in Allcroft Road, probably in the late 1870s.

Street and Inverness Street today. Other costermongers pitched stalls in Kentish Town Road and Chalk Farm Road. There were large numbers of market stalls in Somers Town. In 1856 St Pancras Vestry debated whether to remove the refuse from stalls in Brill Row, Skinner Street, Brewer Street and Chapel Street on Saturday nights or Sunday mornings, or leave it until Monday mornings. However, the Highways Committee didn't want any street trading there at all and pressed the police to clear the streets. This evidently had little effect, for 14 years later the Vestry was urged by local ratepayers *not* to evict stallholders as their absence would reduce trade in the area. In 1889, after fierce debate, Chalton Street market was extended rather than reduced. There were efforts in the 1880s to remove costermongers from the lower end of Hampstead Road, but once again the Vestry was told that their removal would be detrimental to the permanent shops there. In the end the police won the day and had them moved to Drummond Street instead.

No-one knew better the advantage of having a street market outside his shop than John Sainsbury. His first boyhood job was in a grocer's shop in New Cut, a busy market street near Waterloo station. He began in Drury Lane,

109. Leather Lane in 1876.

but for his second shop (and home) he moved to Queen's Crescent, Kentish Town in 1876, a decade or so after the street was built. Here he had a market stall as well. Two years on, Sainsbury opened another shop two doors away, and they also had bacon stoves and warehouses for cheese, eggs and butter in Allcroft Road. It was a hard environment. Alfred Grosch has left in the local archives a description of the area in about 1900. 'People', he said, 'were brutal and pugnacious' and that 'when money went on drink others suffered, usually children. Barefoot, hungry children, clad in rags were a common sight as they racked over the refuse heaps of Queen's Crescent in search of half rotten fruit.'

Today's Leather Lane market in Holborn, possibly originating in the 17th century, sells a wide variety of goods, but usually has specialised in food and produce. Once the local market of a working class district, it now caters as well for office workers.

Industrial Holborn

The building of Kingsway and Aldwych in the early years of the 20th century consolidated the commercial nature of Holborn. While the neighbouring borough of Finsbury was still, and always had been, a largely industrial area, full of craftsmen, clothing manufacturers, printers and distillers, Holborn remained dedicated to commerce rather than manufacture. Partly this was due to the impossibility of such enterprises on the Bedford Estate, or in the precincts of Lincoln's or Gray's Inns which made up a lot of the borough, but also because Holborn, so near to the City and so entwined with the legal profession, had been used for ancillary office space for a long time. The only industry of any size in Holborn was in the Hatton Garden gold and jewellery quarter, which developed from the last half of the 19th century, and tobacco manufacture – Richard Lloyd's Old Holborn factory (later a tobacco warehouse for Gallaher's) at the junction of Clerkenwell Road and Leather Lane, being the best known. There was, too, a large brewery (see below).

The diamond trade has its roots in the 16th and 17th centuries. At that time raw diamonds were most likely to come from India and be processed and resold in Antwerp. By the end of the 17th century English merchants had captured the trade of shipping diamonds out of India away from the Portuguese and Dutch, and when in the late 1860s diamonds were found in large quantities

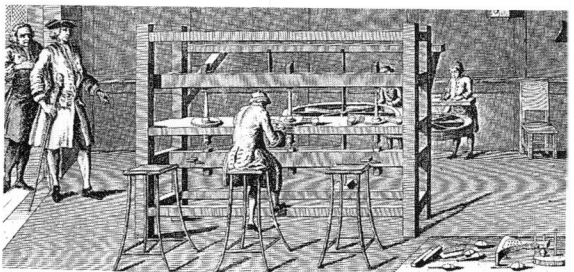

110. *Diamond cutting in 1730.*

in the British-owned South Africa, the infrastructure of dealing in them was already in place in London. In Holborn and Clerkenwell a work force of craftsmen, familiar with jewellery, goldbeating, clocks and watches, already existed and Hatton Garden became the centre for the new trade of cutting diamonds. Dutch workers were also encouraged to come to Hatton Garden and by 1885 there were 67 diamond cutters working there.[7]

Virtual control of diamond supply in South Africa was eventually won by De Beers, one part of which had been formed by Cecil Rhodes, whose ancestors had farmed much of St Pancras and Hornsey.

A large brewery was on the site of the Bourne Estate off Clerkenwell Road. This was established by the end of the 17th century when Morgan Hinde owned a building which according to Strype, was 'very large and gracefully built of brick'. It was bought by Richard Meux and Mungo Murray in 1757 who built there the Griffin Brewery, one of the largest in London. They were joined in 1795 by Andrew Reid, whose wealth enabled them to expand. The company built a vast vat, 60 feet in diameter, 23ft high and holding 10,000 barrels. Two hundred people dined in it before it was used. Reid eventually took charge and Meux moved to the Horseshoe Brewery on the site of the Dominion Theatre, Tottenham Court Road (where a vat burst in 1814 killed eight people and destroyed several houses). Later, Reid went into partnership with Watney, Combe. The brewery in Holborn closed in 1899.[8]

Offices in Kingsway

The number of offices in London had increased considerably by the time that Kingsway and Aldwych were built. The legions of male office workers in England increased fivefold between

1861 and 1911, but the number of women office workers increased 500 times. Although this was partly due to the relaxation of views about women working in commerce, there were still concerns about the moral dangers that might befall them in the work place. It was not until 1872 that the Post Office, one of the larger employers of female office labour, experimented with having women and male clerks in the same room. A senior official was very pleased with the scheme for, he said, 'It raises the tone of the male staff by confining them during many hours of the day to a decency of conversation and demeanour which is not always to be found where men alone are employed'. In this respect office life has not changed much. But concern for the welfare of such women continued and was the reason for the building of the numerous mock-Tudor flats on the Holly Lodge Estate in Highgate in the 1920s, by the Lady Workers' Homes Ltd, and the construction by the Prudential Assurance Company of Furnival House in Highgate, a residential block for female employees (note the naming after the ancient institution previously on the site of its Holborn headquarters), in 1916.

There was also interest in the welfare of young male clerks. The YMCA, founded in 1844, was especially involved and its early activities were in the City of London, not in the poorer suburbs. In 1880 the organisation purchased Exeter Hall in the Strand, before buying a site off Tottenham Court Road in 1912 and taking over the redundant Royal Amphitheatre in High Holborn during the 1st World War.

The development of the typewriter and its accompanying aid, shorthand, towards the end of the 19th century fuelled the increase in women office workers, especially as it was considered socially demeaning for men to do that kind of work. Street directories from before the 1st World War indicate just how the western side of Holborn, not only the newly built Kingsway/Aldwych area, but Bloomsbury as well, had become populated by offices. It was no accident that Pitman's Secretarial College was sited in Southampton Row.

While office workers in Bloomsbury found themselves in stylish old houses with discreet brass plates announcing publishers and professional organisations like the Architects' Association in Bedford Square, those in Kingsway were in buildings *designed* as offices. There were as well some large older office blocks in Holborn, notably those of Prudential Assurance and its

rival Pearl Assurance in High Holborn. The first part of the redbrick Prudential Building was built by Alfred Waterhouse in 1879 (rebuilt 1932) and extended twenty years later, probably the last great Gothic revival building in the country. The company was founded in a small way in Blackfriars in 1848 where the 29-year-old Henry Harben (1823-1911) began work as an accountant in 1852. It was he who led the company to a dominant position and made life assurance an everyday necessity. By 1905 he was chairman and a wealthy man. A resident of Hampstead, a member of its vestry and borough (the first mayor) and Hampstead representative on the old Metropolitan Board of Works, it was Harben who paid for the building of Hampstead Central Library in Arkwright Road in 1897. He also donated £50,000 to erect a convalescent home for working men in Littlehampton in the same year. There is still a Prudential presence in the building, but much of it has migrated to the glass corner of Hampstead Road and Euston Road.

Pearl Assurance began in one room of a house in Commercial Road in 1864, specialising in industrial insurance. By 1875 it had become well known in life assurance and at one time leased Adelaide House on London Bridge where the words 'Pearl Offices' took the place of numerals on the large clock face overlooking the river. But far more space was soon needed and Pearl commissioned its own building in High Holborn, designed in baroque style by Percy Moncton in 1912-14. It cost £158,365. Until the mid 1930s it was possible to see from the upper floors both Crystal Palace to the south and Alexandra Palace to the north. The building was extended by degrees, lastly to take in the site of the Holborn Empire in 1960-62, but such is the speed of change in offices that the building was inadequate in the 1980s and difficult to adapt to computerisation. The company moved out to Peterborough in 1990 and the building, while retaining its old façade and dome, is being converted into a hotel inside.

Kingsway was officially opened in 1905. Together with Southampton Row, it provided a much needed north-south route from Euston to Waterloo Bridge, and at the same time involved the demolition of many slums in the area south of High Holborn. Most of the new buildings were offices, some with shops beneath, or else hotels.

Hotels indeed were becoming an important part of the Holborn economy. Two splendid new ones were built in Russell Square – the Russell

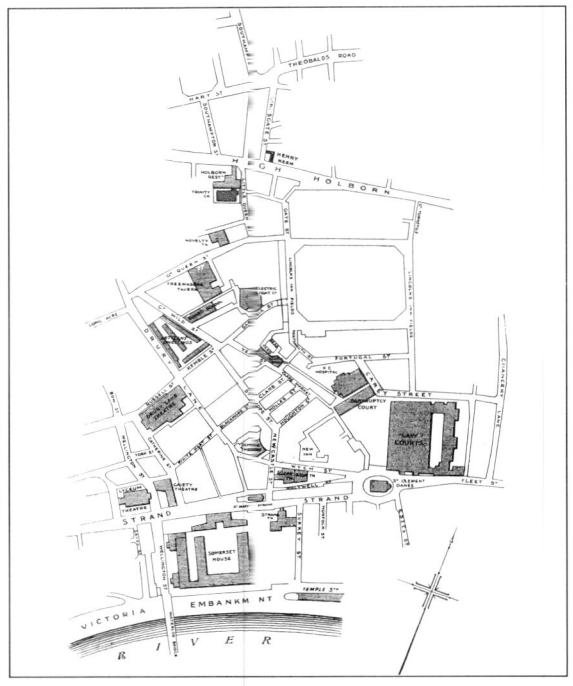

111. The Holborn area before the construction of Kingsway.

112. The Gower Hotel near Euston Square.

(1898), and the Imperial (1905-11). They were both the work of Charles Fitzroy Doll, an architect who was also twice mayor of Holborn and one of the commissioners charged with the responsibility of providing libraries in the old district of St Giles. The Russell, a flamboyant, rather French affair is still with us, awash with marble surfaces on the ground floor, but the Imperial, equally ornate but rather more Empire, was superseded (from 1966) by what must be, along with the Holiday Inn on King's Cross Road, the ugliest hotel building in Holborn. A pity.

Travel and tourism were becoming organised – Thomas Cook opened his first office at 59 Great Russell Street in 1862. But even earlier than that, in 1844, *The Builder* magazine said of Bloomsbury that '…houses are now being rapidly deserted – are converted or converting into shops, lodging houses and chambers, and in a few years, when age begins to stamp its mark upon them, the last traces of aristocratic, commercial or professional opulence will vanish from among them.'

The steward of the Bedford Estate in the 1870s noted that Gower Street had 'lodging-house dry rot', but could not prevent it. To these were added the Thackeray, Bonnington, Royal and

West Central, a new breed of hotels which made in 1935 the closure of the the Midland Grand at St Pancras inevitable. Sumptuous though the Midland might have been, the public preferred central heating to coal fires, and they wanted bathrooms en suite.

[1] *From Primrose Hill to Euston Road*, published by the Camden History Society, p.52 (1995).
[2] Wendy Trewin, 'Shopping in Camden' in *Camden History Review* 11 (1984).
[3] Those photographs which apply to Camden may be seen in the Local Studies and Archives Centre at Holborn Library.
[4] Althea Ridge, 'W. Flint: Ironmongers of Kentish Town' in *Camden History Review* 12 (1984).
[5] Ben Eley, 'Shopping in Camden' in *Camden History Review* 11 (1984).
[6] Ena Baker, *ibid*.
[7] Caroline M. Barron, *The Parish of St Andrew, Holborn*, p.132 (1979).
[8] *Streets of Old Holborn*, published by the Camden History Society, p.56 (1999).

CHAPTER FIFTEEN

Towards a Fresh Start

The Metropolitan Board of Works (est. 1855) and the London School Board (1870) were often considered profligate, spending, it seemed to the vestries, revenue from local ratepayers without restraint. Some vestries, including St Pancras, were unsympathetic to any metropolitan organisation whether it was in charge of policing, sewers, poor relief or fire fighting. This wariness of centralisation, widespread in London, was crystallised in a book called *Local Self-Government and Centralization* (1851) written by a Highgate resident and constitutional lawyer, Joshua Toulmin Smith.

Vestries were notoriously slow to respond to public need or pressure, and were often parsimonious when they did so – those of St Pancras and Hampstead have an uneven record in this regard. But there is no denying that for all the instances of cheeseparing, many of the facilities and functions of modern local government were

in place before our local vestries became the boroughs of Hampstead, Holborn and St Pancras in 1900. The vestry (later town) halls were already built: St Pancras had a simple affair in Pancras Road by 1840 which was enlarged beyond recognition in 1874; Holborn built grand Italianate offices at the junction of Gray's Inn Road and Theobalds Road in 1878, complete with a hall to take 900 people; and in the same year Hampstead completed *their* Italianate building in Haverstock Hill, famously described as 'crushingly mean' by Pevsner. Numerous facilities, including the provision of public baths and washhouses, to improve public health existed. Medical officers of health were appointed, together with inspectors of nuisances to enquire into sanitary problems. Slaughterhouses, cowhouses and the like were visited and licensed. The rebuilding, or rather the invention, of the London sewerage system by Joseph Bazalgette in the 1860s, had an effect on umpteen square miles of London. The destitute were catered for, if unhappily, in workhouses and when ill, in infirmaries. There were soup kitchens for harsh times and lodging-houses that were improvements on the old privately run slums. Though London vestries did not have the power until 1890 (and then only in a limited form) to build

113. The St Pancras Vestry Hall in Pancras Road before its transformation after 1874.

114. Hampstead Town Hall c.1905.

their own dwellings for the poorer classes, there were numerous 'Five per cent charities' in the field, which had erected the first blocks of flats in the capital. Board schools for the compulsory education of poorer children were being built at a speedy rate – for example, in St Pancras seven Board schools were opened in 1874 alone; Fleet Road school, the first Board school in Hampstead, was opened in 1879.

Adult education was still a matter of private initiative, but by the end of the century four notable adult centres had been established in Camden. A 'Technical Institution' was opened in Prince of Wales Road in 1892 for the 'promotion of industrial skill, general knowledge, health and well being of young men and women belonging to the poorer classes'. This was rebuilt in 1929 and reopened as the North Western Polytechnic. In 1890, the novelist Mary Ward (1851-1920) was a founding member of a settlement at University Hall, Gordon Square for religious teaching and social work. They persuaded newspaper owner and philanthropist, John Passmore Edwards, to finance a new building in Tavistock Place in which working class people could obtain adult education. The Mary Ward Centre, as it was called following her death, is a handsome Arts and Crafts building, designed by A. Dunbar Smith and Cecil Brewer. Mrs Ward (better known then and since as Mrs Humphry Ward) opened there the country's first play centre and the first school for disabled children, and from the 1920s the Tavistock Little Theatre used the premises.

The best known of the new educational ventures for adults was the Working Men's College, founded 1854 by Frederick Denison Maurice at 31 Red Lion Square, moving to Lord Thurlow's old house at 45 Great Ormond Street three years later. Here it stayed, a few doors from the Society for the Protection of Ancient Buildings at 55-57, until 1905, when it moved to the corner of Camden Street and Crowndale Road, very near to where Maurice had helped Frances Buss found her North London Collegiate School for Girls. The College's new home had thirty classrooms, laboratories, a gymnasium and a music room, and attracted teachers of the calibre of Ford Madox Brown, Dante Rossetti, Ruskin and Lowes Dickinson.

And in 1882, Westfield College, for the further education of women was founded in Maresfield Gardens, Hampstead, before acquiring the mansion called Kidderpore Hall in Kidderpore

115. The second Working Men's College, in Great Ormond Street.

Avenue, the former home of a nabob, John Tell, made wealthy by trade in Kidderpore and Calcutta. The formidable Constance Garnett was principal of the College from its formation until 1913.

Road improvements, begun in the 1840s with the construction of Endell Street and New Oxford Street, continued apace: Holborn Viaduct (1869), Clerkenwell Road (1878), Shaftesbury Avenue (1886), and Charing Cross Road (1887) removed substantial numbers of slums in Holborn and the building of Kingsway at the turn of the century took away many more. Theobalds Road was widened and aligned to the new Clerkenwell Road, also in 1878. The construction of Charterhouse Street to connect to Smithfield Market had repercussions in the rookery of Saffron Hill. Dickens, never short of a memorable description, noted that in this rookery were 'numerous public houses and in them the lowest orders of Irish were wrangling with might and main. Covered ways and yards which here and there diverged from the main street disclosed little knots of houses where drunken men and women were positively wallowing in filth.' Another welcomed road improvement in Holborn was the demolition of Middle Row, a block of shops and dwellings 200

116. *Middle Row in High Holborn, just west of the Holborn Bars. The church of St Giles is in the background.*

ft long and between 25-50ft wide, which occupied a large part of the roadway of High Holborn just west of the Holborn Bars – a notorious cause of traffic congestion.

But though slums were demolished, slum dwellers remained and the density of population did not decrease for some time. In Holborn and the City the number of persons per dwelling increased from 9.5 in 1851 to 9.7 in 1881. There was considerable overcrowding, and legislation to oust it was often impossible to implement. As the medical officer of health for Hackney pointed out, if he were to enforce the provisions of the 1866 Sanitary Act, 10,000 people would have to live on the streets.

But in the meantime, open spaces for the public were won and were being extended (*see pp.109-116*);. Cheaper and more frequent transport not only made getting to work easier, but encouraged a migration from the centre of town particularly to the Lea valley. Hospital care was more freely available to the impoverished, and charities with long and specific names so beloved of Victorians cared for orphans, cripples, distressed servants, governesses, dogs and

horses. As early as 1833 St Pancras Vestry had agreed to support a scheme to encourage young women to emigrate to 'New South Wales and Van Dieman's Land'. But three years later ratepayers in Fitzrovia were up in arms against a proposal of the Poor Law Commissioners to press for the emigration of children. The suggestion, they said, 'is most repugnant to humanity and calculated to destroy those affections between parent and child which are happily engendered by nature, and emigration would be a cruel punishment on poverty'. The Directors of the Poor in St Pancras did not agree, however, and held out the carrot that the cost of sending a child to the colonies was only equal to one year's stay in the workhouse.

One indication of the increasing confidence of St Pancras and Hampstead vestries as governing bodies was their determination to be direct suppliers of electricity. This stemmed in part from the unhappy history of gas supply by private companies in the metropolis, and when it became possible to manufacture electricity with not too large an outlay, particularly for street lighting, it seemed sensible to many vestries to

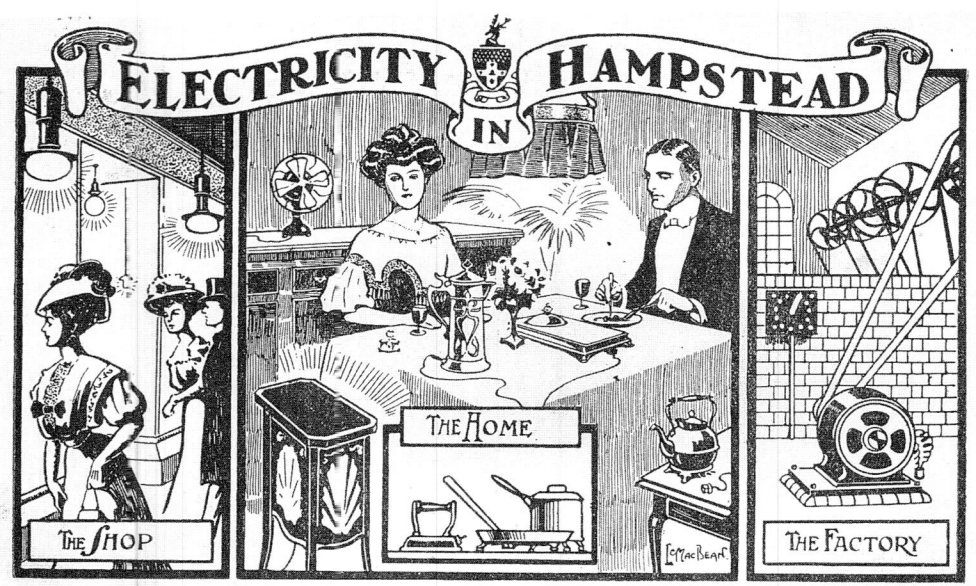

117. *A postcard issued by Hampstead Council to advertise the wonders of electricity (supplied by the Council)*

do it themselves. Criticism of gas companies had crystallised in London in the late 1850s when it was proposed that parts of London should be allocated to particular gas companies both to avoid competition and duplication of pipework. This was a sensible proposal but the vestries claimed that it would create monopolies and increase prices. Even so, when the Metropolitan Board of Works proposed to manufacture gas, St Pancras was strongly opposed as were many other vestries. Despite continued criticism, gas supply remained in the hands of private companies until nationalisation after the 2nd World War.

St Pancras decided to supply public electric lighting in 1874, some time before it was practicable to do so with the use of incandescent lamps. The Vestry was very keen to prevent the gas companies from being involved in street lighting by electricity, and was instrumental in the passing of the Electric Lighting Act of 1882. It was the first vestry in London to obtain powers to manufacture electricity and it sent representatives to a gathering of principal municipal corporations advocating haste in the matter so that the public would be 'saved from having another authority, like the Gas and Water companies, interfering with the public streets [and] the creation of a new monopoly would be prevented'.

There was some delay in taking advantage of

the new powers St Pancras had obtained. The foundation stone of the vestry's first generating station, at 47 Stanhope Street off Hampstead Road, was not laid until November 1890. This supplied the street lights of Tottenham Court Road and Euston Road in 1892. The second London vestry in the field was Hampstead. In 1893 tenders were accepted for an electricity depot and in 1894 Finchley Road became the first highway in Hampstead to be lit by electricity. The choice of Finchley Road was no accident, because the Vestry located its first generator at the Vestry's former stone yard in nearby Lithos Road. Both undertakings after the 2nd World War were transferred to the London Electricity Board.

The adoption of the Public Library Act of 1850 was much more tardy. No developments in the constituent parts of Camden took place in this field until the 1890s and in St Pancras not until the new century.

The vestries of St Andrew and St Giles adopted the Act in 1891 and appointed Commissioners to set up library services – in St Giles, one of their number was Charles Fitzroy Doll, architect of the Russell and Imperial hotels. The two vestries went very much in tandem. St Andrew's, catering for a population of nearly 33,000 opened its first library in January 1893 at 10 John Street, off Theobalds Road. St Giles, with a much larger population, opened a temporary library at 110

Southampton Row in April the same year, replacing it with a purpose-built library in High Holborn in March 1896 – this building, next to the former Holborn Town Hall of 1908, still survives, though empty for some years.

The Commissioners for St Andrew's made a useful list of the occupations of borrowers at John Street. The two largest categories were 'clerks' and 'females of no occupation'. In the year 1897-98, just before the creation of the Borough of Holborn, they lent out 52,987 books whereas in High Holborn the figure was nearly 234,000.

In Hampstead the first branch library was opened in 1895 at 48 Priory Road, a private house converted for the purpose. This was replaced by a purpose-built library in Cotleigh Road in 1901. In 1897 another two libraries were provided. One was in Antrim Grove, which was built on the cheap and had to be demolished in the 1930s, and the other, the Central Library at the corner of Arkwright Road and Finchley Road, designed by A.S. Tayler. This was mostly paid for by Sir Henry Harben. The reference library collection there was based upon the purchase by the Vestry of the 8000-volume library of the scholar, Professor Henry Morley. West Hampstead branch library opened in 1901 in Westbere Road. Bombed in 1940, it was replaced in 1954 by a new library in Dennington Park Road. Heath branch library opened in Worsley Road in 1907, but transferred to a new building in the grounds of Keats House in 1931. No library was provided for Hampstead Town itself, probably because of the availability there of the Hampstead Subscription Library.

Successive votes of ratepayers organised by St Pancras Vestry (or at least those ratepayers entitled to vote on such matters) were opposed to providing libraries, and as a consequence the first St Pancras Borough Council inherited none at all. However, armed with new powers as a borough authority, the ruling St Pancras Progressive Party, elected in 1903, initiated a programme of building libraries, hotly opposed by the Moderate (later called Municipal Reform) members of the council. The Progressives were a fusion of Liberals, Socialists and Fabians, and the Moderates a mix of ratepayers and Conservatives. One of the Moderate councillors, Mr Westacott, a Camden Town estate agent, voiced the opinion that 'Books of reference can be seen free at the British Museum by all who care to take the trouble' and implied that those who

read works of fiction should not be encouraged to do so.

St Pancras Vestry had not been alone in its reluctance to open libraries. Many other authorities dragged their feet and they were encouraged out of this by the generosity of Andrew Carnegie, a Scotsman who had become an American millionaire. He offered vestries sums of money to provide libraries, but with some strings attached. In the case of St Pancras he offered funds if the borough council (as it then was) supplied a free site, but the only one which could be found was at Chester Road, Highgate New Town, in an inaccessible part of the borough. This branch opened in October 1906.

A row over the provision of a central library was to go on for many years. Once again, Carnegie offered a donation and the Borough chose a site in Prince of Wales Road opposite what became the North Western Polytechnic. It was owned by Horace Regnart (*see p.126*) a Progressive member of the Council, and it cost £15,000, a sum which the Moderates were unable to stomach, especially as it was owned by another member of the Council. One of the first decisions of the council elected in 1907, when the Moderates regained power, was to stop work on the central library though the site had already been cleared. Despite protest meetings and further discussions with Carnegie representatives, the project did not proceed. The council block, Una House, was later built on the site and no more libraries were opened in St Pancras until after the 1st World War.

The Press
With the awakening of corporate identities in the various parts of Camden came also a burgeoning of local newspapers, free at last from the expense of stamp duties. One of the first to take advantage of this new financial freedom was the *Hampstead & Highgate Express*, which was first published in 1860. Its earliest editions are not extant and the circumstances of its foundation – where and by whom – are still unknown. When the first known proprietor, George Samuel Jealous, died in 1896 his paper noted that he had bought the *Express* in 1862. Jealous was a printer, a Liberal and a philanthropist, who edited the paper from that year until his death. For much of that time the *Express* was a scant affair of four pages and was increased to eight pages only under John Hayns, editor from 1896 to the late 1920s. In common with other papers of the

118. The St Pancras Gazette at 80 Camden High Street in 1904.

period, the front page was given over to advertisements, and much of the rest to almost verbatim reports of meetings of the vestry, societies and other established groups. It did not rock the municipal boat. And neither did the *St Pancras Gazette* (previously known as the *Camden & Kentish Towns Gazette*) owned by Mr Widdicombe, a member of St Pancras Council and of the Municipal Reform party. This paper carried reports only of Conservative meetings and therefore any other political life in St Pancras until the paper was sold in 1936, may only now be garnered from council minutes and other sources. The *Gazette* became the *North London Press*, during the last war. When Camden borough was formed the paper changed its name to the *Camden Journal*, but in 1980 its proprietors, Courier Press, decided to shut down the paper and transfer journalists to other papers in the group. This provoked a 2-year strike by journalists in the group and was not resolved until the title was sold to Eric Gordon, the present editor of the *Camden New Journal*, and a colleague for a £1 nominal fee. After a feasibility study paid for by the GLC and Camden Council, the *Camden New Journal*, then a co-operative venture,

emerged as a free sheet in March 1982. Mr Widdicombe would not like it.

The *South Hampstead Advertiser* began in December 1880. It went through various name arrangements involving Hampstead, St John's Wood and Kilburn, before settling down as the *Hampstead News* when it was owned by the Hampstead printing firm, Baines & Scarsbrook, who published from Fairfax Road. (The Baines family included F.E. Baines, Hampstead vestryman and compiler of *The Records of Hampstead*.) The *Hampstead News* sold at the almost free-sheet price of a halfpenny. As F.E. Baines noted in his book, 'It has met a want of the district, as a considerable proportion of the houses change their tenants every three or four years, who consequently take so little interest in local matters that they will not *purchase* the local paper.' The *News* (which ceased publication in 1971) and Baines and Scarsbrook were sold in the 1950s to London Counties Press which ran both businesses from a converted villa and a factory in Tottenham Lane, Crouch End, where also was published the *Hornsey Journal* (which, by an odd twist of circumstance, had been founded by George Jealous) and the *North London Press*. Towards the end of its life the *Hampstead News* was similar to, apart from a page or two, the *North London Press*.

The full list of Camden's local newspapers shows that many of them constantly changed their names to keep up with building development and new customers. A different and more recent kind of adjustment was that of the *St Pancras Chronicle* (founded 1900) which changed its name to the *Camden and St Pancras Chronicle* in 1963. This enabled the new title to publish for a larger area if it wished, but it made sense anyway because 'St Pancras' as an identifying location had diminished over many years and would shrink even further with the forthcoming abolition of the old borough name. Since then it has dropped 'St Pancras' altogether.

The *Kilburn Times* was first published in 1868 by Rowland Bassett, consisting of four pages, and though it covers part of Camden, it has always been published outside of the borough. The *Holborn Guardian* began as the *North Londoner* in 1869; this journal became two papers – the *Holborn Guardian* and *St Pancras Guardian* in 1875; the latter ceased in 1925, but the Holborn paper, based on quite a small population, struggled on until 1989.

A plentitude of churches

Though the Church of England was losing its grip on education, it was certainly responding with vigour to the inroads made by the evangelising non-conformist sects. So many new Anglican churches were built locally in the second half of the 19th century that it would be tedious to read a list of them, but some were notable for their nature and architecture. A good number, such as St Peter's Belsize Park and St Paul's Camden Square, were adornments to estate development, but others were straightforward missionary attempts to entice the masses away from atheism, disaffection and evangelicals. One such was Holy Trinity in Hartland Road, Kentish Town, which still survives. This was the domain of the energetic Rev. David Laing, appointed vicar of this new parish in 1849 before the church was even built. Laing was of a new breed of Anglican minister, determined to know his very large potential congregation personally. Beginning with an audience of 23 in a temporary structure, once the church itself had been finished in 1850 he often preached to a thousand. He organised schools both daily and on Sundays; he visited the sick and ran meetings and clubs in the evening. Taking very little money from pew rents, he was in bad financial straits himself by 1857 and moved on to the easier and more financially rewarding life of St Olave, Hart Street in the City. But his church remained an active flagship in alien territory, vying for custom with congregationalists, baptists and methodists.

Holy Trinity, designed by Wyatt and Brandon, was a conventional neo-gothic structure, but that of St Martin's, in Allcroft Road, Gospel Oak, was decidedly odd, and is today a must for students of Victorian architecture. Designed by E.B. Lamb in 1869, it served a growing area, one which the vicar described as being 'very similar to an East End parish...The applications to myself for many purposes are almost ceaseless'. The vicar's implied weariness of such a local congregation may have been the reason for the later success of a mission within his own district led by a young civil servant, Charles Mackeson, whose remarkable energy led to the building of another local church and the creation of a new parish. In a temporary building at first, the missionary version of what was eventually to be All Hallows, Savernake Road, held 14 services a week; there was in addition a Sunday School which called on 90 teachers, three Bible classes, a District Visiting Society, a Temperance Union

119. *St Martin's Church, Allcroft Road, c.1905.*

and a Social Gathering for Working Girls and Women as well as one for men on Saturdays. Despite a regular congregation of between 1500 and 2000, money was very short indeed and the present church was built over a long period, culminating in consecration in 1901.

Another church built specifically for a working class congregation, at least in its original form, was St Luke's, Oseney Crescent in Kentish Town. It had its beginnings in the determination of the notable St Pancras vicar, the Rev. Thomas Dale, to create many more churches in the area. A new parish of St Luke's, King Cross was created in 1849 for a congregation which met in St Pancras Vestry Hall on Pancras Road. Soon, a temporary iron church was erected on the site of the smallpox hospital at King's Cross then owned by the Great Northern Railway, subject to it being moved when needed for railway purposes. When King's Cross station was opened in 1852, St Luke's had moved across the road to a site supplied by the Skinners' Company. Foundations were laid but lack of money prevented much more until a renewed effort resulted in consecration in 1861. But the railway struck again, this time the Midland and its need of the site on which to build St Pancras Station. So, once again, but this time with adequate compensation, the church moved, to Oseney Crescent on a site presented by Christ Church, Oxford whose estate surrounded it. The new church was designed by Basil Champneys, son of the vicar of St Pancras who commissioned it. Nepotism it may have been (and John Johnson, the architect of the previous St Luke's complained that it was), but the locals got a handsome building out of it.

The need to compete for the hearts and minds of the poorer classes was not an issue in the centre of Hampstead – there were far fewer poor and not many nonconformists. On a Sunday in 1851 when a census of churchgoers was made, about half the population of Hampstead was at church that day, of which well over three-quarters were Anglicans. Instead, the problem for the parish church of St John's in Church Row was to keep its affluent custom. In this it was rivalled – irritated is probably a better word – by the well-to-do congregation at the Well Walk Chapel, a building that was a remnant of Hampstead Wells days. That congregation was pressing for its own church and, what is more, its own parish. The Lord of the Manor, Sir Thomas Maryon Wilson, patron of St John's and already at odds with the residents of New End over his plans for development of heath lands, strongly opposed their proposal for a new church. He was to be faced by John Gurney Hoare, who lived at The Hill in North End Way, and who happened coincidentally to be one of Wilson's leading opponents in the Heath debate. It was the extended Hoare family which, in fact, put up most of the money to build Christ Church in what is now Christchurch Hill. Designed by Samuel Daukes in Early English Gothic on the site of some old tea gardens, it was completed in 1852.

Just as the spire of Christ Church is a landmark from Hampstead Heath, so St Stephen's on Haverstock Hill marks the southern end of Hampstead proper. Built 1869-73 to the design of S.S. Teulon, this is a prominent church in all senses. It is bulky but with delicate touches, is a rich example of the use of brick and has a wonderful interior. Unfortunately it gradually deteriorated and developed serious cracks in 1969 when excavations for the new Royal Free Hospital were made.

The first post-Reformation Catholic church in Camden was that of St Mary in Holly Place, Hampstead. The original building, erected in 1816 for a congregation which had grown around the mission of Abbé Morel (1766-1852) in the

1790s, was, before the Catholic Emancipation Act of 1829, an unostentatious building. By 1850, when a Catholic revival was in progress, the building was stuccoed and the statue over the entrance added, and in 1878 the whole building was enlarged into the Byzantine affair it is today.

While expansion of this Catholic church took place in Hampstead, the 13th-century chapel of the old Bishop of Ely's palace in Holborn (see p.17), was bought at auction (the vendors were the Welsh Episcopalians). Though Catholic worship began in the church again in 1874, the building needed a great deal of restoration – fortunately the west window of 1300 survives – and it was not until St Etheldreda's Day, 23 June 1879, that the official reopening of St Etheldreda's took place.

The number of Italians in Holborn increased from 629 in 1861 to 2029 in 1901. Most of them were in the Hatton Garden/Back Hill area, and there was another settlement in nearby Clerkenwell. The Italian skills were prominent in clock and barometer making, in the production of figurines and plaster work, but they were also to be paramount in the sale of ice cream in which Italian street vendors became as familiar to Londoners as the itinerant Italian musicians and barrel organ entertainers. In the 1840s the Italian patriot, Guiseppe Mazzini, had founded a free school for Italian children in Hatton Garden. What the community didn't have was an adequate church. This was remedied in 1863 with the opening of St Peter's Italian Church in Clerkenwell Road, designed by J.M. Bryson. Inside, it is a replica of San Cristogno in Trastevere in Rome. The Italian community today, though much diminished and dispersed, still celebrates here on the Sunday nearest to 16 July, the Procession of Our Lady of Carmel: this travels along a traffic-free Clerkenwell Road with decorated floats in an event which was begun in 1883.

An extraordinary building in Gordon Square is what was once the Catholic Apostolic Church founded by the Rev. Edward Irving (1792-1834). Irving was a wildly romantic figure to his many female admirers at the Scottish Presbyterian Church in Regent Square. Oliver Wendell Holmes described him as 'a black, savage, saturnine long-hair'd Scotchman with a most Tyburn-looking squint to him'. The ladies went in for 'babbling paltry inanities', which was not very Presbyterian, and he was expelled from Regent Square. This led to his formation of the Catholic Apostolic Church, whose most notable building, of cathedral spaciousness, designed by Raphael Brandon (1851-4), is now the University Church of Christ the King. Despite its size, it is, however, an unfinished building, being two bays short and without a spire which would have been nearly as high as St Paul's.

The most influential (and largest) congregational church in London was the Lyndhurst Chapel at the junction of Haverstock Hill and Lyndhurst Road. This building, now a recording studio, is a magnificent collation by Alfred Waterhouse, erected 1883-84, with a hexagonal church inside. It was the domain in its formative years of the Rev. Horton who appealed to the largely prosperous merchant class of the opulent houses then being built in Hampstead. But he was a man who reminded them of their responsibilities. In 1887 he told them that 1 in 5 people died in a poor house, lunatic asylum or hospital and that 939 out of 1000 left no appreciable property. The latter statistic probably made more of an impression on his congregation than the former. This congregation was also responsible for the foundation of a mission which built Lyndhurst Hall in Warden Road, amongst the slums of West Kentish Town, which today still houses community services.

The Bloomsbury Central Baptist Church in Shaftesbury Avenue is the leading church of the Baptist movement in London. It was designed 1845-48 by John Gibson and paid for by Sir Samuel Peto MP, a man made rich from railways, who also converted the old Diorama in St Andrew's Place, Regent's Park, into a Baptist chapel. When Peto sought to build the church in Shaftesbury Avenue, the Crown Commissioners who owned the land were dubious because they assumed that, as it was a Baptist building, it would have no spire and be architecturally dull. In fact Peto provided them with two spires, both demolished in 1951 after war damage.

Pubs and performers

The spurt of church building in the last fifty years of the 19th century was accompanied by a vociferous temperance movement. But the same years saw also the rebirth of the English public house in a massive rebuilding of early inns as large breweries acquired control of numerous public houses. Many of Camden's best pub buildings are of that period, retaining, if they are lucky, original engraved and bevelled mirrors, wood panelling, splendid fittings, ornamental ceilings and decorative fascias. They

may not now retain their old names, but that is another matter.

In that half century pubs developed a recognisable format and character, much of which has disappeared with the rampant branding and commercialisation of the past twenty years. They cast off the wretched gin palace reputation and if they did not quite become respectable in the eyes of those who would look after our morals, then they became more socially acceptable to many more people who just wanted a drink, rather than to get drunk. They were not the usual haunt of the middle classes, who preferred to *dine* and drink, but they were increasingly used by tradesmen and clerks. They became regular meeting places for clubs and societies, particularly masonic-type societies with such odd names as the Association of Foresters. This improvement in the image of public houses was partly a result of the class divisions constructed within the buildings. There were saloon bars for the more affluent, 'public' bars for manual workers, and 'private' bars for women and people who did not care for much company. Children, incidentally, were admitted to all bars, and the sale of beer to those under thirteen was not precluded until 1886. In the public bars the favourite drinks were mild ale and stout, in the saloon bar, bitter, with whisky, rather than gin, the most popular spirit.

Temperance won some victories. No pubs, except the North Star on Finchley Road (opened in 1850 before development began), were built on the Maryon-Wilson estate west of Hampstead Village; few pubs exist on the estates of Eton College and the Church Commissioners. But the temperance enthusiasts were too late or ineffective to prevent a generous provision of public houses in the rest of Camden and had to rely instead on the culling of common beershops by local magistrates. These down-market establishments had mushroomed when in 1830 duty on beer was abolished in an attempt to wean the masses off gin. A licence to sell beer was easily obtained, and almost any property could be turned into a beerhouse. It was not until 1869 that beershops came under the control of magistrates who gradually put them out of business, but the consequence was that the beershop custom transferred itself to the licensed public houses whose owners, it seems, were free to enlarge their premises without hindrance.

In the latter part of the century, as breweries vied for sales, the ownership of public houses

120. The Bull and Gate in Kentish Town, rebuilt in 1871, shown here in 1904.

became paramount. Large sums were invested in the purchase and conversion of existing houses. One such example is the Assembly House near Kentish Town underground station, grandly rebuilt in 1896 with a large billiard room, designed by the Camden High Street practice of Thorpe and Furniss. It contains decorative glasswork by William James of Kentish Town. By the same architects is the Boston, just over the borough border at Tufnell Park, a much abused landmark. Treadwell and Martin designed the well-known Rising Sun in Tottenham Court Road, also in 1896. Three years later another Rising Sun in Euston Road was rebuilt by the appropriately named Shoebridge and Rising practice. Other outstanding examples of this period are the Lamb in Lamb's Conduit Street (again with much wonderful glass and a 'snob-

screen'), the Load of Hay on Haverstock Hill of 1863 (which has had a long-standing association with boxing), the Bull and Gate, Kentish Town (1871), the Mother Red Cap (now the World's End) at Camden Town, the Chalk Farm Tavern in Regent's Park Road (now the Lemonia restaurant), the Red Lion (1890) and the Black Lion (1898) both in Kilburn High Road. In all this rebuilding, the Old Bell in Holborn, the last galleried inn north of the Thames, was demolished in 1897.

Public houses in the 18th century relied heavily on outdoor facilities, such as tea gardens and sports to bring in additional custom. A good number of 19th-century pubs instead provided music or music hall, while the Edinburgh Castle in Mornington Terrace fielded a museum of curiosities, such as relics of Lord Nelson, a great

121. *The Euston Palace of Varieties, in its latter days known as the Regent Theatre, was at the junction of Euston Road and Tonbridge Street, a site now occupied by the extension to Camden Town Hall. Designed by Bertie Crewe, it opened on Boxing Day 1900, but was used as a cinema as from 1932. It closed in 1950.*

auk's egg and a Babylonian brick. When the collection was sold in 1908 it contained a bugle which (allegedly) sounded the charge at the Battle of Balaklava, and a display of 80,000 butterflies.

The Bedford Music Hall stemmed out of the Bedford Tavern, a drinking place and tea gardens noted for occasional balloon ascents, between Camden High Street and Arlington Road. The music hall opened in 1861, described in *The Era* magazine as a 'small and inconvenient building, entered only from a court'. But some improvements were made as the *Camden & Kentish Town Gazette* in 1870 pointed out: 'When some eight years ago it first sprang into existence it was nothing better than a long, ugly room badly lighted and badly ventilated, penny-gaffy in its

appearance and most decidedly penny-gaffy as regards the nature of its entertainments. It did not however, long continue in this condition, for soon it took upon itself a gallery, which originally stretched solely across its lower end, but which ultimately came to be extended along its two sides. By this time it lost much of its Whitechapel character...' It was the interior of this building that Sickert painted so often. The lack of frontage on the High Street was remedied in 1899 when a new Bedford Palace of Varieties was opened to the design of Bertie Crewe.[1]

Finch Hill and Paraire, architects of numerous pubs, were responsible for the Holborn Empire at 242-5 High Holborn, which developed out of the Seven Tankards pub in 1857 under the

122. The Royal Amphitheatre in Holborn, in 1867.

ownership of Edward Weston. Weston's Music Hall, as it was usually called in the earlier part of its life, had galleries but no auditorium until 1887. The *Building News* in 1857 described it as being 103 feet long, with the back wall mirrored so as to enhance the feeling of space within the building. It was the same Edward Weston who began the pleasure gardens called Weston's Retreat off Highgate Road in 1863 (*see p.83*), a venture that was closed within two years.

The Empire was rebuilt entirely in 1906 to the design of the prolific theatre architect, Frank Matcham. This building survived until the last war, when it was seriously damaged; it was later demolished and its site taken by Pearl Assurance next door.

Two rivals in Holborn were the Duke's Theatre at 42 High Holborn (once again a Finch Hill & Paraire building) from 1866 until 1880 when it was burnt down, and the Holborn Theatre at 85 High Holborn, which existed under a bewildering number of names, from 1867 to 1887, but which had begun as the Royal Amphitheatre for the sale of horses or for equestrian and circus entertainments. It later became a boxing stadium and used by the YMCA, and was bombed in the last war.

The lively night life of Holborn at this period, before the growth of offices condemned it to evening isolation, is confirmed by the opening

of Holborn Restaurant in 1874 at 218 Holborn (at the south-west corner of High Holborn and Kingsway). This very large building, designed by Archer and Green, had a vast, galleried dining hall, and numerous other dining rooms particularly beloved of the nearby Freemasons.

In the St Giles part of Holborn another well-known theatre developed from a public house. The Winter Garden at 167 Drury Lane was on the site of a 17th-century place of entertainment. Public houses with exotic names such as the Turkish Saloon or the Great Mogul preceded the Middlesex Music Hall which opened there in 1851. This was rebuilt in 1911 as the New Middlesex Theatre of Varieties, a building designed by Frank Matcham. From 1919 it was known as the Winter Garden Theatre and became a theatre (specialising in musical comedy) rather than a music hall. *The Era* described it as a 'striking object lesson in the advance of refinement in the public amusements of the people of this country'.

The Winter Garden lasted until 1960 when the Rank Organisation closed it so that the site could be redeveloped for offices. A condition of planning permission was that a theatre was incorporated on the site. This resulted in the singularly unappealing New London, designed by Sean Kenny, which has for much of its life been home to Andrew Lloyd-Webber's *Cats*.

123. Holborn Restaurant, c.1954.

Two other theatres of this period are worthy of note. The Camden Theatre, at the junction of the High Street and Crowndale Road, had its opening night in December 1900 with Ellen Terry as guest of honour. The architect of this flamboyant building was William Sprague, who with Frank Matcham had built many of the great theatres in London. The Camden was considered the finest theatre in the northern suburbs. It held 3,000 people. A marble staircase led to a crush bar furnished with deep red upholstery, and the auditorium and public rooms were decorated by Waring and Gillow in Louis XIV style. The *Camden and Kentish Town Gazette*, when reviewing a production of the musical *The Geisha* in 1901, said that 'the opera was presented at our beautiful local theatre on a scale of magnificence and completeness which would do credit to a West End theatre, but this is nothing new at the Camden Theatre, being rather a continuation of the policy with which the proprietors started their enterprise, viz. to offer nothing to their patrons but standard work, which has received the unmistakeable approval of critics and public.' Despite such a safe policy, by 1924 the Camden was a cinema and it probably survives today (as a night club) because the BBC took it over from 1945 in an era when cinemas and theatres were being routinely demolished.

The Scala Theatre in Charlotte Street had a much longer history, being descended from concert rooms in 1772 and the Cognoscenti Theatre of 1802. It had a troubled history before it was demolished in the early 1900s and rebuilt with an ample use of marble. The new building, designed by Frank Verity and opened in September 1905, had distinctive marble staircases leading from the dress circle to the stalls, passing beneath the boxes. It was built, however, at the wrong time, as cinema was just getting into its stride. Despite some productions of quality, it became a mixed screen and stage venue and was often booked for productions by amateur companies, although oddly enough it revived as a theatre during the last war. It was also used for a visit by Chessington Circus. The animals were not to appear during blackout hours or during air raids and were, in any case, to be 'animals of good character'. The Scala, however, was in the wrong location as a theatre or cinema, and it was closed in 1969 and demolished soon afterwards.

[1] Info. taken from Marian Kamlish, '...the Alhambra of Camden-town' in *Camden History Review* 19 (1995).
[2] See extensive article by Joan Barraclough, 'The Scala Theatre, Charlotte Street: long-lived , but not always lucky', in *Camden History Review* 20 (1996).

CHAPTER SIXTEEN

The new Boroughs

The formation of the boroughs of Hampstead, Holborn and St Pancras in 1900 occurred as party political labels became significant in local affairs. This followed such a trend on the London School Board from the 1880s, and on the London County Council, formed in 1889. At the inception of the LCC in 1889, the Progressives – a mix of Liberals, Socialists and Fabians – took power. Their opponents called themselves Moderates, which encompassed Conservatives and other right wing politicians. The Labour Party was not formed until 1900 and did not secure its first elected representation on the LCC until 1907.

Though party politics at local level had arrived they were not quite so clear cut as they are today – one member of the LCC in 1889, for example, was asked to stand as a candidate in St Pancras by both the Liberals and the Conservatives, and this was not felt to be too abnormal. George Bernard Shaw, who served on St Pancras Vestry from 1897 and then on the borough council for its first three years, wrote that on the vestry, 'Every member can vote as he thinks best without the slightest risk of throwing his party out of power and bringing on a General Election… I never had to vote on any question otherwise than on its specific merits.' Shaw himself was a member of the Fabian Society, a group which sought the gradual and legal transition of society from capitalism to socialism. The Fabians' roots were firmly in Camden. They began as a gathering at the lodgings of Edward Pease at 17 Osnaburgh Street, off Albany Street, in October 1883 (a blue plaque on the wall of the White House now commemorates the Fabians). Pease, a member of a well-known Quaker family, had recently made the acquaintance of Henry Hyndman and his left-wing Democratic Federation – a blue plaque now records Hyndman's residence at 13 Well Walk, Hampstead from 1916 until his death in 1921 – and William Morris. The Federation sought to subdue capitalism or promote Socialism by much less gradual means than those that appealed to the Fabians. Those attending the first Fabian meeting included clerks, an architect, some journalists,

Havelock Ellis and six women. Shaw did not become a member until May 1884 and as we have seen (*p.120*) he and other Fabians were also members of the Hampstead Historic Society which met at Wyldes, Hampstead at the same period.

The early LCC was regarded as a socially acceptable body to serve on. It attracted two dukes, 38 other members of the peerage and several cabinet ministers, while Lord Rosebery himself was the first chairman a few years before he became prime minister.[1] For all these illustrious names much of the impetus at member level came from lesser-known councillors determined to transform the sorry condition of London – these included radicals of the calibre of John Williams Benn, the grandfather of Tony Benn. As the LCC gradually found its assertive feet it began to worry the Conservative government of the day and when the boroughs were created by an Act of 1899 it was probably with the intention that their enlarged powers should curtail the activities of the LCC.

The Progressives on the LCC were in power from 1889 to 1907, and in this their fortunes roughly mirrored those of the Liberal Party nationally. And so it was in St Pancras, where the Progressives took power in 1903 and were trounced in 1906. In Hampstead the Progressives did quite well in this heyday of their fortunes though they did not win power in the vestry, nor elect an LCC member. In the 1904 LCC election the top Conservative got 3252 votes and the top Progressive 2893, a creditable performance in what was to be a largely Conservative borough until the 2nd World War.

Before the 1st World War the new boroughs did little more than consolidate the activities they inherited from the vestries. St Pancras made a minor foray into public housing. It erected Goldington Buildings at the southern end of Royal College Street in 1904, and an interesting development of 84 dwellings at Flaxman Terrace near St Pancras New Church in 1908. While Goldington Buildings were firmly in the Artisan Dwellings style, Flaxman Terrace, designed by Joseph & Smithern, were of an entirely different

124. *Goldington Court (formerly Buildings) in 1999*

125. *Ossulston Street Estate, built by the London County Council 1927-37.*

architecture; the Brookfield flats in north Kentish Town of the 1920s, built on St Pancras Church land, were a reversion to Artisan style while the estate of houses around it was similar to the LCC 'Becontree' style. In Holborn, the LCC built the Bourne Estate on the site of the Griffin Brewery, and as their architects' department got into its stride it designed, from 1927, the handsome Ossulston Street estate, Somers Town, in a style which owed much to contemporary Viennese housing. Eventually, the LCC built 514 dwellings in Somers Town but there was still much to do to rid that area of slums. St Pancras Council was inactive in the matter and made the formation of what was then called the St Pancras Housing Improvement Society necessary.

The Society (now the St Pancras Housing Association) was formed in Charrington Street in 1924, a product of the energy of Father Basil Jellicoe and the organising ability of Edith Neville. Jellicoe, a nephew of the famous Admiral and head of the Magdalen College, Oxford Mission in Somers Town, took the view that no real impact could be made in the area without civilised housing. Edith Neville, the daughter of a judge and with private means, gave all her time unpaid to social work. She was also secretary to the St Pancras Council of Social Service and Warden of the Mary Ward Centre in Tavistock Place. The Association's aim was either to convert sub-standard properties or build new dwellings in their place, and still make a small profit. Early shareholders included the future Edward VIII, Stanley Unwin, Sir Hugh Walpole and the Carreras tobacco company. The Association was adept at the early use of star names to endorse their

appeals – John Betjeman, J.B. Priestley, Yvonne Arnaud, Jack Hawkins, Gladys Cooper and Flora Robson all raised money for the cause.

At the end of the 1st World War the transition of poor housing to slum property speeded up as a result of the government's Rent and Mortgage Restriction Act, which encouraged landlords to let their properties go unrepaired. In 1925 the Association made its first purchase – eight awful houses in Gee Street (now Polygon Road) for £2800. To pay for this and the rebuilding of the properties, £7,000 was needed and was quickly raised. The old houses, built for single families, often contained five families, and had no water supply other than a tap in the back yard near the outside lavatory. Irene Barclay, a surveyor who managed the Association's property from the outset, relates in her history of the Association how outraged a St Pancras councillor was at the suggestion that the Council should raise its rate by a 1d to make a corresponding effort to ease the slum problem. The Municipal Reform party had regained control in 1922 and had reverted to the parsimony of the old vestry. (When the Children's Libraries Movement acquired 13 Cranleigh Street in north Somers Town in 1921 and opened it as the David Copperfield Library for use by poor children, the new council declined to accept it as a gift or to play any part in its running.)

126. *Leonard Day House and Priestley House on the Athlone Street Estate of the St Pancras Housing Association.*

127. *The Pryors on East Heath Road, drawn by E. Stamp in February 1902. It was replaced by two blocks of flats.*

From such small beginnings the St Pancras Housing Association went in for larger enterprises such as the estate around Drummond Street (1926-36), the Athlone Street scheme in West Kentish Town (1933-37), and at the invitation of the LMS Railway, groups of flats on the Company's spare land at York Rise, Kentish Town (1937-38). Many other of the Association's developments are dotted around the St Pancras area.[2]

Somers Town was not just a matter of building houses, as the Association realised from the start. Of advanced views for the period, it wanted to create communities which not only kept together, but which understood the basic rules for good health. It was following in this the example of the St Pancras School for Mothers, a charity set up to counter the high infant mortality rate of the area, which met in the People's Hall, Chalton Street. From 1907 it provided meals for expectant mothers and gave cooking demonstrations in people's homes. (From 1921, Marie Stopes – a former pupil of Miss Buss at the North London Collegiate School for Girls – ran a birth control clinic in Whitfield Street, Fitzrovia.)

Hampstead, whose housing problems were mild by comparison, built three blocks of flats in Garnett Road 1905-06, but no others until 1935, when the 290 dwellings of the Westcroft estate were built safely out of sight in Cricklewood on the site of a former home for retired horses. This did not please the Hampstead Tenants' League which demanded that the council rehouse its working class residents within the borough.

Between the wars the residents of Hampstead were more preoccupied with the spread of mansion flats in the borough, though this had begun much earlier. In 1884 a large house in Belsize Park Gardens was demolished to make way for Manor Mansions; in 1893 Alfred Bax (father of the future composer, Arnold Bax), put up Ornan Mansions on his Ivy Bank estate. The more contentious Gardnor Mansions in Church Row involved the demolition of a run of the original houses in 1898. The Hampstead Heath Protection Society, formed the year before, would not have protested at this since it limited itself to the Heath and its fringes, and the Hampstead Antiquarian and Historical Association, formed in 1898, was too late to do so. The Protection Society was however concerned about the demolition of the old house, The Pryors, in East Heath Road and the erection of two blocks of flats on the site (by Hall and Waterhouse), which were thought to be a great disfigurement of the Heath. The Society had more effect when Bellmoor, a house at the top of East Heath Road, was demolished and the new flats (1929) had two floors lopped off the original design. Ironically, this house had been the residence of Thomas Barratt, author of the grand 3-volume *Annals of Hampstead* (1912) and hero of a number of battles to save open space in the area.

Between the wars Hampstead became 'valuable' in the eyes of estate agents, turning it from a quiet, respectable if slightly inaccessible suburb, into a part of the metropolis. In 1900, though built up, it had been a quiet town, so simple in its facilities that when the town of Mafeking in South Africa was relieved that year the news was relayed, for want of any other destination, to the fire station in Heath Street and then transmitted by word of mouth. Within hours Heath Street and High Street were crowded with people and flags, and the *Hampstead & Highgate Express* reported that the news of rejoicing in the village of Highgate could be heard across the Heath.

128. A moorish room in Bellmoor, East Heath Road, 1893.

This tranquility could not, of course, last especially once the Northern line had reached Belsize Park and Hampstead in 1907. The Protection Society was unable to save Telegraph Hill in 1913 and in 1933 realised that its interests lay not just with the Heath, but in old Hampstead as well. Schemes were mooted for blocks of flats in Keats Grove and Downshire Hill, both of which were chased away with the help of the Society, but it did not in 1936 prevent planning permission for the building of flats at the foot of Haverstock Hill by Chalk Farm station. In the 1930s a great swathe of Belsize Park near the underground station was rebuilt with flats, some above shops. The Blue Star petrol station replaced Norway House off the High Street and the Greenhill flats in Prince Arthur Road were built in 1935. People had difficulty in selling old houses. George Romney's old house in Holly Bush Hill, owned by the architect Clough Williams Ellis, failed at auction in 1931 to make its reserve price of £12,500 when bidding stopped at £7,500.

Across the Heath, some parts of Highgate succumbed. In 1923 mock-Tudor flats were built on Baroness Coutts' old Holly Lodge estate. In 1934 South Grove House at the brow of Highgate West Hill was demolished and replaced by flats, causing the Highgate Literary and Scientific Institution to buy adjacent Church House to preserve the character of Pond Square. Most notably, the White House off Albany Street was built as self-service apartments in 1936.

Other developments included the moving out of the Foundling Hospital in 1926. Most of the grounds were bought by a speculator who proposed to move Covent Garden Market to the Hospital site and transform the adjacent streets into ancillary market buildings. Fortunately, nothing came of this plan and the grounds of the hospital were saved for many generations of children by Harold Harmsworth (Lord

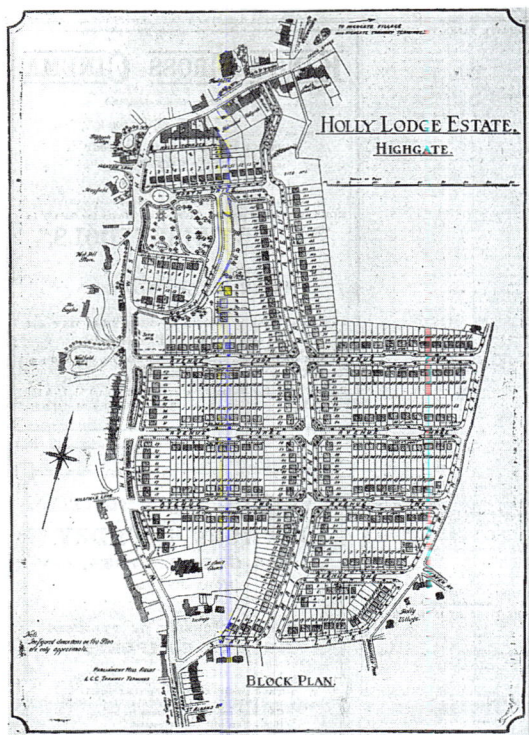

129. *The original layout of the Holly Lodge Estate, as published in the Hampstead & Highgate Express in December 1923. The blocks of flats built by Lady Workers' Homes Ltd, were a later addition.*

130. *Between-the-wars picture of children playing at the Harmsworth Memorial Playground.*

131. *The Isokon flats in Lawn Road.*

Rothermere). The Harmsworth Memorial Playground, usually called Coram's Fields Playground, was opened in 1936. A year later, the art treasures of the old Hospital were housed in a neo-Georgian building in Brunswick Square.

St Pancras Council built itself a much-needed new Town Hall in 1937, full of marble and wood panelling at first floor level (where councillors meet and the mayor has his parlour), but depressingly tedious elsewhere, and the Society of Friends built themselves an award winning headquarters in Euston Road opposite Euston Station in 1927. In Hampstead some architecturally outstanding houses were erected. These included Sun House at 9 Frognal Way (1935), by Maxwell Fry, and 66 Frognal (1938) by Connell, Ward and Lucas. Two other developments caused considerable comment. In Lawn Road, a combination of Jack Pritchard and Wells Coates built the 'Isokon' flats, but their role went further than usual in that the flats were fully

furnished with items designed by them. The flats, the architects said, could set people free of 'permanent tangible possessions'. And despite the protests of the Heath and Old Hampstead Protection Society, Erno Goldfinger demolished three small old houses at the foot of Willow Road and built in 1938 what were then regarded as monstrosities in the Bauhaus style, nos 1-3 – he lived at no. 2, now open to the public.

Potentially more serious from a conservationist's point of view was the purchase by the government in 1920 of a large part of Bloomsbury on which to build a new University of London. But the government of 1926 changed its mind and resold the site to the Bedford Estate. This prompted Sir William Beveridge, Vice-Chancellor of the University, to go to America and return with a cheque for £400,000 from the Rockefeller Foundation so that the land could be bought back again. The foundation stone of Charles

132. Keats House, opened to the public in 1925.

Holden's remarkable Senate House, then the tallest building in London, was laid in 1933 and the building was occupied by 1936. The new site was, topographically, the best that could be had, for the area, which contained the British Museum, was already an academic quarter. Not much of value was lost of the old streets at this stage, but with so much to bring together on the site, so many colleges and institutions, the nature of the area was changed considerably after the 2nd World War as the university expanded.

There were some embellishments in this difficult period punctuated by wars, recession and unemployment. The year 1925 was a notable one: both Keats' House and Kenwood House (see *p.113*) came into the public domain. Keats' House is actually two houses knocked together, in one of which Keats lodged 1815-16, and the other for a time housed Fanny Brawne and her family. Keats' House was saved mostly with American money. It was opened to the public by Sir Arthur Quiller-Couch, the poet, in May 1925 when the guests included a granddaughter of Fanny Brawne.

In 1920 the Everyman Theatre opened in Hollybush Vale in a drill hall which of late had been used as a 'Palais de Whist'. It was founded by Norman MacDermott, who was advised by George Bernard Shaw to throw his money on to horses rather than risk changing the playgoing habits of the English. It had a tiny auditorium and small backstage, so that in the first production – a period costume play – the hoops of the actresses dresses became jammed in the narrow spiral staircase that led down to the stage. The most famous production here was Noel Coward's *The Vortex* in 1924 (directed by and featuring the master himself). It was not without incident: one actress stormed out because of

Coward's behaviour to her, and Lord Cromer, then responsible for reading new playscripts for the government, declined to include a reference to two young ladies going away together. He said that it implied that the two were lesbians, to which Coward replied that he wished he had thought of that himself.

The Everyman was an important theatre between the wars. Performers included Edith Evans, Carleton Hobbs, Ellen Terry and Claude Rains, but cinema still claimed it eventually, but at least it was a memorable victor. In 1933 it was bought by Jim Fairfax-Jones, lawyer turned cinema buff, who specialised in foreign films – a rare venture. His wife Tess ran the Foyer Gallery where Paul Klee was given his first public show. Against all odds, and through the most difficult of years, the Everyman has survived as a renowned repertoire cinema.

Camden has a close association with the beginnings of cinema. An early pioneer of the medium, William Friese-Greene (1855-1921) lived at 136 Maida Vale and worked from 20 Brooke Street in Holborn (he is buried in Highgate Cemetery). Friese-Greene was the first to print a moving picture photographed on celluloid Chronologically, the first cinema in Camden was the Dara in Delancey Street, Camden Town, a converted skating rink. According to research by Mark Aston, thirty cinemas had opened for long or short spells in Camden by the end of the 1st World War. These included the Hampstead Playhouse in Pond Street, which opened in 1913. Here, talking pictures arrived in 1930 but a full orchestra was retained for the silent screen feature that was still shown. The most notable buildings came in the 1930s. These included the Odeon, Haverstock Hill (1934) where facilities included earphones for the hard of hearing, the Forum, Highgate Road (1934), the Gaumont, Parkway (1937) and the Odeon, Swiss Cottage (1937).

Despite the increasing popularity of cinema, new theatres were still being built. These included the Dominion in Tottenham Court Road (1929), the Cambridge at Seven Dials (1930), and the Phoenix in Charing Cross Road (1930). Another addition in 1928 was the conversion of the Hampstead Conservatoire at Swiss Cottage to the Embassy Theatre. The Conservatoire was founded in 1885. From 1896 to 1905 its director was Cecil Sharp who is better known for his foundation of the English Folk Dance and Song Society whose 1931 headquarters in Regent's

133. Hampstead Conservatoire at Swiss Cottage, c.1905.

Park Road commemorate his name. The Embassy Theatre survived fewer years than the Conservatoire. It was saved from conversion to a cinema in 1932, when a former manager secured a lease to house a permanent theatre company, and though never profitable it somehow survived as a theatre venue until taken over by the Central School of Speech and Drama in 1956.

Despite its size, one of the best known theatres in Camden was what became Unity Theatre. This opened at the redundant St Jude's National School, Britannia Street off Gray's Inn Road in 1935 before moving to a former mission hall in Goldington Crescent in 1937. It was thought of for much of its career as a Communist theatre, and certainly Communists were dominant amongst its membership and probably a lot of its audience as well. But to describe it merely as 'Communist' reduces it. More accurately, it was a 'political theatre' in which many of the issues of the 1930s, before we became more sceptical about 'isms', were acted out and discussed. It was socialist, of course, reverential to the Soviet Union and firmly based on the trade union movement, but there were also influences from the less firmly labelled left wing. The era

itself was politically energetic and unpredictable – the establishment of the Soviet Union, the Spanish Civil War, the rise of Fascism here and in Europe all made the 1930s a remarkable political decade in which passions and enthusiasms ran high. Unity's most famous early production (April 1936) was a short play by Clifford Odets called *Waiting for Lefty*.

Fascism indeed was on the local doorsteps. Many rallies and meetings took place in St Pancras and Hampstead. In 1936 a fascist meeting at Hampstead Town Hall was addressed by one, William Joyce, later to be famous as the German propagandist, 'Lord Haw-Haw'. In 1937, attacks on shops run by Jews began and in the same year fights between Fascists and Communists broke out at Camden Town underground station.

It was time to batten down.

[1] John Davis, 'The Progressive Council 1889-1907' in *Politics and the People of London. The London County Council 1889-1965*, p.230 (1989).
[2] Information on the St Pancras Housing Association has been drawn from Irene Barclay, *People need Roots* (1976), and Malcolm J. Holmes, *Housing is not Enough* (1999).

CHAPTER SEVENTEEN
A sober time

A Rush of Housing

Events and experiences of the 1st and 2nd World Wars have been deliberately omitted from this book. Much has already appeared in publications and articles – available at Camden's Local Studies and Archives Centre – and it seems unnecessary to reshape them. The end of both conflicts brought hope, if not of a Utopian future, at least of improvements in the quality of life and of better housing. In the years after the 1st World War, the LCC was active in this field, but the boroughs of Hampstead, Holborn and St Pancras hardly stirred.

More determination and political will, encouraged by both Labour and Conservative governments, were evident after the 2nd World War. A great deal of housing was put up in a hurry. Unfortunately much of it was built on the cheap and designed at a time when architectural style was at a very low ebb. It would be difficult to think of many buildings in Camden of this postwar period, domestic, commercial or public, that one would want to retain.

Holborn Council had little land available for estates and concentrated its efforts north of Theobalds Road. But in the 1950s the opportunity of bomb damage was taken to extend Holborn's commercial capability by the construction of some awful office blocks at the western ends of Theobalds Road and High Holborn and, at the same time, to introduce a disfiguring and hostile traffic system. In 1950 came two government buildings, Ariel (later Adastral) House and Lacon House, and in 1955 Mercury House all three in Theobalds Road; in 1959 State House was built in High Holborn. Mercifully, Ariel and Lacon Houses have now been demolished and at the time of writing their replacements are still under plastic. Mercury House has since been 'modernised' and State House, which had little to recommend it and was not made any more acceptable by a Barbara Hepworth statue outside, has also been demolished.

Inevitably, Labour-run St Pancras built most housing. Aneurin Bevan opened 126 flats in St Pancras Way in 1948 and in the same year the

134. Clarence Way flats in 1999.

Council was negotiating with the Crown Commissioners to buy land east of Albany Street on which the Regent's Park Estate was developed. In 1952 blocks around Clarence Way were finished, which included the 1000th flat the Council had built since 1945. In 1955 the Council bought the Christ Church estate in Kentish Town, then in disrepair, and went on to improve rather than demolish. The biggest task lay in West Kentish Town where it was judged in 1957 that most of the housing was not worth keeping.

It is true that much of West Kentish Town was in a sorry state. It had a history of sub-standard building, indifferent landlords letting out to poor people, a lack of repairs between the wars and an absence of upkeep as rent control made any profit unlikely. Blight was intensified as it became obvious that the Council was to buy up much of it at knock-down compulsory purchase rates. The neighbourhood, with exceptions such as the 'Crimea' area around Raglan Street and Willes Road, slid further down a spiral of dereliction.

Repair and conversion of such property was not even considered by the Council. The councillors and officers of that era had seen the improvements in living conditions and public health that came from new housing estates, particularly those of the pre-war LCC, and at that time the creation of estates seemed the way forward. They were then the solution of conventional wisdom and thus, when in 1958 St Pancras proposed a 20-storey block at Gospel Oak, it expected plaudits, not opprobrium. And when in 1962 it announced the wholesale redevelopment of the Gospel Oak area, few voices opposed it. As late as 1964 it was noted that a 6-roomed house in Weedington Road had 14 occupants, with one kitchen and one outside lavatory. What could be more deserving of demolition?

There were some misgivings about the amount of property the borough council was buying, but on the other hand there was also pressure from some private tenants for it to do so. In 1952 the tenants of Langbourne Mansions on the Holly Lodge Estate, property of the Lady Workers' Homes, had been asked *voluntarily* to pay more rent. This was because rent control did not enable the owners to make a reasonable profit, let alone an excessive one. Consequently, the flats were sold to a property company which adopted a policy of emptying the flats as tenants died or left, presumably with some great scheme in mind. It was reported in 1963 that of the 639 flats on Holly Lodge, 209 were empty and that no attempt was being made to fill them. Tenants became very worried indeed and the Council was urged to buy the properties. It did so and became owners on Christmas Day 1964.

In Hampstead, work began soon after the war on flats in Upper Park Road and Parkhill Road. In 1955 construction commenced on blocks in Broadhurst Gardens and, at the time of absorption into Camden, it was hoped that the high-rise flats proposed on the Chalcots estate would eradicate much of the Hampstead housing list.

During this period, many Camden residents were persuaded out to New Towns such as Basildon and Stevenage. Simultaneously, or in their wake, went with them quite a lot of Camden's industry, large and small. Carreras had moved to Basildon by 1960 and Gilbey's decided to leave for Harlow in 1961. These companies had good practical reasons for going but it is true to say that industry was made to feel unwelcome in inner London by boroughs and the LCC, who were themselves in thrall to the Abercrombie plans for London (1943-44). And in St Pancras the business rate was hiked up as far as it might go so as to keep the domestic rate down.

Large schemes

The Abercrombie plans were commissioned during the war to provide a blueprint for the Greater London area once the conflict had ended. They laid heavy emphasis on separating industry and residences, and on the construction of new roads. The road proposals were largely ignored or found to be either impractical or detrimental, but an obsession for major new highways remained at the LCC and its successor, the Greater London Council. An example of the LCC approach was the Euston underpass. This ugly and divisive feature entailed the destruction of a great deal of local property, caused blight on what was left and led inevitably to the cluster of office blocks which are now on the northern side of Euston Road. A mini-Croydon centre was formed, and redevelopment here resulted years later in the demolition of Tolmers Square, for which a hard battle was fought.

The actual and potential problems of traffic congestion brought about other mixed blessings. Finchley Road was widened up to Hendon Way; a one-way system was introduced in Camden Town in 1964 hot on the heels of that introduced in Tottenham Court Road and Gower Street. Absurdly, the Ministry of Transport in 1962 proposed a lorry route through Highgate Village to ease congestion on Archway Road and many people had to waste time and money fighting this ridiculous proposition. Other people a year later had to band together to save the North London Line from Beeching's closures.

Hampstead Council turned to the matter of civic buildings soon after the war ended. The Town Hall at Belsize Park, the baths in Finchley Road and the war-damaged central library in Arkwright Road were no longer adequate. In 1949 the Council decided to relocate its major public buildings at Swiss Cottage on the island site where today's library and baths now stand. As part of this plan, the St Dunstan's School for the Blind and St Columba's Hospital moved out in the 1950s. Basil Spence, then fresh from building the new Coventry cathedral, was chosen as overall architect and work began only on the baths and library in 1962, for it was certain by then that Hampstead as a borough was near its end and a new town hall was not required there.

New Libraries

Libraries, in fact, came fast and furious in this period. The thriller writer, Peter Cheyney, opened a new East Holborn branch in Gray's Inn

Road in 1947. This was a stop-gap, and was closed when the borough opened a central library in Theobalds Road in 1960, designed by S.A.G. Cook, the Borough Architect. In St Pancras, which in 1945 boasted just the purpose-built branch library in Chester Road, and a converted house in Camden Street, a whole series of new buildings were produced or planned. Branches in Robert Street and Sharpleshall Street were opened in 1961, Dr Jacob Bronowski declared open the Kentish Town branch in 1962, and Victor Gollancz did the same in Camden High Street in 1964. Hanging in the air was a proposal for the long-desired central library which in 1955 St Pancras Council decided to build on the site of the old Bedford Theatre in Camden High Street. This plan was abandoned by the Conservatives when they came to office in 1959, with a proposal to build it instead in Euston Road.

Political changes

In 1945 Santo Wayburn Jeger was elected as Labour MP for South East St Pancras. In 1950, when constituency boundaries were redrawn, he became MP for Holborn & South St Pancras until his death in 1953, when his widow, Lena Jeger, took over the seat. With the exception of the years 1959-63, she was MP for the constituency until elevation to the House of Lords in 1976. During the years she was out of office, the Conservative MP was Geoffrey Johnson-Smith.

Hampstead's usual political stability was shaken in 1950 when the local Conservative Party decided to deselect its sitting member, Charles Challen. In his place they chose Henry Brooke, who had previously been MP for West Lewisham 1938-45 and who was a Hampstead resident. Amid much controversy, Challen threatened to stand as an unofficial Conservative but was eventually dissuaded. Though Hampstead was Conservative in its borough council majority and in its choice of representatives to the LCC and Parliament, it was a centre of left-wing ferment. Arthur Goss, for a period the proprietor of the *Hampstead & Highgate Express*, together with Sheila Jones of the Hampstead Labour Party, founded what became the Campaign for Nuclear Disarmament in the late 1950s, and the Hampstead branch was its largest. Sidney Silverman, a Labour MP who lived in Finchley Road, led the campaign to abolish capital punishment. In this his campaign secretary was Peggy Duff who was later to be secretary of the CND and a member of St Pancras Council. Just

as controversially, Roy Shaw, secretary of the Hampstead Labour Party (and now Millennium Mayor of Camden), persuaded his party in 1957 to nominate Dr David Pitt – the first black candidate in Parliament's history. He didn't topple Henry Brooke, but his vote was respectable and he went on to become the first black member of the House of Lords.

At Parliamentary level St Pancras North made a calm transition from Labour MP George House, who died in 1949, to Kenneth Robinson, who later became a Minister of Health. The headlines, though, were made by the borough council.

After the 1956 local elections the Labour council was much more left-wing as many of the old leaders, traditional trade union councillors, gave way to a militant group led by the charismatic John Lawrence. There were suggestions at the time that the new leaders were either actual or covert members of the Communist Party, especially when in 1958 the Red Flag was hoisted above the town hall. This caused a sensation, especially in the *Evening Standard*, and embarrassed the Labour Party nationally. In fact Lawrence became leader of the Council by chance when in 1956 he opposed (as he would do) the traditional sharing of aldermanic seats with the opposition. His view prevailed on the Labour group and the leader of the party resigned in protest, allowing Lawrence to be elected.

The militancy of the Council was entwined with the passing of the 1956 Rent Act, put together by a Conservative government and implemented from 1957 by the Housing Minister, Henry Brooke, MP for Hampstead. The Act sought to abolish rent control and allow landlords to charge a market rate. The downside of rent control has already been noted – properties deteriorated for want of proper economic return – but on the other hand an increased rent was a serious matter to a large section of the population at a period when the rise in price of a loaf of bread would make front page news. Opposition to the Rent Act was an easy rallying cry, but more seriously for St Pancras Council the consequent rise in value of property freed from rent restrictions, made the aim of the Council to buy up houses more expensive. The deficit on the St Pancras housing account, bearing in mind that the Council refused to increase rents to tenants, was rising inexorably and eventually, failing to do anything about this, a surcharge was placed on many members of the Labour group.

Lawrence was a charming agitator, but he also

was a former Trotskyite who had now become an embarrassment to the national party. The Red Flag, the failure to act on the rent deficit, and the much publicised decision not to adopt any measures which would provide civil defence in the event of another war, made his suspension and eventual expulsion from the Labour Party inevitable. A number of other Labour councillors who failed to give assurances of future correct behaviour were expelled at the same time. These included Jock Stallard, later to be Labour MP for North St Pancras and Lord Stallard.

Lawrence was succeeded as Leader by Charles Ratchford, a councillor since 1940. He was a dogged, good natured and honest man, more driven by his memories than future visions, but he was not an inspirational leader. He had little ability to re-present his party, which was hounded out of office by a public tired of the Lawrence affair, in 1959. The new Conservative administration raised the temperature even more, for under its leader, Tony Prior, a differential rent scheme for council tenants was introduced. Apart from raising rents generally (though a small number actually went down), it also revived among older people memories of pre-war means tests. Though the Labour opposition consistently fought the scheme, the most public protests came from the United Tenants' Association led by a mix of hard-left activists who included Don Cook, a trade union shop steward of Kennistoun House in Leighton Road. The Association urged tenants to withhold rents, and a great many did at first until eviction notices were sent out. In June 1960 the *St Pancras Chronicle* reported that only three tenants were left withholding rent. The scene was set for evictions. Extraordinary scenes occurred in Leighton Road where Cook's first floor residence was surrounded by barbed wire and supporters day and night. Support arrived from all directions – from the fire brigade union which refused to take part in any eviction, and from marchers from London and elsewhere to the town hall where the police had difficulty in containing them. Television, radio, cinemas and newspapers featured the stand-off as main stories, but Cook and Arthur Rowe, who had a flat in Silverdale on the Regent's Park Estate, were both evicted in a fairly bloodless early-morning encounter. The battle over differential rents was over and no attempt was made to reverse the scheme once Labour came back into power in 1962.

New enterprises

What became the principal arts organisation in Hampstead was formed while the war still raged. Richard Carline, whose home then was in Pond Street, founded the Hampstead Artists' Council in 1944, with the active participation of Fred and Diana Uhlman. An early home was found in part of a house owned by William Empson in Hampstead Hill Gardens. The object of the Council was to regularly sponsor small exhibitions and one-man shows and to strengthen the ties between artists and the district in which they lived. Some exhibitions were held in Wilson's bookshop in Hampstead High Street, others at Burgh House, John Barnes and the town hall, and murals were painted in a British Restaurant (a war-time local authority restaurant). In 1949 the first open-air exhibition, which became an annual event, was held at the top of Heath Street.

In 1955 the HAC moved to Burgh House where it expanded under the leadership of Patricia Angadi. In that year the HAC took part in the first Hampstead Festival of the Arts and in 1958 a major exhibition was held at the Everyman Cinema which included works by Klee, Hepworth, Nicholson and Anthony Gross.

Just as in Hampstead the first tentative steps were being taken by the borough council to involve itself in arts activities (albeit under the aegis of the 'Entertainments' Committee), St Pancras was proceeding by a similar route. The St Pancras Arts and Civic Council was formed in 1947 with the support of Krishna Menon, then on St Pancras Council. The first St Pancras Arts Festival was held in 1954, though this followed on from much smaller affairs which had flourished since 1947. Though well-supported by a sometimes bemused borough council, the Festival's subsequent success was the result of the enthusiasm of William Taylor the Borough Librarian and Leonard Marcus his deputy.

In 1946 the Hampstead Music Club was formed. Kenwood House was reopened to the public in 1950 and concerts in the grounds were initiated the following year. Lady Binning left Fenton House, the oldest house in Hampstead, to the National Trust in 1952.

In 1959, James Roose-Evans began the Hampstead Theatre Club at the Moreland Hall, Hollybush Vale with professional, but virtually unpaid, actors. They rehearsed in an upper room at the Three Horseshoes opposite, which was at one time to be their auditorium had it been possible to meet the fire regulations. Roose-

Evans was here following on from MacDermott's Everyman Theatre (*see p.153*) and at one time seemed likely to follow it into oblivion. Fortunately, Hampstead Council provided the Club with a prefabricated building on the Swiss Cottage site and, if development there had not been interrupted by the creation of Camden, it would probably have merited a purpose built theatre in due course.

The first production at Swiss Cottage in December 1962 was Chekhov's *The Seagull*. Years of financial worries followed. (Sir) Max Rayne paid off the Club's debts in 1963 and remained a committed friend, but the Club has always been short of money despite its many successes and transfers to West End stages. In 1964 the entire weekly wage-bill for the non-acting staff and James Roose-Evans, was £116.

By the time that Camden began in 1965, the conservation movement had gained strength. The Holborn Society had been formed in May 1954 and the St Pancras Civic Society in 1953 (this became the Camden Civic Society from 1965). Hampstead, of course, already had the well-established Heath & Old Hampstead Society which had, since 1960, been opposing the proposal by the LCC to demolish the old tollhouse by the Spaniards Inn; this was eventually suc-

cessful, but on the other hand it did not impinge much on the design of the building which replaced the Vale of Health Hotel. St Pancras Council had made two notable forays into conservation: one was the preservation in 1953 of a Georgian house discovered when a building was demolished in Euston Road. With the financial help of the firm, Car-mart, it was restored only to be demolished when the Euston underpass was constructed. More importantly the Council rescued and restored from 1956 the delightful Woburn Walk behind St Pancras New Church. Local societies were sometimes augmented by national lobby groups, particularly the Victorian Society, and it was this society which fought and lost the campaign to save the Euston Arch in 1962. The demolition of the Arch was one of the most unnecessary and outrageous acts of institutional vandalism of the post-war period. This splendid structure, standing in front of the old Euston station, was judged to be an impediment to traffic movement at the rebuilt station and, on the whim of British Rail, and with the connivance of the LCC, it was dismantled: Herbert Morrison, who had with pleasure ceremoniously begun the demolition of the old and beautiful Waterloo Bridge in 1936, would have been pleased. Triumphant though British Rail

135. Woburn Walk in 1922. It had deteriorated still further before restoration by St Pancras Council in the 1950s.

was, it was a pyrrhic victory, for the public by then was so incensed that when the British Transport Commission wanted to pull down St Pancras Station as well it lost hands down. Henceforth, not much of value was demolished without a fight.

Strangers to the shores

The ethnic nature of some parts of Camden was already changed in the 1950s. In Hampstead an influx of European Jews before and during the war brought numerous talents, especially artistic ones, to the area This raised the ire of two women in Belsize Park Gardens, who in 1945 persuaded 2000 people to sign a petition to expel foreigners from the area to ease the housing shortage. It was supported by Hampstead's MP, Charles Challen. No doubt it also found favour with Oswald Mosley who addressed a meeting of one hundred people at Stanfield House in the High Street the following year.

There were sufficient Greek Cypriots in Camden Town by 1948 to make All Saints church in Camden Street their place of worship. The first groups of Cypriots came in the 1930s to escape the poverty of the island and worked mainly in the hotels and restaurants of the West End – Camden Town was as good as anywhere to settle as a community, but it is not yet known why it was chosen. After the war they opened their own cafés and restaurants, even taking over traditional English fish and chip shops. They also specialised in dry-cleaning, shoe mending, off licences and clothes manufacture. There were further waves of settlement in the 1950s and early '60s which, inevitably, joined the older one in Camden Town. More came in 1974 when Turkish occupation of the northern part of Cyprus occurred

The Merger

Throughout the early 1960s the imminence of the borough's merger into new, enlarged authorities was in the air and, after 1963, when it was certain, made forward planning difficult. The redistribution of London authorities and the enlargement of the metropolis was not a new idea. In November 1950, at a celebratory dinner to mark the fifty years since the first meeting of Hampstead Council, Lord Radcliffe, who lived in Cannon Place, declared, "There will have to be a recognition of a Greater London outside the present county. There might then have to be an amalgamation of areas.' Ten years later a Royal

Commission proposed the merger of Hampstead and St Pancras, neither of which was keen. Willesden in 1962 made an attempt to poach 250 acres of West Hampstead (as well as slices of Paddington and Hendon) to avoid a merger with Wembley, and this may have convinced Hampstead councillors that a link with St Pancras might be preferable if merger was inevitable. At any rate Hampstead and St Pancras councils signalled that same year their agreement to a marriage, though St Pancras Labour Party, then out of power, still opposed the whole scheme. By that time too, Holborn, previously earmarked to join Shoreditch and Finsbury, was included in what became Camden.

The first three-party talks began in May 1962, just before the last municipal elections took place. These returned Labour to power in St Pancras and gave them a larger share of the vote in both Holborn and Hampstead. Even then St Pancras Council stood out against the merger and passed a resolution in June which claimed that the 'best interests of … local government will be served by maintaining the existence of the metropolitan boroughs…', though the party was not averse to slimming down the LCC by transferring some of its activities, especially housing, to the boroughs. This was not the unanimous view of the Labour group, many of whom saw advantages to a greater rateable base in an enlarged borough. What the Labour group was really worried about was that the Conservatives might take control of Camden, though it could take comfort in the fact that the Tories of Holborn and Hampstead feared the reverse.

The London Government Bill was passed in July 1963. It created the Greater London Council together with new London boroughs which included Camden. Arguments were over and the transition to Camden had to be achieved in harmony if only for the sake of the staff. Negotiations continued between the three leaders. Alderman Leslie Room of Hampstead, quiet, distinguished and courteous, Charles Ratchford of St Pancras, a modest but sometimes passionate ex-railwayman of little formal education but with a quick ability to assimilate paperwork, and William Ridd of Holborn, a business man and a gregarious person, very much in charge of the old Holborn council. These early meetings needed compromise and a readiness to make an agreement. It is as well that John Lawrence was not still leader of St Pancras.

CHAPTER EIGHTEEN

Camden Days

The first elections for the new borough of Camden took place on 7 May 1964, though the three old boroughs and their councils continued to function until May 1965, winding up business that had little consequence for Camden. The result in 1964 was a close-run thing, as most people predicted. The tally of 34 Labour councillors and 26 Conservatives disguises the fact that had the four seats of Priory Ward in Hampstead gone to the right, then the result would have been a tie. At that stage, when there were no sitting aldermen in place to tip the post-electoral balance in the selection of mayor and aldermen, the political beginnings of Camden could have been very messy indeed.

The Labour Party appropriated eight of the ten aldermanic seats to give itself a working majority and an insurance against a bad result in the next election. Charles Ratchford made the transition to Leader of the Council and Leslie Room became Leader of the Opposition. Samuel Fisher was made mayor, chairmanships were distributed and business began. St Pancras Town Hall became Camden Town Hall (an ugly extension was built in 1977-8 by the Council's own architects). The Engineer's (Works) department went to Hampstead Town Hall, architects and planners to Holborn Town Hall, and the Librarian to Swiss Cottage Library until St Pancras Library was completed. The new Health, Welfare and Children's departments were housed, together with the Housing Department, in the unlovely Bidborough House in Bidborough Street.

It was early decided not to have a coat-of-arms and to have instead a symbol. This was commissioned from Wolff Olins, a Camden Town design company, and their motif of clasped hands has generally been used by Camden since.

Politically, the two parties worked together fairly harmoniously (too harmoniously for some ex-St Pancras councillors used to a more fractious atmosphere) and within a year or two Camden had the reputation in London for being the most progressive of the new London boroughs.

High profile arts

Camden's early reputation was partly founded on its participation in high-profile arts activities. The Camden Arts Festival capitalised on the remarkable reputation of the St Pancras Arts Festival. The visually prominent baths and library (albeit nearly finished before the merger) opened at Swiss Cottage in November 1964. The Camden Arts Centre was begun in the old central library at Arkwright Road, a joint venture between the Council and the Hampstead Artists' Council, who were then led by Jeannette Jackson and Bernard Gay. Not only was there an art school (opened 1965), but professionally staged exhibitions, the first of which in 1966, *The Artist at Work*, was opened by Anthony Blunt. The Council also became involved with Charles Marowitz at the Open Space Theatre, Drama Centre, the acting school in the old Methodist church in Prince of Wales Road, the Contemporary Dance Theatre at The Place in Dukes Place, and with Arnold Wesker in the formation of Centre 42 at the Roundhouse. The Council was also keen to put the Hampstead Theatre Club on a firmer financial footing.

The Roundhouse Centre 42 project sprang from resolution 42 passed at the Trades Union Conference in 1960 urging greater participation by the trades union movement in the arts. It was sufficiently anodyne to be passed, but it was taken up seriously by a group led by the left-wing playwright, Arnold Wesker, which believed that the arts should be more freely available to the general public. Not very much happened as far as the TUC was concerned, but Wesker did not give up. He needed a base in which some of the ideals of Centre 42 could be practised, a place for social intermixing and artistic performances. Coincidentally, the lease of the old train shed called the Roundhouse, at Chalk Farm, came up for sale. Louis Mintz, already a patron of the arts, wanted to buy the lease via his company Selincourt. He was persuaded to do this but to donate it afterwards to the Centre 42 project. This he did in July 1964 and in 1965 the Round House Trust was set up with Wesker as its artistic director and George Hoskins (who claimed to have been responsible for the re-establishment of coffee-bars in London in the 1950s) as administrator. In 1967 the freehold of the building was obtained.

Wesker's hopes for the Roundhouse were unfortunately beyond the resources they had to achieve them. The building was in a bad condition after over a century in use as a warehouse – to rescue its fabric was a heavy enough expense. The not unreasonable aims of Wesker included a flexible auditorium, dressing rooms, showers, dark room, work room, restaurant, a social area for youth clubs and even quarters for artists. When an appeal for funds flopped Hoskins allowed outside organisations to hire the venue and in 1969 the first drama productions were staged there. This was not what Wesker had envisaged and he was increasingly worried about Hoskins' insistence on commercialising the building to provide funds to bolster up the larger venture. In 1970 Wesker directed his own play, *The Friends*, there. Booked in for 12 weeks, it was a financial disaster and was taken off in six. Hoskins brought in Kenneth Tynan's *Oh! Calcutta!*, which was an enormous box-office success, and Wesker resigned.

The project, now minus the Centre 42 label, continued but still with money problems. Outside productions such as *Rabelais* and *The Grand Magic Circus* made full use of the atmosphere of the place, but the output was of mixed quality. In 1977, when Hoskins became ill, Thelma Holt was brought in from the Open Space Theatre to be administrator. Gradually she diminished the motley of productions going on there, giving it a more distinctive arts direction, and even produced herself a memorable *Bartholomew Fair*. A partnership with the Royal Exchange theatre in Manchester (which also has a circular auditorium) was established, but gradually the Arts Council lost interest and Camden dropped out altogether so that Holt left in 1983. Since then the building has been the subject of many projects and still has an uncertain future.

Another theatre was established in Camden in April 1971 with the opening of the Shaw Theatre as part of the new St Pancras Library. The Library building had an unusual history. When the Labour Party lost control of St Pancras Council in 1959 one of the first decisions of the Conservative administration was to switch the location of a proposed central library away from Camden Town to Euston Road. The borough already owned some run-down shops there and had the money and the powers to buy an island site. Elidir Davies, architect of the National Theatre of Wales, was appointed for the scheme and he engineered a deal with developers so that the library and theatre were to be built virtually free of charge while the developers were permitted to pile offices on top. In fact, Camden incurred a lot of costs as the project was turned into a central library for Camden instead of just St Pancras. In truth, the building was a disappointment and the Shaw Theatre (after George Bernard Shaw), was too cramped. When a theatre was included in the original 1959 scheme, its role was to be a 'civic theatre' – regarded as a good thing in those less sophisticated days, and it was envisaged as not much more than an assembly hall with advanced facilities. The theatrical world had moved on a great deal by 1971 and the old concept was out of date, which is why Elidir Davies, a theatre architect, had been brought into the project. A permanent theatre company at the Shaw was regarded as too expensive, and the prospect of it being used by touring companies was not inviting. So, the National Youth Theatre, which had already made its mark under Michael Croft, was invited to be the resident company with modest financial help from Camden. The Shaw must rank as one of the shortest-lived purpose-built theatres in London. It was closed in 1993, the same year as the central library was stripped and reduced to a branch library operating out of the Town Hall extension across the road. Recently the old building has been reclad and is now the Shaw Park Plaza Hotel. A bizarre name.

Branch Hill and other developments

Angry debates occurred on Camden Council over the question of Branch Hill Lodge and its grounds. For many years both the Heath & Old Hampstead Society and Hampstead Council had fought off plans to develop this estate – the LCC had proposed housing on the site as early as 1951. In 1965 the Society persuaded the owner, Lord Glendyne, to sell the site to Camden at a cheap price and on a 'gentlemen's agreement' that the house would become an old people's home and the open land would be added to the Heath. Glendyne died shortly afterwards and Camden promptly announced a plan for 90 maisonettes on the open land. In the event this plan did not materialise but 42 semi-detached houses were later built on the site. In 1983 Camden rezoned

136. Branch Hill Lodge at the end of the 19th century.

the open area as residential in the hope of attracting private buyers. By 1972 Camden had
also bought Spedan Tower, the old home and
grounds of the store owner, John Lewis, but nine
years later, strapped for cash, the Council resold
it to a private developer for over £2 million.

Other major Camden Council developments
have been the redevelopment of West Kentish
Town, the Alexandra Road estate in West Hampstead, the troubled Maiden Lane estate off York
Way, the secluded estate on old railway land
near York Rise, Kentish Town and the Brunswick
Centre in Bloomsbury. It also bought 100 houses
on the 19th-century St Bartholomew's Estate in
Kentish Town.

Out of Camden's hands, for it had few powers
in the matter, was the growth of the Royal Free
Hospital, Hampstead, which was officially
opened in 1974. The bulk of the building, which
spoils many views from the Heath, was beyond
even the energy of the Heath & Old Hampstead
Society to ameliorate.

But Camden *was* a willing partner in the devastating plan for Covent Garden initiated by the
Greater London Council in 1968. This proposed,

137. The Brunswick Centre, Bloomsbury.

once the fruit and vegetable market had moved
out, to raze 60% of the area, rehouse 2,000 people
and uproot many businesses. A major road,
parallel to the Strand, was planned and hotels
and business centres were to be built in this
'exceptional opportunity' for replanning a central part of London. There was to be a 'line of

163

character' from Leicester Square to Lincoln's Inn. And there was also a rise in car parking spaces from zero to 1½ million square feet. It positively encouraged traffic to come in and owed much of its ethos to the Abercrombie plans of the 1940s. A combination of the Covent Garden Community Association and public opinion quashed this undesirable scheme, leaving Covent Garden to be mostly regenerated privately with a minimum of demolition.

Large development does not always make a profit. The YMCA found that redevelopment of its headquarters and main hostel off Tottenham Court Road in the 1970s nearly bankrupted the Association, mainly due to numerous industrial disputes. Centre Point, the skyscraper which stands at the junction of Charing Cross Road and St Giles High Street, stood empty for years, though fortunately for Joe Hyams, the developer, it got more valuable as the years went on even though unoccupied. This was because office rents were rising fast and potentially the rent income of the building rose. Centre Point was a classic example of planners making a mess of things. In a deal with the LCC, Hyams had agreed to buy adjacent land for a traffic roundabout in exchange for permission for his tall block. In the event the LCC did not build its roundabout.

The Euston Centre on Euston Road was a collusive effort by the LCC and the developer,

Joe Levy. It took a long time to put together and build. The LCC found that the route of its proposed Euston underpass contravened a number of planning consents it had already given to Levy, who owned some of the plots of old shops and houses along its route. It would have cost a great deal to have breached those consents and in a deal unknown to the public Levy was encouraged and aided to buy up the rest of the property he needed to make a large office development possible and to hand over the land necessary for the new underpass layout.

The fate of the empty King's Cross railway lands has been discussed virtually since Camden was formed and a resolution is nowhere in sight. In the 1950s and 1960s coal sales reduced and the main function of the goods yards at King's Cross diminished; more and more freight was carried by road and other business was lost.

Development of this land was complicated by a number of preservation orders and Conservation Areas. The Regent's Canal, which flowed through the yard's lower reaches, was a Conservation Area by 1974 – indeed Camden had earned much praise for the restoration of the towpath within the borough. A number of buildings along the canal's banks, and the gasholders were listed. There was too the Camley Street Natural Park, created by the London Wildlife Trust in 1983 on the site of some old coal drops. This gained much public support and its removal or

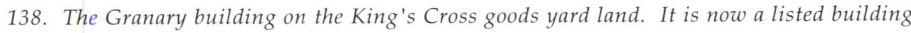
138. The Granary building on the King's Cross goods yard land. It is now a listed building.

relocation was an emotive issue. Putting these features aside there was in any case no consensus as to how this very large site should be used. The Greater London Council, shortly before its demise, had engaged in public consultation about possible uses, but the site was so large that it was meaningless to gather man-in-the-street preferences.

Initiative for wholesale redevelopment, with offices and luxury homes at its core, came from the developers of the successful Broadgate Centre at Liverpool Street. Camden Council, keen to see regeneration in the area, was alarmed by the nature of the scheme and by its possible electoral consequences. British Rail, which owned much of the site, eventually selected the London Regeneration Consortium as developers – this was a partnership of the National Freight Corporation, which also owned a chunk of the site, and Rosehaugh Stanhope, the developers of Broadgate. In turn, LRC appointed Norman Foster Associates as architects for the scheme. Foster's plan included a central park straddling the canal, and a glass structure which pulled together King's Cross and St Pancras stations after the closure of Pancras Road. The plan slowly made its way through the consultative processes, but in the early 1990s the office property market collapsed (as did many other markets) and the developers went bankrupt. Not much has happened since.

During the later stages of all this, and before the scheme collapsed under the weight of its own cost, a new factor arose – the Channel Tunnel link. It was proposed that instead of the link terminating at Waterloo, the new dedicated line from the coast would cross the Thames to Stratford and then go west into St Pancras, thereby connecting to numerous and possibly profitable routes to other parts of the country. The railway line would have to come through the King's Cross railway lands, requiring a fundamental rethink of the layout of the development. An ancillary benefit of the Tunnel link to St Pancras would be that the financial potential of the largely derelict Midland Grand Hotel in front of St Pancras station (now called St Pancras Chambers) would be enhanced. British Rail cleaned and made watertight the exterior of Scott's Gothic fantasy during this period, but apart from some restoration, the interior remained as it was. Parts of the building had been badly knocked about by the former occupants, British Transport Commission's own architects' department, and

the rest seemed unconvertible into either hotel or offices. The Tunnel link and the restoration of the hotel were then thrown in doubt when railways were privatised, since when it has never appeared certain or even very likely that the link would reach Euston Road at all. St Pancras Station (and its hotel) is owned by London Continental Railways, whereas all other stations now are owned by Railtrack. More recently, there has been a definite plan to convert much of the hotel back into a hotel, turn the mansard floors into loft apartments, and restore the public rooms to their old glory. But it is still a plan.

Next door to the Midland Grand the British Library, designed by Colin St John, was at last opened in 1998. The saga of its building does not bear retelling, as it is so embarrassing, but its opening could have significant repercussions in the area. Originally, it was proposed to build it south of the British Museum, on that small grid of streets of cafés, specialist bookshops, galleries and pubs that delights any visitor to the Museum. Instead, Anthony Crosland, then the appropriate Minister, insisted that the Library should be built on the less constricted but far less welcoming site of the Somers Town Goods Depot.

Because of that decision the lower end of Bloomsbury kept its character, but the question is whether the Library can now influence for the better the nature of the King's Cross area in tandem with the restoration of the Midland Grand? So far the Library has made no difference to the environment – there has been no rash of cosy eateries, or second hand bookshops, or nice pubs that one might expect to open in the wake of such an important academic building. And despite the building of substantial numbers of new upmarket apartments to the east of York Way, around the canal, the area directly to the east and south of King's Cross remains resolutely seedy, where drug selling and prostitution are commonly visible.

If developments were getting larger, the role of conservationists was burgeoning also. Planning applications were routinely forwarded from Camden Council to the appropriate local societies for their comments, stretching to the limit the time that volunteer members had to deal with them thoroughly. The Highgate Society, formed in 1966, had planning application paperwork from both Camden and Haringey, and occasionally from Islington, to respond to.

There were a number of *cause célèbres* for the local societies to campaign for. One was the

139. An interior in Witanhurst.

140. One of the attractive villas lost in the private redevelopment of Primrose Hill Road in the 1970s.

future of the large mansion called Witanhurst at the top of Highgate West Hill. It was firmly settled that the house (built in *c*.1920) was to remain, but what about the grounds? Plans to build on them emerged as soon as the last personal owner, Paul Crosfield, departed. Over the years both the Highgate Society and the Heath & Old Hampstead Society combined to fight a variety of schemes, bemoaning the loss of trees in the ample gardens at the back of the house, but by 1982 the battle had been lost and luxury houses were built, though not as many as originally proposed. The two societies were also concerned about other large mansions on the fringes of the Heath as they changed hands at prodigious prices. Witanhurst itself was sold in 1984 for £14 million, allegedly 'to an Arab sheikh or king', and nearby Beechwood (a handsome house built by Basevi) went to the Emir of Qatar for £8 million the following year. St Columba's Hospital, near the Spaniards Road, was sold in 1987 by 'a sheikh' for a rumoured £7 million, having paid £2.5 million for it in 1980. At the time of writing The Elms in Fitzroy Park is on the market for £7 million.

One of the most important issues for conservationists was not a building but the Heath itself. When the GLC was abolished in 1986, who should own it, who would run it? The first proposal from the government was extraordinarily inept, bearing in mind that most of the Cabinet must have known the character of the area. It was to hive off Kenwood House and its grounds to English Heritage, and split the rest of the various parts of the Heath among the appropriate boroughs.

Geoffrey Finsberg, by then Hampstead's MP, suggested that the Heath be taken over by the City of London, a proposal that aroused the ire of many local residents and councillors. But alternative suggestions that it should be administered by an authority comprised of local borough representatives, or even just by Camden, were not very convincing. The City had more experience of managing open spaces than any of the boroughs. It had owned since the 19th century Highgate Wood and Epping Forest, amongst other open spaces, which it had bought at a time when county and local authorities had no power to save them from builders. In the 1980s the City's role is more political than social for in much of the 20th century it has been fighting off attempts to merge it into London boroughs or otherwise reduce its autonomy. The City needs to be useful to survive and the management of the Heath, in the absence of an overall

London authority, suited its image very well. In fact, the City has looked after the Heath far better than the LCC or the GLC ever did and has been far more responsive to local opinion. Not the same could be said about English Heritage which has been remarkably high-handed in its management of Kenwood.

In 1977 the crumbling Pergola Walk off North End Way, designed by Thomas Mawson in 1906, was given on long loan to the Greater London Council by the Industrial Orthopaedic Society which owned the Manor House Hospital in adjacent Inverforth House. Not much attempt was made by the GLC to improve the Pergola and eventually it was closed. After a thorough restoration by its new owners, the City of London, it was reopened in May 1995.

Other concerns in Hampstead and Highgate were the futures of Burgh House and Lauderdale House. Burgh House in New End Square was built in 1703 and was soon the residence of the Hampstead Wells physician. It took its name from the Rev. Allatson Burgh, who lived here until his death in 1856. From 1858 to 1881 it was the headquarters of the Royal East Middlesex Militia, who had barracks in Willow Road. After the 2nd World War, Hampstead Council, which erected the adjacent council flats called Wells House on the site of the bombed second Long Room, bought the house for a community centre. It was sadly neglected, so much so that it was closed in 1977 because of dry rot. A vigorous campaign to restore it to public use, chaired by David Sullivan, resulted in it being vested in the Burgh House Trust in 1979, when it reopened as a meeting place; it also featured the Hampstead Museum, run by Christopher and Diana Wade.

Lauderdale House on Highgate Hill, backing on to Waterlow Park, was given to the London County Council by Sir Sydney Waterlow in 1889 and served as the park tea-room. In 1961 the LCC began extensive restoration but a serious fire in 1963 gutted much of the interior. Changes of ownership – from LCC to Greater London Council in 1965, and to Camden in 1971 – encouraged a neglect of the fabric until 1978 when the Lauderdale House Society was granted a licence to run it as a community and arts centre. Financed by the 1889 endowment and fire insurance money, serious restoration began – the ground floor in 1978, the staircase and cupola 1983-85, and the Long Gallery in 1993. During this work much of the earlier history of the house has been uncovered.

There was also concern at the deteriorating state of Highgate Cemetery. By 1975 it was more gothic than its builders would have liked – covered by impenetrable undergrowth and overrun by sycamores, vandalised and used for 'black magic' parties. The cemetery company closed its gates and the Friends of Highgate Cemetery organisation was set up in 1975 to care for the cemetery ground. Restoration work, using substantial grants from English Heritage and young labour from the Manpower Services Commission, continued for years. In 1981 two members of the Friends bought the Cemetery for £50 and later the freehold was vested in Highgate Cemetery Charity. The Friends have continued to look after the Cemetery and it is now a popular north London tourist attraction.

Conservationists and ordinary residents alike were equally appalled at another disastrous plan put forward by the GLC in 1965. Usually called the 'Motorway Box', it was intended as a massive ring road circling inner London on both sides of the Thames. Within Camden it stretched from Kilburn to York Way and included a six-lane motorway on the line of East Heath Road, an intersection at Pond Street, and a stretch from Belsize Park to Swiss Cottage. There was also a spur which ran through the Chalcots Estate and Chalk Farm to Camden Town where, after crossing Gloucester Crescent, a three-level interchange would feed cars into central London. It was estimated that in Camden alone, 7000 people would be displaced but of course the blight and ugliness of it would affect many thousands more. This arrogant scheme was a perfect example of how planners can ignore communities and, indeed, aesthetics, in search of a logical solution to a problem. It was eight years and a wasteful public enquiry later before the plan was abandoned by the GLC.

Shopping changes

One of the most remarkable changes in Camden and elsewhere since 1974 has been in shopping. At that time, multiples already held sway in the high streets, but they did not destroy competition – rather the reverse, for their presence allowed independents to cluster nearby in the knowledge that the general public would shop in the street. When Sainsbury's opened its supermarket in the old Finchley Road baths in 1973, it was considered a large store but not detrimental to other businesses. But when it reopened at the O2 Centre further north in the road in 1998, it was so vast that it did serious damage to local trade. As evidence of a switch to one-stop shopping, John Barnes, beloved of generations of Hampstead residents, closed in January 1981 in the face of the weekend exodus to Brent Cross.

On the whole, Camden Council has been sensible in its policy towards large supermarkets. It acknowledges their appeal and realises that great damage will be done to the local economy if residents go out of the borough for their weekly shopping. Therefore, while the new Sainsbury shop at Camden Town, the Safeway store on old railway land at Chalk Farm and the O2 Centre may cause some local traffic congestion, that is better than people travelling miles to visit other superstores. It is a pity that one was not established on the industrial estate opposite Kentish Town station, which might have revived the flagging fortunes of that area of Camden.

Supermarkets aren't always the reason for the decrease in independent shops in Camden, especially in Hampstead. Rent levels are also to blame. As Hampstead itself became an estate agent's haven, so boutiques and restaurants came in to pay the rents asked to occupy many of the prime sites in Hampstead High Street. The fairly modern phenomenon of eating out, or taking out, that has affected almost all areas of London has transformed Hampstead. The Heath & Old Hampstead Society, which in 1960 complained of numerous eating places and night clubs in Heath Street and High Street, has witnessed an explosion of such places. The Society with some of the public behind it, fought a long and unsuccessful campaign to keep out McDonald's, although the restaurant was obliged to do without its usual awful fascia. Further evidence of the strength of modern multiples was the demise in 1988 of Ian Norrie's High Hill Bookshop, a business lovingly expanded over the years, which gave in quickly to the arrival of Waterstone's in the old Woolworth's building. Highgate Village in particular has deteriorated as a shopping centre, where there are now more estate agents than anything else.

But other things flourish. Who would have imagined that what began as a craft shopping centre on the banks of the Regent's Canal at Camden Lock would become one of the most popular tourist attractions in London? It was begun in 1973 by Peter Wheeler, Bill Fullwood and Eric Reynolds who, under the umbrella of Northside Developments, took on a lease of the lock basin when the Motorway Box threatened to obliterate it. It included a number of fairly derelict premises previously occupied by Dingwall's, a packing case manufacturer. The Lock market began with stalls selling mainly craft products, extended to workshops for craftsmen, good food stalls and clothes stalls and the famous Dingwall's music and dance hall. The motorway threat to the site was lifted and business grew rapidly. A new market hall, designed by John Dickinson, was opened by Simon Callow in August 1991. The first event here was an exhibition celebrating the first 200 years of Camden Town, organised by Camden's Local Studies and Archives Department and the Camden History Society which had been formed in 1970.

So successful was Camden Lock Market that the whole stretch of Camden High Street from the Underground station and beyond the railway bridge became a commercial extension of it. More stalls were put into the Stables running along Chalk Farm Road, and a recognisable style of three-dimensional shop front advertising has emerged. So many people arrive at the Underground station at weekends that London Transport has been obliged to restrict passenger traffic in the station.

During the development of the Camden Lock Market the canal has been more extensively used for sight-seeing. John Jones had begun running passenger boats along the canal from here in 1951, and in 1968 Paddy Walker began the *Jenny Wren* boat trips from the canal bridge at Chalk Farm Road in 1968. Walker was also to co-operate with Viscount St Davids in opening the nearby Pirates' Castle on the canal in 1977 to teach young people the art of mucking about in boats. The surprising architect of this castellated building was Richard Seifert, who also built Centre Point. In about 1986 Northside began their own services. There are frequent boats to Little Venice, and regular trips to Limehouse and the river Lea.

Architectural newcomers
The most visible new Camden building, 580ft high, is what began as the Post Office Tower (now Telecom Tower) off Cleveland Street. Completed in the mid-1960s, its chief architect was Eric Bedford. When it first opened it had a viewing gallery and revolving public restaurant, but the explosion of an IRA bomb there in 1971 led to their closure.

141. The NW1 Restaurant in Hawley Crescent.

142. The Glass Building in Jamestown Road.

Other new buildings of distinction are the TVam building in Hawley Crescent, Camden Town, designed by Terry Farrell, opened in 1983; with the demise of TVam, the building was occupied by MTV as from 1988. Next door is the NW1 Restaurant, designed in 1997 by Crouch End architects, Papaloizu, which took the place of an old garage. Across the road in Jamestown Road is the recently built Glass Building, designed by Piers Gough; and the ITN building in Gray's Inn Road is always popular during the annual Open House week. In Hampstead there is the Kingswell development in Heath Street (recently refurbished) by Ted Levy, Benjamin & Partners who also designed the pleasant office block on the Swiss Cottage civic site and the West Hill development in Highgate; Old Brewery Mews was the work of Dinerman, Davison & Partners and in Downshire Hill, Michael Hopkins designed a handsome glass house. Then there is, of course, Sainsbury's store in Camden Road, designed by Nicholas Grimshaw on the site of the ABC factory, which closed in March 1982. It is a building which has many admirers, but some would say it overwhelms the street and looks grubby already.

Gains and Losses
St Stephen's church, Haverstock Hill was made redundant and still stands derelict after many years – new proposals for its use appear regularly. Opposite, the stylish Lyndhurst Congregational Chapel has been handsomely restored and converted as a recording studio by Chrysalis plc. The old North Western Polytechnic in Prince of Wales Road became part of the University of North London and left for Holloway; the building has a handsome interior which has been converted sensitively into a Pizza Express and apartments. The wretched Blue Star garage in Hampstead High Street was razed and handsome shops and offices erected in its place. The Freud Museum opened in Maresfield Gardens in 1986; the Saatchi Gallery in Boundary Road began in 1984, showing Charles Saatchi's extensive collection of modern artists; the Parkway cinema was saved from closure; the Screen on the Hill cinema replaced the Odeon, Haverstock Hill, and while the Forum in Highgate Road closed as a cinema it has for many years been a hugely successful music venue. And in 1999 the full Egyptian glory of the old Carreras building in Hampstead Road was restored to a grateful public.

Many times there are advantages to delays. We are fortunate that British Rail were so lethargic in developing their goods yards at King's Cross and Camden Town, for otherwise they would be covered by the awful architecture of the 1960s and 1970s. In these two areas of Camden most changes will happen over the next ten or fifteen years. There is to be considerable redevelopment between Parkway and the canal, and across the road north of the Underground station. The future of the King's Cross railway lands is less certain, but it seems likely that some new plan will emerge to transform these virtually derelict acres. Also, the Middlesex and University College hospitals are to merge into one building to be erected at the junction of Gower Street and Euston Road.

A diverse population

The 1991 census showed that Camden's population was still declining, though at a slower rate – it is now about 180,000. Malcolm Holmes has compiled some fascinating population figures of the areas which today make up Camden, back to 1801, when the total was 102,610. In 1821, the population was roughly the same as it is today – an astonishing statistical comparison given the enormous of amount of building that has occurred since that earlier date. Part of the reason for this has been the depopulation of Holborn which is now down to about 22,000. Overcrowding in previous times may be imagined from the 1891 figure of 373,311 – well over twice today's number. Since then there has been a steady decline, most particularly in the 1960s when there was a steady migration to New Towns and outer suburbs, and a great deal of demolition of substandard housing. There was, too, a fall in the birth rate.

The 1991 census also shows how ethnically diverse the population of Camden now is. And it reveals some surprises. For example, the borough has the highest number of people in London born in Germany – no doubt reflecting the refugee Jews before and after the last war. The Cypriot population is not as large as is generally perceived – twelve other London boroughs have a larger number of Cypriot-born people than Camden (1318). It is anecdotal that the younger Greek Cypriots have moved out of the borough in recent years, especially to Haringey, leaving the older generation in Camden, mainly in Camden Town. There were 920 Poles, 1116 Spanish and 539 from parts of the former USSR. There were 3054 from the Caribbean, 2633 Chinese, 6021 Bangladeshi and only 760 Pakistani. There were over 2700 people from Australia and New Zealand. It is estimated that within Camden's population over 140 different languages are spoken. This has made for problems in Camden's schools, which have been administered by Camden since the abolition of the Inner London Education Authority. Here, there is a wide diversity of first languages spoken ranging from Bangladeshi and Somali, to Portuguese, Gujarati, Tagalog, Farsi, Urdu and Mandarin.

Problems in Recession

In the Camden Council elections of 1967 the Conservatives swept into power by 38-22. It was to be their only period of control in Camden for since then the electorate has consistently returned a Labour majority and the Conservatives have been whittled down further by a Liberal Democrat presence. There have been unhappy periods for the Labour administration, especially in the 1980s when central government curtailed the powers of local authorities by rate capping and encouraged the sale of council dwellings. Whatever the justification of the 'right-to-buy' policy, it frustrates any effort by local authorities to build housing because within years any house may be bought by the sitting tenant at a relatively cheap price and is lost to the public housing pool. There is now no incentive for local authorities to build houses for rent – that field of activity is now the prerogative of housing associations and the like. For a time in the 1980s Camden attracted widespread criticism for its politicial militancy and a perceived recklessness in expenditure, but of late it has re-established itself in local authority circles despite a persistent shortage of money and a vastly increased role in social work, dealing with problems that hardly existed in 1965 when Camden began. It could also be said, with some justification, that many of Camden's present financial difficulties have been caused by the willingness of the Council to tackle urban issues that are new to London generally.

Camden is undoubtedly more vibrant than at its formation, making it in many ways more difficult to administer. It has more visitors and tourists to accommodate; it has soaring house prices and a lack of accommodation for less affluent people. There are chronic parking problems and the Underground lines that go through the borough are overloaded. There are shops and clubs that open all night, but there is also a need for less urban stress, noise and activity to make the enjoyment of city life possible. There are social problems caused by poverty, and there are others as a consequence of consumerism. There are more arts and social welfare organisations than can be sustained properly by one borough council, but the number of these is an indication of the energy and activity in the area. Camden is still, as it has always been, a microcosm of London.

Further Reading

Camden

Aston, Mark, *The Cinemas of Camden* (Camden Council, 1997).

Flood, Aidan, *The Irish in Camden* (Camden Libraries 1990).

Hassiotis, Anna, *The Greek Cypriot Community in Camden* (Camden Libraries (1989).

Wistrich, Enid, *Local Government Reorganisation: The first years of Camden* (1972).

Camden Town, Chalk Farm, Primrose Hill, Regent's Park

Camden History Society, *From Primrose Hill to Euston Road* (1995).

Richardson, John, *Camden Town & Primrose Hill Past* (1990).

Saunders, Ann , *Regent's Park from 1086 to the Present* (2nd edn 1981).

Whitehead, Jack, *The Growth of Camden Town AD1800-2000* (1999).

Hampstead

Baines, F.E. (ed), *Records of the Manor, Parish and Borough of Hampstead* (1890).

Barratt, Thomas J., *Annals of Hampstead* (3 vols) (1912).

Bentwich, Helen, *The Vale of Health on Hampstead Heath 1777-1977* (reptd by Camden History Society 1977).

Camden History Society, *The Streets of Belsize* (ed. Christopher Wade 1991).

Camden History Society, *The Streets of Hampstead* (rev. edn, ed. by Christopher Wade 1984).

Camden History Society, *The Streets of West Hampstead* (ed. Christopher Wade 1992).

Camden History Society, *Buried in Hampstead* (ed. Christopher Wade 1986).

Carswell, John, *The Saving of Kenwood and the Northern Heights* (1992).

Farmer, Alan, *Hampstead Heath* (1984).

Hampstead Annual 1897-1907.

Hampstead Scientific Society, *Seventy five Years of Popular Science 1899-1974* (1974)

Ikin, Christopher, *Hampstead Heath Centenary 1971* (1971, revised and reptd 1985 by High Hill Press).

Kennedy, J., *The Manor and Parish Church of Hampstead* (1906).

Knox, E.V., *The Adventures of a School* [Heath Mount School] (n.d.).

MacDermott, Norman, *Everymania: The History of the Everyman Theatre, Hampstead 1920-26* (1976).

Newton, E.E., *Fifty Years of Progress in Hampstead 1860-1910* (1910).

Norrie, Ian, *The Heathside Book* (1962).

Park, John James, *The Topography and Natural History of Hampstead* (1814).

Port, Michael, *Hampstead Parish Church. The Story of a Building through 250 years* (1995).

Potter, George W., *Hampstead Wells* (1904, reptd 1978).

Richardson, John, *Hampstead One Thousand AD986-1986* (1985).

Rosslyn Hill Chapel. A Short History 1692-1973 (published by the Chapel (1974).

A Short History of St John's, Downshire Hill, Hampstead (published by the Church n.d.)

Service, Alastair, *Victorian and Edwardian Hampstead* (1989).

Sullivan, David, *The Westminster Corridor* (1994).

Thompson, Professor F.M.L., *Hampstead. Building a Borough 1650-1964* (1974)

Venning, Philip, *Wyldes: A New History* (1977).

Victoria County History, Middlesex, Vol. IX, *Hampstead and Paddington Parishes* (1989).

Wade, Christopher, *Hampstead Past* (1989).

Wade, Christopher, *For the poor of Hampstead, for ever. 300 years of the Hampstead Wells Trust* (1998).

Woodford, F. Peter, *A Constant Vigil. 100 years of the Heath and Old Hampstead Society* (1997)

Highgate

Barber, Peter and Oliver Cox and Michael Curwen, *Lauderdale Revealed. A History of Lauderdale House, Highgate … 1582-1993* (1993).

Heart of a London Village. The Highgate Literary and Scientific Institution 1839-1990 (1991).

Hinde, Thomas, *Highgate School. A History* (1993).

Lloyd, John H., *The History, Topography and Antiquities of Highgate* (1888).

Prickett, Frederick, *The History and Antiquities of Highgate* (1842).

Richardson, John, *Highgate: Its history since the Fifteenth Century* (1983).

Survey of London, Vol. XVII, *The Village of Highgate* (1936).

Holborn

Barker, T.C., *Three hundred years of Red Lion Square* (Camden Libraries 1984).

Barron, Caroline, *The parish of St Andrew Holborn* (1979).

Byrne, Andrew, *Bedford Square. An architectural study* (1990).

Camden History Society, *Streets of Bloomsbury & Fitzrovia* (1997).

Camden History Society, *East of Bloomsbury* (compiled by David Hayes 1998).

Camden History Society, *Streets of Old Holborn* (Steven Denford and David Hellings 1999).

Chancellor, E. Beresford, *The Romance of Lincoln's Inn Fields* (nd).

Clinch, George, *Bloomsbury and St Giles* (1890).

Colpi, Terri, *The Italian factor: the Italian community in Great Britain* (1991).

Field Lane Foundation, *The Field Lane Story* (2nd edn 1972).

Godber, Joyce, *The Harpur Trust 1552-1973* (1973).

Lehmann, John, *Holborn: an historical portrait of a London borough* (1970).

Parton, John, *Some Account ... of St Giles in the Fields* (1822).

Survey of London, Vol. III, *St Giles-in-the-Fields* (Pt I) (1912).

Survey of London, Vol. V, *St Giles-in-the-Fields* (Pt II) (1914).

Tames, Richard, *Bloomsbury Past* (1993).

Thomson, Gladys Scott, *The Russells in Bloomsbury 1669-1771* (1940).

Williams, E., *Early Holborn and the legal quarter of London* (1927).

Kentish Town

Richardson, John, *Kentish Town Past* (1997).

Tindall, Gillian, *The Fields Beneath* (1977).

St Pancras

Bailey, Nick, *Fitzrovia* 1981).

Barclay, Irene, *People need roots* [St Pancras Housing Association] (1976)

Brown, Walter Edward, *The St Pancras Poor 1718-1904.* (1905).

Brown, Walter Edward, *From Open Vestry to Borough Council* (1905).

Brown, Walter Edward, *St Pancras Open Spaces and Disused Burial Grounds* (1902).

Burchell, Doris, *Miss Buss' Second School* (1971).

Clarke, Linda, *Building Capitalism. Historical changes and the Labour Process in the Production of the Built Environment* [Somers Town] (1992).

Clinch, George, *Marylebone and St Pancras* (1890).

Denford, Steven L.J., *Agar Town: The Life & Death of a Victorian 'Slum'* (Camden History Society (1995)

Holmes, Malcolm J., *Housing is not enough* [St Pancras Housing Association] (1999).

Hunter, Michael and Robert Thorne, *Change at King's Cross* (1990).

Lee, Charles E., *St Pancras Church and Parish* (1955).

Miller, Frederick, *St Pancras Past and Present* (1874).

Nichols, R.H. and F.A. Wray, *The History of the Foundling Hospital* (1935).

The North London Collegiate School (1950).

Palmer, Samuel, *St Pancras* (1870).

Survey of London, Vol. XIX, *Old St Pancras and Kentish Town* (1938).

Survey of London, Vol. XXIV, *King's Cross Neighbourhood* (1952).

Survey of London, Vol. XX1, *Tottenham Court Road and Neighbourhood* (1949).

Wates, Nick, *The Battle for Tolmers Square* (1976).

Wiswould, Samuel, *An Account of the Charitable Foundations, Bequests...to the Parish of St Pancras....* (1863).

General

Barton, Nicholas, *The Lost Rivers of London* (rev. edn 1992)

Bebbington, Gillian, *London Street Names* (1972).

Howard, Diana, *London Theatres and Music Halls 1850-1950* (1970)

Camden History Society publications
(other than those noted under the previous headings)
Camden History Review, Nos. 1-22
Camden History Society Newsletter Nos. 1-175

INDEX

An asterisk indicates picture or caption